THE VISUAL IMAGINATION
OF D. H. LAWRENCE

For J.G.M.A.

THE VISUAL IMAGINATION
OF D. H. LAWRENCE

KEITH ALLDRITT

Northwestern University Press
Evanston
1971

© KEITH ALLDRITT 1971

First published 1971 by
Edward Arnold (Publishers) Ltd.
41 Maddox Street, London W1

First published in the
United States of America 1971
by Northwestern University Press
1735 Benson Avenue, Evanston, Illinois 60201

Library of Congress Catalog Card Number: 76-155801

ISBN: 0-8101-0356-7

Printed in Great Britain by
W & J Mackay & Co Ltd, Chatham

CONTENTS

PREFACE

THE chief subject of this essay is the visual element in the style of D. H. Lawrence's major novels. My aim is to draw attention to the considerable but usually un-remarked and unappreciated achievement represented by Lawrence's actual writing, his way with the English language. The visual is, of course, but one feature of Lawrence's prose style, but it is the most characteristic and the one which most clearly reveals the tradition to which his art belongs.

The main critical method I have employed is the analysis of certain selected passages. This is the only way in which it is possible to reveal the various kinds of visual writing which are so important in creating the effect of each novel. At the same time I have also found it illuminating to concentrate upon certain proper nouns that occur in the prose. For the many specific references to paintings and painters are as crucial to the overall effect of each novel as any other individual item of the style. Lawrence's imagination, as his several essays in art theory and criticism attest, was powerfully affected by his very considerable experience of paintings. And the many references to painting and sculpture in the novels often serve to complement or enhance a certain passage in the writing. Also, art objects are important subjects in the novels and the painter is often a major character. Cyril Beardsall, Paul Morel, Will and Gudrun Brangwen are all to varying degrees practising painters, and to consider Lawrence's view and treatment of them is to come by insights that can clarify the meaning and effect of the novels. For Lawrence, as for Blake and Ruskin (two "painter-poets" with whose work he was closely acquainted), a painting or sculpture can be the most vivid and revealing evidence of a state of consciousness or of the tensions of a social order or of a historical turning point. And in his major novels works of art continually figure as specific indications of such larger subjects. Nevertheless, in seeking to elucidate such matters I will try to avoid that narrowly thematic approach which misses most of the effect of Lawrence's art. Despite the many departures from the actual texts, the prime and directing concern of this essay is Lawrence's use of words, his way of writing. Visual art is a subject of these novels, but it is also, more importantly, a key influence upon their style.

The sort of stylistic criticism which I intend allows only a very restricted coverage of an *oeuvre* as voluminous as that of Lawrence. The particular novels which I have singled out for attention are those written between 1910 and 1920. I share the now orthodox view first established by F. R. Leavis that these are the years of Lawrence's finest achievement in the novel form. I also believe that during these years we can trace a very revealing development in Lawrence's visual style. This development begins with certain basic categories and configurations inherited from diverse nineteenth-century sources and continues in a sucession of very original styles of fiction, the last of which, in *Women in Love*, is significantly affected by Lawrence's experience of modernism in painting and sculpture. In the novels written after the Great War there is a marked deterioration brought about by the sudden deficiency of cultural confirmation for Lawrence's characteristic mode of seeing.

To those who have assisted me in the writing of this book I should like to express my gratitude. My biggest debt is to my wife Judith Alldritt, who has shared all the work of revision and improvement. Sherman Paul undertook a very careful reading of the manuscript and supplied a great deal of helpful criticism and advice. To him I am indebted for many stimulating discussions of Lawrence and for a sustaining friendship which now extends over more than a decade. I am also grateful for the many constructive suggestions provided by John Goode. I am happy to have an opportunity to record the help of the Canada Council. It was during a leave fellowship awarded by the Council that the greater part of the writing was completed. I have also been helped by financial support from the Committee on Research of the University of British Columbia.

ACKNOWLEDGEMENTS

The author and publisher gratefully acknowledge permission given by the Estate of the Late Mrs Frieda Lawrence, Laurence Pollinger Ltd. and The Viking Press Inc. to reprint extracts from *Sons and Lovers*, *The Rainbow*, *Women in Love*, *Phoenix: The Posthumous Papers of D. H. Lawrence*, *Phoenix II* and *The Collected Letters of D. H. Lawrence* edited by Harry T. Moore; and by the Estate of the Late Mrs Frieda Lawrence, Laurence Pollinger Ltd. and Alfred A. Knopf Inc. to reprint extracts from *The White Peacock*.

ONE
THE MATURING STYLE

The subtle, steady rush of the whole
Grey foam-mist of advancing Time
As it silently sweeps to its somewhere, its goal,
    Is seen in the gossamer's rime.

Is heard in the windless whisper of leaves,
In the silent labours of men in the field,
In the downward-dropping of flimsy sheaves
    Of cloud the rain skies yield.

"COROT"

THE LANDSCAPES OF
"THE WHITE PEACOCK"

I N 1914 Bertrand Russell described the contemporary intellectual situation in the following terms:

> Evolutionism, in one form or another, is the prevailing creed of our time. It dominates our politics, our literature, and not least our philosophy. Nietzsche, Pragmatism, Bergson, are phases in its philosophic development, and their popularity far beyond the circles of professional philosophers shows its consonance with the spirit of the age.

By way of characterising Bergson's philosophy, Russell gave a brief account of this concept of evolutionism:

> Life, in his philosophy, is a continuous stream, in which all divisions are artificial and unreal. Separate things, beginnings and endings, are mere convenient fictions; there is only smooth, unbroken transition. The beliefs of today may count as true today, if they carry us along the stream; but tomorrow they will be false, and must be replaced by new beliefs to meet the new situation.[1]

Though it would not be a very useful critical endeavour to try to bind Lawrence's fictions to the thought of any one philosopher, it is clear enough that evolutionism in the broad sense in which Russell defines it here is the leading assumption of all the early novels. From *The*

[1] Bertrand Russell, *Our Knowledge of the External World*, quoted in Wyndham Lewis, *Time and Western Man* (London, 1927), p. 201.

3

White Peacock, begun in 1906, to *Women in Love*, completed around 1919, Lawrence's main category of perception and the main subject of his novels is process. Unlike Jane Austen writing exactly a century before, Lawrence has no pre-Romantic sense of the world as stasis. For him everything is to be seen as growth, change, movement, development—the basic principle of life being, as he maintained in a letter of 1911, "a vast, shimmering impulse which waves onwards towards some end, . . ."[2] Lawrence's most vivid realisation of process is to be found in the sequence comprising *The Rainbow* and *Women in Love* in which the story of four generations of a family serves to convey the development of English society, culture and consciousness during some seventy highly critical years. The novels which precede the Brangwen saga can, to some extent, be seen as preliminary sketches for this major enterprise. One likely reason for the lapse in Lawrence's creative energy, specifically as a novelist, after *Women in Love* may have been his sense of having already achieved his long envisioned task of placing and explaining the life of his generation in terms of the historical forces conditioning both psyche and society. (It is significant that of all the novels Lawrence wrote during the twenties the only one that shows anything of the tremendous verbal energy of the early books is *The Plumed Serpent*, a work in which Lawrence's old concern with process and history expresses itself in the new form of a prophetic vision of the future.)

Lawrence's first novel, *The White Peacock*, was begun during his first year as a student at Nottingham Univer-

[2] *The Collected Letters of D. H. Lawrence*, ed. Harry T. Moore (London, 1962), p. 76. Except where otherwise stated, all subsequent references to Lawrence's letters are to this edition.

sity College and finished at the end of his first year as a schoolmaster in south London. The several faults of this book have been often remarked. The unconvincing middle-class setting, the stilted dialogue and the colourless and imprecise depiction of character all betray the youth and inexperience of the author. Another very important weakness is Lawrence's uncertainty about the meaning of the story he has to tell. This deficiency is of especial interest here because it helps to reveal an early and immature stage in the dialectic which characterises Lawrence's vision as a novelist. It illuminates a certain incoherence between his ideas and his specific perceptions.

In *The White Peacock* Lawrence attempts to explain the events related in terms of some very differing notions of process. One is established by the historical perspective with which the book opens. This is the first paragraph of the novel:

> I stood watching the shadowy fish slide through the gloom of the mill-pond. They were grey, descendants of the silvery things that had darted away from the monks, in the young days when the valley was lusty. The whole place was gathered in the musing of old age. The thick-piled trees on the far shore were too dark and sober to dally with the sun; the weeds stood crowded and motionless. Not even a little wind flickered the willows of the islets. The water lay softly, intensely still. Only the thin stream falling through the millrace murmured to itself of the tumult of life which had once quickened the valley.

The implication of this is plain enough. The life of the valley is neither as robust nor as intense as it was in the medieval period. Over the years it has become grey, dark, sober, sluggish, somnolent. Fish, trees, streams all provide evidence of a process of stagnation and decay. This principle is made to apply to the human as well as to the natural life of the valley. A little further on the narrator rebukes the main character, George Saxton, for being sleepy and not fully alive: "Your life is nothing but a doss. I shall laugh when somebody jerks you awake." The strategic positioning of this idea seems calculated to compel us to regard what follows, the story of Lettie Beardsall and her two suitors, as an instance or a consequence of this principle of progressive devitalisation. And certainly the growing improverishment of the life of the valley is a distinct influence upon the events related. The determination of the local squire ("head of an ancient, once even famous, but now decayed house") to preserve the rabbits for his own financial advantage and the resulting damage to farm crops are a main cause of the break-up of the Saxton family. Nevertheless the major theme of the novel, which has to do with Lettie's flirtation with the young farmer George Saxton and her subsequent marriage to Leslie, the mine-owner's son, who is richer and socially more acceptable, is not clearly related to the opening assumption. The sexual dislocation that is caused by the failure of both Leslie and George to be sufficiently vital and authoritative in the face of the female initiative is merely asserted and never explained. Lawrence may suggest that Lettie is a "modern woman" and tell us that "she read all things that dealt with modern women", but the precise nature of her modernity is never made clear. Similarly, the leading metaphor of modern woman as a peacock, "all vanity and screech and defilement" (which is introduced by the gamekeeper Annable and then charitably modified by Cyril into the *white* peacock in order to imply a lack of consciously malicious purpose) comes to seem unjustifiably portentous and adolescent.[3] And in the absence of satisfactory explanation, the endless series of miserable marriages,

[3] The schema of metaphors, allusions and images in the novel is very carefully worked out. See Robert E. Gajdusek, "A Reading of *The White Peacock*" in *A D. H. Lawrence Miscellany*, ed. Harry T. Moore (London, 1961), pp. 188–203.

which is intended presumably to give general validity to the experience of the three main characters, is gratuitous. The historical forces that figure so prominently in *Sons and Lovers* are in this novel only dimly surmised and unconvincingly declared.

Another idea of process advanced in the novel concerns the development of the individual. For the events of the story are also interpreted by the narrator as illustrative of the growth into adulthood. In these terms the book is a record of the successive experiences of fear, then pain, then nostalgia at the fact of expulsion from Nethermere, which is equated with the world of childhood and youth. These three citations give something of this emphasis:

> I thought of the time when my friend should not follow the harrow on our snug valley side. . . . My heart clung passionately to the hollow which held us all; how could I bear that it should be desolate!

> The long voyage in the quiet home was over; we had crossed the bright sea of our youth. . . . It was time for us all to go, to leave the valley of Nethermere whose waters and whose woods were distilled in the essence of our veins.

> I went home to Woodside early in September. . . . Nethermere was no longer a complete, wonderful little world that held us charmed inhabitants. It was a small insignificant valley lost in the spaces of the earth. The tree that had drooped over the brook with such delightful romantic grace was a ridiculous thing when I came home after a year of absence in the south.

This sense of gradual and ineluctable alienation from the vivid life of youth is carefully maintained and developed throughout the book. But again the idea is essentially decorative rather than functional. It is in no way relevant to the problems of human relationship at the centre of the novel. Nor is it a sufficient explanation of the lives of the characters. In the final analysis it serves only as a

7

prop for the self-conscious melancholy of the narrator and usually heralds, as is evident from the quotations, a marked deterioration in the quality of the writing. This representation of growth into maturity is as peripheral to the vital issues of the book as the ideas concerning the course of history.

There is, however, another issue of psychological development which is treated more successfully. This is the question of the nature of seeing. An important event in the development of the story, though one whose significance is not altogether fully elucidated, is Cyril's discovery of "reproductions of Aubrey Beardsley's 'Atalanta', and of the tailpiece to 'Salome', and others". The effect upon Cyril is complex:

> I sat and looked and my soul leaped out upon the new thing. I was bewildered, wondering, grudging, fascinated. I looked a long time, but my mind, or my soul, would come to no state of coherence. I was fascinated and overcome, but yet full of stubbornness and resistance.

Cyril finds the drawings on the day immediately after the funeral of Annable; and this may in part explain their strong effect upon him. For like Annable's idea of the white peacock, the pictures express what is for Cyril a new and completely unfamiliar way of looking at the world, and specifically at woman. The more familiar image of woman is that found in Pre-Raphaelite painting. Cyril, for instance, says to Emily, somewhat uncolloquially, "You are like Burne-Jones's damsels. Troublesome shadows are always crowding across your eyes and you cherish them." And such references abound.[4] There

---

[4] In one of his studies of nineteenth-century art William Gaunt remarks upon the way in which the new interest in painting on the part of the Victorian middle class helped to create this concern with images of woman. He writes: "Some women became like Pre-Raphaelite pictures. They imitated the composite ideal which Dante Gabriel Rossetti had evolved from Elizabeth Siddal and Jane Morris, sad eyed, brooding with passionate melancholy, with full drooping

is little doubt that the characteristic Pre-Raphaelite image signifies for Cyril what it does for Annable—a spiritual, sentimental and emotionally destructive manner of seeing. Leslie Tempest voices what appears to be the general masculine opinion in the book: "Hang thin souls, Lettie, I'm not one of your souly sort. I can't stand Pre-Raphaelites. You—You're not a Burne-Jones—you're an Albert Moore. I think there's more in the warm touch of a soft body than in a prayer."

The Beardsley pictures are as important an experience for George Saxton as they are for Cyril. From the moment he sees them, the pictures become an equivalence for his own intense physical desire for Lettie. ("And the more I look at these naked lines, the more I want her. It's a sort of fine sharp feeling like these curved lines.") With his emotions now more clearly formulated by the pictures, George decides to arrange one last meeting with Lettie in order to attempt to persuade her to marry him instead of Leslie. But when he sees her, her dress and appearance do not conform to the Beardsley image. And the subsequent conversation expresses George's failing determination to see her in his and Beardsley's terms:

> "You have been putting white on—you, you do look nice—though not like—"
> "What?—Who else?"
> "Nobody else—only I—well I'd—I'd thought about it different—like some pictures."

---

lips and a long columnar neck. On the other hand for those who were not medievally minded there was another type which seemed to derive from the highest art—the classic. There was the stately beauty depicted by Frederick Leighton and Edward Poynter, the aristocratic Romans of Alma-Tadema, the ladies painted by Albert Moore who sat on marble benches, in flowing draperies, doing nothing in particular. . . . Thus it came about that the Beatrice of Dante was reincarnated in Kensington and the ballrooms in the London season were full of eligible Dianas and stately Minervas."
William Gaunt, *The Aesthetic Adventure* (Harmondsworth, 1957), p.77.

> She smiled with a gentle radiance, and asked
> indulgently, "And how was I different?"
> "Not all that soft stuff—plainer."
> "But don't I look very nice with all this soft
> stuff, as you call it?"—and she shook the silk
> away from her smiles.
> "Oh, yes—better than all those naked lines."

In this conversation we have one of the thematic as well as the narrative climaxes of the novel. For the most discernible cause of George Saxton's subsequent deterioration is his failure to hold true to his newly discovered mode of perception, that is to say, to an image of woman that is more a true equivalence of his feeling than Pre-Raphaelite woman, Annable's white peacock or any of the others proposed in the book. The incident shows his inability to save himself from a disabling way of seeing. His consciousness is lacking in the vital capacity to develop and evolve. The hero of Lawrence's next major novel, *Sons and Lovers*, is confronted by essentially the same demand.[5] Paul Morel is also faced with the need to evolve beyond the orthodoxies of mid-Victorian feeling, orthodoxies which again find expression in certain visual images and configurations. He differs from George Saxton, however, in that he is ultimately capable of this

[5] Of Lawrence's second novel, *The Trespasser*, little needs to be said. It is a rewriting of a story by one of Lawrence's fellow teachers at Croydon. Lawrence was ill during the period of composition and the book shows evidence of haste and fatigue. Nowhere else in Lawrence's work do we find writing of this quality:

> Meanwhile the flowers of their passion were softly shed, as poppies fall at noon, and the seed of beauty ripened rapidly within them. Dreams came like a wind through their souls, drifting off with the seed-dust of beautiful experience which they had ripened, to fertilise the souls of others withal. In them the sea and the sky and ships had mingled and bred new blossoms of the torrid heat of their love. And the seed of such blossoms was shaken as they slept, into the hand of God, who held it in His palm preciously; then scattered it again, to produce new splendid blooms of beauty.

personal, psychological and cultural evolution. For him perception is not just a passive registering or an easy recourse to and acceptance of familiar images. It is an act of moral energy that entails a continuing responsiveness and fidelity to a seen world that is in continual change.

Reference to certain moments in the history of painting as a way of treating the important theme of developing perception is something we shall encounter in all Lawrence's major novels. In each of them the evolving consciousness of main characters is rendered in significant part through the presence or discovery of certain art images. This characteristic of Lawrence's fiction must be attributed to the particular cast of his mind and sensibility. We know that from boyhood Lawrence experimented with painting, both making copies and undertaking original works.[6] And the dialogue of *The White Peacock* alone is sufficient to remind us of the prominent part played by painting in the talk of the group of Eastwood "pagans" that centred upon the young Lawrence. It also alerts us to something which we must consider more fully later on, the pronouncedly visual emphasis in the culture of the late Victorian England in which Lawrence grew up.

Visual categorisation is not just a theme in Lawrence's novels; it is a distinctive feature of their style. It is as much a part of Lawrence's mind as a novelist as of the minds of his created characters. And Lawrence's own visual imagination also undergoes evolution and development. In *The White Peacock* the most striking visual category is landscape description. In *Sons and Lovers* it is the characters who make the deep impression on the

[6] See Ada Lawrence and G. Stuart Gelder, *Young Lorenzo* (Florence, 1931), pp. 65–7.

reader's mind; in *The Rainbow* it is the great numinous tableaux and scenes. But in this first novel what stays with us are the detailed descriptions of the way in which landscape and country life change with the sequence of the seasons. The human element in the book is in comparison imperfectly observed, incoherent and unengaging. The descriptions of the landscape and of the natural life of Nethermere are what make this a book of some distinction, even if it is not one of Lawrence's major novels.

This particular form of seeing, this consciousness of landscape, sometimes expresses itself in the virtuoso performance of the set-piece as, for instance, in the description of the country funeral or in the account of potato planting in the opening section of the chapter entitled "A Poem of Friendship". Sometimes it is there in a couple of bridging sentences of closely observed detail. Most frequently, however, it takes the form of a consciously planned paragraph such as this:

We turned aside, and climbed the hill through the woods. Velvety green sprigs of dog-mercury were scattered on the red soil. We came to the top of a slope, where the wood thinned. As I talked to Emily I became dimly aware of a whiteness over the ground. She exclaimed with surprise, and I found that I was walking, in the first shades of twilight, over clumps of snowdrops. The hazels were thin, and only here and there an oak tree uprose. All the ground was white with snowdrops, like drops of manna scattered over the red earth, on the grey-green clusters of leaves. There was a deep little dell, sharp sloping like a cup, and white sprinkling of flowers all the way down, with white flowers showing pale among the first inpouring of shadow at the bottom. The earth was red and warm, pricked with the dark, succulent green of bluebell sheaths, and embroidered with grey-green clusters of spears and many white flowerets. High above, above the light tracery of hazel, the weird oaks tangled in the sunset. Below, in the first shadows, drooped hosts of little white flowers, so silent and sad; it seemed like a holy communion of pure wild things, numberless, frail, and folded meekly in the evening light.

This passage well exemplifies one of Lawrence's greatest gifts—his ability to actualise and to vivify our sense of the beauty or, to use his own word, the glamour of the seen world. At first sight, the subject of the paragraph, spring flowers, may seem unpromising. But this passage is not merely a literary exercise. To attend to the words is to see that the writing is founded upon experience rather than upon literary models. It is directed by a keen determination to record fully and accurately a specific moment of perception. And what is seen is reproduced with an astonishing but convincing abundance of detail.

The chief stress of the paragraph is upon colour; for instance, upon the colour of the snowdrops as they appear when suddenly discovered in a certain light and atmosphere. And colour is always carefully realised in terms of texture ("velvety green sprigs of dog-mercury", "the dark succulent green of the bluebell sheaths"). This essential emphasis is maintained by the continuing prominence of adjectives of colour and texture as the writing moves from the focal particular of the flowers to the dusk light and the surrounding trees which create the setting. The description of the cup-shaped dell, "with white flowers showing pale among the first inpouring of shadow at the bottom", shows Lawrence's fidelity, even at the cost of a slightly gauche syntax, to the actual phenomenon seen. The primacy of the object and the accuracy carry through to the last sentence in which the feeling elicited by the sight of the flowers is described. The result is that there is no question of sentimentality here. The access of reverence and compassion that is conveyed is not a matter of authorial self-indulgence. The response is as immediate and as authentic as the perception itself. In the *White Peacock* there are many passages of similar quality. Others might be cited to give better evidence of the botanical knowledge underlying Lawrence's descriptions. There are others which show his equally precise rendering of larger subjects involving sky, weather and terrain. But in all of them there is the same vibrance, the same intensity of response.

This first novel initiates that insistence upon landscape which will continue to manifest itself in every one of Lawrence's subsequent (and visually more various) novels. As we know from his discursive writings, Lawrence was always interested in landscape as an art form. Perhaps the best evidence is one of his travel books, *Sea and Sardinia*, in which we find him commenting particularly upon a whole series of landscape, types and the kind of feeling which they predicate. This, for instance, is his comment upon Italy: "But Italian landscape is really eighteenth-century landscape, to be represented in that romantic-classic manner which makes everything rather marvellous and very topical: aqueducts, and ruins upon sugar-loaf mountains, and craggy ravines and Wilhelm Meister waterfalls: all up and down."[7] Here, of course, Lawrence is thinking of the major convention of one of the phases in the history of taste which was simultaneously literary and artistic.[8] But the kind of descriptions which we find in Lawrence's fiction recall a later period in which landscape was again of interest to writers as well as to painters. To be reminded of the landscapes of Poussin, Lorrain and Salvator Rosa is to be aware that those which we find in Lawrence's novels derive from that later and different tradition which he knew from his study of Constable, Turner and the English watercolourists and from his reading of Wordsworth and

[7] *Sea and Sardinia* (New York, 1954), p. 83.
[8] A detailed account of this period of taste is to be found in Elizabeth Wheeler Manwaring, *Italian Landscape in Eighteenth-Century England* (London, 1965).

Ruskin. The feeling for landscape as motion, force and process which is the main feature of this tradition is also a main feature of Lawrence's art. In fact this type of landscape description is the most discernible way in which Lawrence conveys his characteristic sense of man's involvement with a natural order larger and more imposing than anything that can be rendered in merely social terms.

The landscapes in *The White Peacock* are interesting both intrinsically and as the first expression of Lawrence's genius. But in this first novel he is unable as yet to bring his great powers of seeing to bear upon subjects which, though real and important to him, were unusual to the novel form. Thus the mining landscape which we know to have been a very important part of Lawrence's early visual experience is mentioned only very infrequently and cursorily. Lawrence removes it from his field of vision for the same reasons of literary convention that he removes his characters from the working-class milieu that he knew best. A very important part of Lawrence's maturing as a writer is the development of his ability to make his unusal powers of perception focus upon a wider area of reality. In *Sons and Lovers* Lawrence extends his landscapes and fills them with more convincing human figures. But there, as in the later novels, whether the thematic categories of process are psychological, social or historical, an adequate definition of the content must include this pervasive concern with landscape and the natural order in all their unceasing mutation.

"SONS AND LOVERS": INTERIORS AND INDIVIDUALS

CYRIL Beardsall in *The White Peacock* is very much an amateur painter. His efforts are those of the dilettante. The only completed works of his that are mentioned are the four watercolour landscapes given as a wedding present to George Saxton and his bride. Paul Morel, the hero of *Sons and Lovers*, takes his art much more seriously and strenuously. Through youth and early manhood painting is for him a very important means of expression. And in later years, it is suggested, it will become a profession and a way of life.

> He was gradually making it possible to earn a livelihood by his art. Liberty's had taken several of his painted designs on various stuffs, and he could sell designs for embroideries, for altar-cloths, and similar things, in one or two places. . . . The applied arts interested him very much. At the same time he laboured slowly at his pictures. He loved to paint large figures, full of light, but not merely made up of lights and cast shadows, like the impressionists; rather definite figures that had a certain luminous quality, like some of Michael Angelo's people. And these he fitted into a landscape, in what he thought true proportion. He worked a great deal from memory, using everybody he knew. He believed firmly in his work, that it was good and valuable. In spite of fits of depression, shrinking, everything, he believed in his work.

The kind of painting described here is the last of several stages in the development of Paul Morel's art as this development is described in the novel. The very first picture that is characterised in any detail is a sketch of one of the women spinners in the surgical garment factory in which Paul works in Nottingham. But the picture could scarcely be called naturalistic or even realistic. The factory girl (who reminded Paul of Elaine in "Idylls of the King" and who "appealed to his romantic side") is fully translated into one of the familiar forms of Victorian romanticism. The sketch portrays Connie "sitting on the stool before the wheel, her flowing mane of red hair on her rusty black frock, her red mouth shut and serious, running the scarlet thread off the hank onto the reel". It is clearly a work in the Pre-Raphaelite style. The next phase of Paul's progress as an artist comes with his new found admiration for his native industrial landscape, an admiration which he has to defend against the more conventional ideas of the beautiful held by his mother and by Clara Dawes. This new perception expresses itself in a "sketch of a colliery at work" which is of special significance to Paul because it is the first to attract the attention of the wealthy art partons of Nottingham. This realistic mode of painting is in its turn replaced by another in which it is Paul's aim to depict that which underlies shape and form, "the shimmering protoplasm in the leaves and everywhere, and not the stiffness of the shape". Paul goes on to tell Miriam that "the shape is a dead crust. The shimmer is inside reality." And when he proceeds to explain his intention in terms of another picture, a group of pine trees caught in the glare of the evening sun, it becomes clear that his purpose is essentially the same as that of the German expressionist painters. "Now look at them," he orders Miriam, "and tell me, are they pine trees or are they red coals, standing-up pieces of fire in that darkness? There's God's burning bush for you, that burned not away."

One function of these references to Paul's painting is to suggest his development in perception and feeling. Another is to establish the all important setting in time of the hero and his evolution. *Sons and Lovers* is primarily a novel about the play of historical forces upon the life of an individual. (And in terms of the development of Lawrence's own thinking, it can be seen as the first stage in his effort to formulate process in terms of history, an effort which is carried further in certain chapters of *Twilight in Italy* and completed in "Study of Thomas Hardy", which is at one and the same time an extension of and a comment upon that more impersonal novel, *The Rainbow*.) Published discussion of *Sons and Lovers* has usually been divided over what the themes of the novel are. Broadly speaking, it can be said that there are those who see the book as primarily an account of an oedipal situation and those who prefer to regard it as a novel of education, a *Bildungsroman*. My own sympathies are with this latter group. For though in Lawrence's rendering of the relationship between Paul Morel and his parents and in his comments upon it there is much to justify the Freudian reading, such an interpretation constitutes something of a restrictive and thus false emphasis. To see the book solely in oedipal terms is to deny its great richness of implication and to incur the risk of reducing the work to a mere sensational case history. To propose Paul's love for his mother as the chief subject of the novel is to be encumbered with a constricting definition. This love is rather the symptom of something else. The situation of Paul Morel is one that is best defined in terms of history and generation. More specifically, *Sons and Lovers* is a portrait of the artist, a *Künstlerroman*; it concerns the struggle of an artist to develop and to hold true to his vision at a particular moment in time.

Throughout the novel, Paul's situation and his particular agony are defined in terms of a pronouncedly historical perspective. Although the main subject of *Sons and Lovers* is the childhood, adolescence and early manhood of Paul Morel, for about the first hundred pages of the book Paul is only a peripheral character. The main focus is upon his parents. And the terrible, destructive conflict between these two constitutes the first and most powerful influence in making Paul what he is. The bitter antagonism between husband and wife originates in the failure of Walter Morel to live up to certain moral and social demands made of him by his wife. These demands are founded upon attitudes which reach far back into English history. In the opening pages of the novel where the first and basic lines of the portrait of Mrs. Morel are established, her character is to a great extent defined by reference to her forebears and to an outlook derived from them. "She still had her high moral sense," we are told, "inherited from generations of Puritans." And her puritanism is traced back directly to distinguished Nottingham ancestors at the time of the Civil War: "Mrs. Morel came of a good old burgher family, famous independents who had fought with Colonel Hutchinson, and who remained stout Congregationalists."[9] But her uncompromising determination, which ultimately destroys Walter Morel, is inherited more immediately from her father; "She was puritan, like her father, high-minded, and really stern." This influence also appears to explain Mrs. Morel's choice of name for her son: "Her father was to her the type of all men. And George

[9] Colonel Hutchinson is a prominent figure in the history of Lawrence's native region. He was a fervent supporter of Parliament in the Civil War and a member of the High Court of Commission that condemned Charles I. He was also allegedly involved in the conspiracy against Charles II known as the Yorkshire plot. For further details of his career, see *The Victoria County History of Nottinghamshire* (London, 1910), vol. I, pp. 343–56.

Coppard, proud in his bearing, handsome and rather bitter; who preferred theology in reading, and who drew near in sympathy only to one man, the Apostle Paul; who was harsh in government, and in familiarity ironic; who ignored all sensuous pleasure:—he was very different from the miner."

Walter Morel has no history, at least no certain history. We are told only that "His grandfather was a French refugee who had married an English barmaid—if it had been a marriage". He lives for the moment, unconscious of himself, unaware. The conflict between husband and wife is inevitable: "She fought to make him undertake his responsibilities, to make him fulfil his obligations. But he was too different from her. His nature was purely sensuous, and she strove to make him moral, religious."[10] One part of the cost of Mrs. Morel's slow victory over her husband is his gradual degeneration into ugliness and brutality. This is what repels Paul from his father and what brings about an intensification of affection between Paul and his mother. Paul's sensitivity is also such that he is quick to appreciate her energy, her principle, her refinement and her interest in books and ideas. Nevertheless, there is always a tacit reservation in Paul's admiration for his mother. Despite his great devotion to her, he is very critical of her outlook and beliefs. There is a tension in his attitude to her which is altogether different from

[10] The conflict between the Morels can be seen as a version of what was to become for Lawrence a crucial episode in the history of the European consciousness. A few years after completing *Sons and Lovers* he was to write in the essay "The Lemon Gardens" in *Twilight in Italy*:

The Puritans made the last great attack on the God who is Me. When they beheaded Charles the First, the king by Divine Right, they destroyed, symbolically, for ever, the supremacy of the Me who am the image of God, the Me of the flesh, of the senses, Me, the tiger burning bright, me the king, the Lord, the aristocrat, me who am divine because I am the body of God.

what may be suggested by the adjective oedipal. We may perhaps express it by saying that from quite early in life the artist Paul Morel is an unconvinced puritan.

The meaning of this difficult but inevitable word as it is used in *Sons and Lovers* is to some extent clarified by the first half dozen paragraphs of the book in which the historical perspective of the novel is clearly established (in *Sons and Lovers* as in *The White Peacock* and *The Rainbow* the narrative is prefaced with a notion of process and history): these describe how the predominantly agrarian order of the Notts. and Derby border country was invaded "by the large mines of the financiers". They tell of the many industrial incursions during the age of Palmerston into the old rural scene that is evoked by references to Robin Hood's Well and "the ruined priory of the Carthusians". The brisk movement of the second paragraph conveys something of the urgency of new activity which suddenly disturbed the quiet landscape of woods, sandstone brooks and cornfields. During this great upheaval the Morel home itself is built. The point is that Mrs. Morel's puritanism is different from that of the seventeenth-century Colonel Hutchinson. It is a puritanism which has behind it the fact and the experience of the industrial revolution. In the novel the puritan tradition is seen as an important part of the impetus behind industrialisation. Mrs. Morel's father was an engineer; more significantly Mrs. Morel herself strongly endorses the notion of industry both in the modern and in the older sense of the word. In *Sons and Lovers* post-industrial puritanism is shown to have certain very distinct connotations. In fact, these form a cluster of concepts which may be said to constitute the themes that control the major episodes of the novel. And since Lawrence himself as narrator names and employs these abstractions, it will not seem too much of a conceptualisation of the novel to list them here. The words are business, class, town and nature. And in respect of all of them Paul's attitudes differ very considerably from those of his mother.

Mrs. Morel takes intense pleasure at the thought of her two sons pursuing their careers in business and industry. But Paul, even before he starts to work at Jordan's, "seemed to feel the business world, with its regulated system of values, and its impersonality, and he dreaded it". After a childhood and youth lived on the margin of the countryside, the industrial routine seems a form of imprisonment, a frightening diminution of personal liberty: "Already he was a prisoner of industrialism. . . . Already his heart went down. He was being taken into bondage. His freedom in the beloved home valley was going now." Mrs. Morel, unlike Paul, is unequivocal in her love of urban life. She was born in Nottingham and likes to talk "Nottingham and Nottingham people". She is also very happy to think of her eldest son working in London and Paul in Nottingham: "Now she had two sons in the world. She could think of two places, great centres of industry, and feel that she had put a man into each of them, that these men would work out what *she* wanted; they were derived from her, they were of her, and their works also would be hers." Concerning this particular feature of Mrs. Morel's character, a small but telling incident occurs when she and Paul first walk to Willey Farm. Once they leave the road and start to walk across the country, Mrs. Morel becomes uncertain of the way; she is unable to detect the path through the wood and Paul remarks to her, "You've got town feet, somehow or other, you have." Paul himself is unable to share wholeheartedly his mother's love for the town. In this respect there is in him a cultural tension. His life is divided between Nottingham where he works and the un-spoiled countryside around Miriam's home at Willey Farm where he spends so much of his early life. There is a similar tension between his need to work long hours at the

22

1 Albert Moore, "The Toilet"　　　　(*By courtesy of the Tate Gallery, London*)

2 Burne-Jones, "Vespetiea Quies" (*By courtesy of the Tate Gallery, London*)

factory and his desire to devote himself more and more to his art.

Mrs. Morel's pretension to involvement in the success-ful business world also expresses itself, as might be expected, in her ideas of class. She can never forget that in marrying a collier she married beneath her, and her main aspiration for her children is that they shall succeed in returning to the bourgeoisie. Regarding her expecta-tions of Paul we are told that "she frankly *wanted* him to climb into the middle classes, a thing not very difficult, she knew. And she wanted him in the end to marry a lady." But again in this matter there is a sharp divergence between Mrs. Morel's feelings and those of Paul. In one conversation between them which takes place after Paul has returned from visiting some wealthy people who are interested in his paintings, he tells his mother: "I don't want to belong to the well-to-do middle class. I like my common people best." In answer to her objections Paul suggests that ". . . from the middle classes one gets ideas, and from the common people—life itself, warmth". Mrs. Morel then proceeds to win the argument by suggesting that Paul go and talk to his father's pals. But her momentary victory does not end the disagreement. Here as elsewhere Paul is making a very serious criticism of his mother both for being an adherent of the middle class and also for being a woman of ideas.

It may well be that the somewhat unnatural intensity of Paul's love for his mother comprises something of an unconscious effort on his part to compensate for his down-right contradiction of her attitudes and hopes. In other words, the element of incestuous feeling in the mother–son relationship is not so much an original cause in the narrative as a consequence of something else. It is a sort of camouflage for Paul's incorrigible dissent from the Victorian puritanism that is such an important part of the nature and outlook of his admired mother. This dissent is extremely radical and extends even to a rejection of the Christian faith itself. Doctrinally and intellectually Paul's situation is one that was very common among intelligent young Protestants in the closing years of the nineteenth century. There is his "beginning to question the orthodox creed", his study of Renan's *Vie de Jésus*, his setting "full sail towards agnosticism" and his connection with the "Socialist, Suffragette, Unitarian people in Nottingham". But this questioning of old ideas which is so painful to his mother is not merely wanton. It is not a denial of commitment but a search for a new commitment that will allow a greater spiritual freedom. Paul never surrenders that concern with principle, that moral scrupulousness and earnestness which in the service of whatever body of belief are the primary characteristics of the puritan mind. He may be unable to accept many of his mother's beliefs and attitudes; he is not, however, likely to become like his father. Puritanism as a way of feeling and as a set of the will is strong in his nature. It is his task to adapt it in such a way as to make it serviceable in his time and generation.

This view of the basic situation in the novel makes the ultimate failure of Paul's two love affairs more readily intelligible. They break down eventually not because they are thwarted by an oedipal relationship between Paul and his mother but as a result of certain difficulties of self-definition which Paul experiences as a result of his own residual, latterday puritanism. These difficulties can be seen most clearly in the story of Paul's love for Clara Dawes. Critics taking a psychoanalytical approach to the book regard Clara and her husband Baxter as Paul's surrogates for his father and mother. And in making love to Clara and fighting Baxter and then eventually restoring them to each other Paul is seen to be acting out certain childhood dreams.[11] This is quite a convincing reading.

[11] See Daniel A. Weiss, *Oedipus in Nottingham: D. H. Lawrence* (Seattle, 1962), pp. 26–37.

Indeed, to judge from the implausibility of the scene in which Paul hands Clara back to her husband, one suspects that Lawrence may have been writing to a thesis. Nevertheless, even if this is the case, even if Frieda did encourage Lawrence to insert some Freudian notions into the final draft,[12] there is no doubt that the Clara portion of the novel has other and richer implications because of its positioning in the deeper thematic pattern.

For all the full and careful individualising of Clara as a woman, she has also to be regarded, mainly because of the inevitable contrast with Miriam, as something of a representative figure. She too is a product of a certain phase of protestant and industrial culture. She is the independent woman able to earn her own living, socially more resistant to conformity than her mother's generation had been, politically conscious and active as a suffragette, and sexually dissatisfied with a husband who attempts to maintain the superannuated role of masculine dominance. Unlike Baxter Dawes, Paul Morel is able to accept Clara's independence and the relationship which develops is the great confirmation for each of them. The failure of this at one time most exhilarated relationship to eventuate in marriage has directly to do with Paul's reluctance to delimit himself. Clara is of course a married woman and this fact always stands in the way of any discussion of the future between her and Paul. But it is also a pretext for evading a far less readily soluble problem. For when the break between them finally occurs, it is occasioned by precisely the same feature of Paul's nature which had formerly distressed both Miriam

[12] Frieda had become interested in the theories of Freud some time before she met Lawrence in the spring of 1912. It seems very possible that she communicated some of her interest and knowledge to Lawrence during the later months of that year when they were living together in Italy and Lawrence was completing the last draft of *Sons and Lovers*. See Frederick J. Hoffman, *Freudianism and the Literary Mind* (Baton Rouge, 1958), pp. 153, 154.

and his mother, a lack of unity and firmness in his character, a certain inconsistency and unreliability.

> Watching him unknown, she said to herself there was no stability about him. He was fine in his way, passionate and able to give her drinks of pure life when he was in one mood. And now he looked paltry and insignificant. There was something evanescent about Morel, she thought, something shifting and false. He would never make sure ground for any woman to stand on.

There is in Paul Morel, as Clara sees, a profound reluctance to limit the fluidity of feeling and personality. Until the very last page of the novel, he finds nothing that deserves, or is able to compel, such a sacrifice. In his work at the factory, in his relationship with his mother, with Miriam and with Clara, Paul has some very instructive experiences of human contact; but none of them is able to elicit from him any sort of commitment or the sacrifice of emotional freedom which commitment entails.

What Miriam brings to Paul's education is considerably different from that brought by Clara. Miriam is invariably associated with the country as Clara is with the town. And far from being in any real sense a modern woman, she represents a somewhat archaic type of femininity. In the very first paragraph describing Miriam, Lawrence identifies the phase of history from which her outlook is derived.

> The girl was romantic in her soul. Everywhere was a Walter Scott heroine being loved by men with helmets or with plumes in their caps. She herself was something of a princess turned into a swine-girl in her own imagination. . . .
>
> Her great companion was her mother. They were both brown-eyed, and inclined to be mystical, such women as treasure religion inside them, breathe it in their nostrils, and see the whole of life in a mist thereof. So to Miriam, Christ and God made one great figure, which she loved tremblingly and passionately when a tremendous sunset

burned out the western sky, and Ediths, and Lucys, and Rowenas, Brian de Bois Guilberts, Rob Roys, and Guy Mannerings, rustled the sunny leaves in the morning, or sat in her bedroom aloft, alone, when it snowed. That was life to her.

Miriam and Clara, then, belong to different traditions of Victorian womanhood. Miriam is in comparison the unliberated woman who makes her lot tolerable by indulging in categories of feeling and sentiment which were first made available and commended in the years around the beginning of the nineteenth century. Towards Miriam Lawrence often displays a stridency that shows him still too close to the relationship for him to give a proper account of it. For although he deplores Miriam's anthropomorphism, it was, after all, "in this atmosphere of subtle intimacy, this meeting in their common feeling for something in nature, that their love started". And though Paul is irritated by the excessive spirituality of the Leivers family which makes them so strained and awkward in the ordinary matters of daily life, they foster his art in a way that others, even his mother, are incapable of doing. "But Mrs. Leivers and her children were almost his disciples. They kindled him and made him glow to his work, whereas his mother's influence was to make him quietly determined, patient, dogged, unwearied." The relationship with Miriam and her family is one of the most important impulses to Paul's development as an artist. Despite the discomfort of the peculiarly high-pitched intensity of the relationship, Miriam "brought forth to him his imaginations". "In contact with Miriam he gained insight; his vision went deeper. From his mother he drew the life-warmth, the strength to produce; Miriam urged this warmth into intensity like a white light."

Paul's ultimate denial of commitment to Miriam Leivers constitutes one of the most painful stages in the

27

novel, because it brings about the end of a very long established relationship and because the effects of repudiation are more damaging, more destructive for Miriam than they are for Clara. Whereas Clara had only desired that Paul subordinate his feelings to the fact of their physical relationship, Miriam wants something more intense and more demanding. She wants Paul to limit and control his consciousness so as to allow his responses to reverberate in unison with her own. She wants a spiritual communion.

> She wanted to show him a certain wild-rose bush she had discovered. She knew it was wonderful. And yet, till he had seen it, she felt it had not come into her soul. Only he could make it her own, immortal. . . .
>
> It was very still. The tree was tall and straggling. It had thrown its briars over a hawthorn bush, and its long streamers trailed thick right down to the grass, slashing the darkness everywhere with great spilt stars, pure white. . . . Point after point the steady roses shone out to them, seeming to kindle something in their souls. The dusk came like smoke around and still did not put out the flowers.
>
> Paul looked into Miriam's eyes. She was pale and expectant with wonder, her lips parted, her dark eyes lay open to him. His look seemed to travel down into her. Her soul quivered. It was the communion she wanted. He turned aside, as if pained. . . .
>
> "Let us go," he said.
>
> There was a cool scent of ivory roses—a white, virgin scent. Something made him feel anxious and imprisoned. The two walked in silence.
>
> "Till Sunday," he said quietly, and left her; and she walked home slowly, feeling her soul satisfied with the holiness of the night. He stumbled down the path. And as soon as he was out of the wood, in the free open meadow, where he could breathe, he started to run as fast as he could. It was like a delicious delirium in his veins.

Paul is unable to commit himself to the kind of relationship which Miriam demands; he cannot tolerate the restriction and the claustrophobia. What begins as an adolescent idyll continues past its proper term and ends as a history of gathering bitterness, failure and recrimination.

None of the three women who in their different ways assist Paul's development is able to command his complete allegiance. On his side there are very serious reservations in each relationship. (With his mother the fact of reservation is all the more painful because of normal filial feeling and because of Paul's sense of special indebtedness owing to the particular family situation.) Paul's career is not principally a matter of tension between alternative relationships, as Freudian critics suggest; it is rather a process involving three stages. The distinct and particular character of each of these stages, the way each develops and grows only finally to die away, creates a considerable part of the unsentimental poignance of the book. In one way the three women may be seen to represent different traditions of thought and feeling, each of which affects him but none of which dominates him. In his mother there is the moral earnestness and the will characteristic of an earlier puritan generation; in Miriam the intense cult of feeling that derives from the Romantic era; and in Clara the moral independence, self-consciousness and confusion of the "new woman". As man and as artist Paul is strongly affected by all of these; he can commit himself to none of them.

At the very end of the book, when his mother is dead and both Miriam and Clara have gone from him, Paul undergoes a period of profound depression. In his new and total isolation he realises he has nothing to live for. Even his painting is not enough of a vital commitment because, as he concludes, "Painting is not living."

> He would not admit that he wanted to die, to have done.
> He would not own that life had beaten him or that death
> had beaten him. . . .

So the weeks went on. Always alone, his soul oscillated, first on the side of death, then on the side of life, doggedly. The real agony was that he had nowhere to go, nothing to do, nothing to say, and *was* nothing himself.

The difficult freedom that Paul has chosen almost ends by destroying him. And only his will prevents him from succumbing to the sense of his own isolation and hopelessness. In the last paragraph of the book, Paul finally wills himself to make the one commitment it is left to him to make; and here we see his uncommitted, unordered and thus fatally vulnerable emotional life brought under control. There comes at last his firm resolve to restrict the free play and movement of consciousness in the interest of survival and of life itself. His physical attitude suggests the new rigidity.

On every side the immense dark silence seemed pressing him, so tiny a spark, into extinction, and yet, almost nothing, he would not be extinct. . . .
But no, he would not give in. Turning sharply, he walked towards the city's gold phosphorescence. His fists were shut, his mouth set fast. He would not take that direction, to the darkness, to follow her. He walked towards the faintly humming, glowing town, quickly.

For Paul Morel youth is the freedom successively to deny the aegis of each of the three characters closest to him. Manhood is the recognition of the dangers of this kind of atomistic individualism.

Paul's earlier reluctance to make commitments is in great part explained by the fact that he is an artist. The narrator defines the artist as a man marked by a duality of consciousness which makes for distance and equivocation in human relationships. He has the normal subjective perception of the ordinary man, but simultaneously there is in him a more objective mode of perception, or what Lawrence in the novel repeatedly calls "the eye of the artist". For example, on one occasion Miriam is upset by the division in Paul's perception of her: "Later she saw him remark her new blouse, saw that the artist approved, but it won from him not a spark of warmth." This severance between personal perception and the artist's perception is what brings about the most painful and violent episode in the book, Paul's fight with Baxter Dawes, the man who stands to him in the relationship of the *homme sensuel moyen* to the artist. After the event, when the two men are to some extent reconciled, Dawes explains that what had so deeply angered him was Paul's laughter when Dawes had encountered him arm in arm with Clara. Paul denies that he ever laughed, "except as I'm always laughing". And when we turn back to the actual incident, we find that this customary laughter is Paul's ironic recognition of his own dual consciousness. Here is the actual incident as Lawrence describes it:

> One evening, as Paul and she were walking along Woodborough Road, they met Dawes. Morel knew something about the bearing of the man approaching, but he was absorbed in his thinking at the moment, so that only his artist's eye watched the form of the stranger. Then he suddenly turned to Clara with a laugh, and put his hand on her shoulder, saying, laughing:
> "But we walk side by side, and yet I'm in London arguing with an imaginary Orpen; and where are you?"
> At that instant Dawes passed, almost touching Morel.[13]

This sumultaneity of perception which makes for ironic laughter is, so the book suggests, what differentiates the

[13] The reference to Sir William Orpen, a fashionable Edwardian painter helps to specify Paul's situation in terms of art history. Even more interesting in this respect is Paul's interest in the applied arts and his designs for Liberty's. The founding of this famous firm in 1875 by Sir Arthur Lasenby Liberty marks an important stage in the repudiation of mid-Victorian taste. *Style Liberty*, in fact, became one of the many synonyms for Art Nouveau. Perhaps Paul's designs may be seen as further evidence of his desire for a freedom and fluidity of consciousness as opposed to the more characteristically Victorian rigidity of his mother's outlook.

artist from his fellow man and what makes him on occasion menacing to them. His rare insight and vision also give added meaning to Paul's name (and to his nickname, 'Postle). This two-fold vision is something which neither his mother nor Miriam nor Clara can readily appreciate. Here, for instance, is a small incident that clearly dramatises the difference between Paul's powers of vision and Clara's. They are walking in the country.

> They came near to the colliery. It stood quite still and black among the corn-fields, its immense heap of slag seen rising almost from the oats.
> "What a pity there is a coal-pit here where it is so pretty!" said Clara.
> "Do you think so?" he answered. "You see, I am so used to it I should miss it. No; and I like pits here and there. I like the rows of trucks and the headstocks, and the steam in the daytime, and the lights at night. When I was a boy, I always thought a pillar of cloud by day and a pillar of fire by night was a pit, with its steam, and its lights, and the burning bank,—and I thought the Lord was always at the pit-top."

This distinction between Clara's conventional notion of "the pretty" and Paul's more comprehensive vision has its exact counterpart in Mrs. Morel's hesitation in sharing Paul's interest in the visual qualities of the colliery when the two first walk to Willey Farm. Miriam has more experience of art but, in the final instance, she too is unable to share Paul's radical impersonality. The following paragraph epitomises their ultimate irreconcilability.

> He was discussing Michael Angelo. It felt to her as if she were fingering the very quivering tissue, the very proto-plasm of life, as she heard him. It gave her deepest satis-faction. And in the end it frightened her. There he lay in the white intensity of his search, and his voice gradually filled her with fear, so level it was, almost inhuman, as if in a trance.

Such incidents reveal the difference between Paul's consciousness and that of each of the women closest to him. And they suggest the extent to which Paul's ultimate isolation is something more than a social and historical matter. *Sons and Lovers* is most essentially about the difficulty of attaining a proper personal freedom and autonomy, but it is also about the particular kind of freedom which is the necessary condition of the artist's life.

Thematic organisation is only a small part of the total effect of a novel. And to concentrate on this alone is often to ignore the very qualities which comprise the distinction of the work. That criticism has for so long been concerned primarily with the themes of this particular novel can be explained by Lawrence's uncertainty, his ambivalence even, in his own interpretations of the story, both as narrator and in his letters. This uncertainty is undeniably an imperfection in the novel. But it does not detract seriously from the great power and memorability of the reading experience offered by the book. There is here a texture and a creative energy in the medium of words that testify to a rare and a major work of literature. The most striking quality of this literary art is its visual richness. It is of a kind that can be suggested by Paul Morel's own paintings. For if the Pre-Raphaelite portrait recalls something of the ethos of *The White Peacock*, the straightforward realism which we may presume informed the sketch of "a colliery at work" helps us to define the new fictional art of *Sons and Lovers*.

When he began writing *The Lost Girl* in Italy in 1913, Lawrence told Edward Garnett, his friend and literary advisor, that it was "all analytical—quite unlike *Sons and Lovers*, not a bit visualised".[14] This stress upon the visual

14 *Letters*, p. 193.

which is to be found in so many of Lawrence's references to *Sons and Lovers* suggests an appropriate refinement of the notion of realism as a definition of the art of this third novel; for it enables us to emphasise the more incisive, the more delicate power of seeing that is at work in *Sons and Lovers* compared with that in other familiar works of realism such as Arnold Bennett's *Old Wives' Tale* or Flaubert's *Madame Bovary*. A passage that illustrates this pre-eminent quality of the writing is the following description of Paul and his mother going through the yard of Jordan's factory on their way to the interview for Paul's first job.

> They emerged into a wide yard, like a well, with buildings all round. It was littered with straw and boxes, and card-board. The sunshine actually caught one crate whose straw was streaming on to the yard like gold. But elsewhere the place was like a pit. There were several doors, and two flights of steps. Straight in front, on a dirty glass door at the top of a staircase, loomed the ominous words "Thomas Jordan and Son—Surgical Appliances". Mrs. Morel went first, her son followed her. Charles I mounted his scaffold with a lighter heart than had Paul Morel as he followed his mother up the dirty steps to the dirty door.
>
> She pushed open the door, and stood in pleased surprise. In front of her was a big warehouse, with creamy paper parcels everywhere, and clerks, with their shirt-sleeves rolled back, were going about in an at-home sort of way. The light was subdued, the glossy cream parcels seemed luminous, the counters were of dark brown wood. All was quiet and very homely. Mrs. Morel took two steps forward, then waited. Paul stood behind her. She had on her Sunday bonnet and a black veil; he wore a boy's broad white collar and a Norfolk suit.

In the novel these two paragraphs are not as conspicuous as they must inevitably appear here. In their proper context they are, for all their rich texture, incidental to the larger narrative course. Nevertheless, although the moment described is not one of the more important ones in the novel, it is still a good and typical instance of Lawrence's specifically visual method. The initial anxiety and the subsequent relief are both related to things seen. And in a way that is characteristic of the many quick and agile shifts in the author's point of view in this novel, the writing moves from what is perceived to the perceivers themselves. The vulnerability of the Morels at this particular instant and the pathos of the whole situation are evoked in the last few sentences when Lawrence steps away from his characters leaving them placed in a completed tableau.

The most striking quality in this passage is the rightness, the correct representativeness of the visual detail. The last two lines, which give us the appearance of Paul and Mrs. Morel, are supported by many previous descriptions of them; but this one sentence alone gives us Mrs. Morel's sense of decorum and social occasion and also (purely in terms of his dress) Paul's awkward, rather painful suspension between the worlds of boyhood and adulthood. Earlier in the passage a very few items of description are sufficient for Lawrence to establish the darkness and dirtiness of the factory exterior and then the surprising and reassuring attractiveness of the interior. And as is so often the case in Lawrence's writing, objects are subordinated to the concern with atmosphere and light. The luminousness of the parcels is what makes the inside of the factory psychologically comforting; and this luminousness is specified by reference to the "subdued" light and the "dark brown wood" of the counters on which the glossy cream parcels lie. One other characteristically Lawrentian feature of this passage is the contextual effect of the third sentence of the first paragraph. It is the sort of pleasing detail that the eye does in fact take in, even on an occasion such as that presented here when perception is influenced by nervousness and apprehension. This kind of added and arresting detail is

35

one of the more readily observable distinctions of Lawrence's creative prose. It is not an extra step in a quest for a more encyclopaedic naturalism. Rather it is the detail which modifies the homogeneity of a given moment of perception. Often (such is the affirmative quality of Lawrence's vision) it is the very detail which constitutes something of colour or grace in an object of perception which is otherwise uninteresting, too familiar, or depressing.

The specific, day to day realities of the family life of the Morels are presented with the same careful accuracy. Lawrence has managed to convey, in a way that no other modern English novelist has, the full density of a close family life. (Only at the beginning of Part Two of the book, when Paul begins his visits to Willey Farm and thus has a standard for comparison, do we realise how fully we as readers have been enmeshed like Paul himself in the constricted life of the Morel home.) This sense of closeness is in great part explained by the deep and unceasing conflict between Morel and his wife and at times between Morel and his children. But it is also enhanced by the unobtrusive presence in the narrative of so many accounts of very ordinary household activities such as ironing, cooking, the laying of meals, going to the market every Friday, baking bread, fetching wages from the pit offices. All these have the involving immediacy that is customary in Lawrence's writing. The following description is an example of one of the activities peculiar to a mining community; it shows Morel and his children making fuses to blast down the coal in the pit.

But the best time for the young children was when he made fuses. Morel fetched a sheaf of long sound wheat-straws from the attic. These he cleaned with his hand, till each one gleamed like a stalk of gold, after which he cut the straws into lengths of about six inches, leaving, if he could, a notch at the bottom of each piece. He always had a beautifully sharp knife that could cut a straw clean without hurting it. Then he set in the middle of the table a heap of gunpowder, a little pile of black grains upon the white-scrubbed board. He made and trimmed the straws while Paul and Annie filled and plugged them. Paul loved to see the black grains trickle down a crack in his palm into the mouth of the straw, peppering jollily downwards till the straw was full. Then he bunged up the mouth with a bit of soap—which he got on his thumb-nail from a pat in a saucer—and the straw was finished.

Here again in this passage of vivid childhood memory we have what Dorothy Van Ghent has called "the authenticity of a faithfully observed, concrete actuality". She ascribes this quality to "Lawrence's controlling sense of the characterful integrity of objects".[15] In terms of Lawrence's medium, the actual words that he uses, this sense can often be traced back to the briefest of phrases; here for instance it is in the words "a crack in his palm" and "peppering jollily". This is precisely what constitutes what I have termed the added detail, that further access of insight so characteristic of Lawrence's visualisation. And in terms of the general movement of the novel as a whole this description has exactly the same function as the detail has within the description itself. It is one of the passages which mitigates the movement from horror to fear and thence to dislike and disgust which governs the presentation of Walter Morel. An important part of Lawrence's genius, specifically as a writer, is that he never permits us to see anything, be it a man or a factory yard, in simplified frames or categories; he constantly alerts us to the full variegation of a perception. The authenticity of the sensuous detail is an important part of the aesthetic effect of the novel. Yet the great abundance of this detail is always kept properly subordinate to the narrative and thematic development. There is here no piling up of

[15] Dorothy Van Ghent, *The English Novel, Form and Function* (New York, 1959), p. 256.

37

detail for its own sake after the fashion of the naturalists.[16] Everything is carefully arranged and patterned to further the articulation of the themes.

One principle of the organisation is provided by the narrative voice, which also constitutes a very striking feature of the art of the novel. The succession of experiences is organised and presented to us through the mediation of a narrator who, though in principle performing the same general office as that of the Victorian novelists, is in practice unusual, particular. Purely in terms of

[16] Nevertheless, there are certain features in the novel that bring this particular fictional aesthetic to mind. And their presence helps, through the comparison they inevitably involve, further to characterise Lawrence's art. Heredity is shown to be a powerful influence upon Paul's life, but the particular ideas of heredity which Lawrence suggests are more intricate than anything in the Rougon-Macquart. Also the lengthy description of Paul's first day at work ending with the sentence, "The day in the factory was just twelve hours long", might seem at first sight to be intended both to make a social indictment and to establish the power of harsh environment. But this, of course, is not the actual effect of this section of the novel. Lawrence's eye is such that the routine of factory and colliery life is seen in infinitely more numerous and richer categories than are to be found in Zola's often "got up" descriptions of work. Indeed, the distinction of Lawrence's rendering of ordinary experience brings out the sentimentality and self-indulgence of much of Zola's writing about the real, the harsh, the sordid. (The work which particularly invites comparison with Lawrence's "colliery novel" is, of course, *Germinal*.) One further feature of Zola's novels which may be of relevance to *Sons and Lovers* is the well known failure of so many women in his books to find happiness or stability with a second husband or lover. A recent critic of Zola who regards this idea as deriving from Michelet's *L'Amour* has described Zola's view in these terms: "What Zola asks us to believe is that a woman, having once cohabited with a man, remains tied to him by indissoluble physiological bonds, even though her affection for him has been destroyed, and even though, having been abandoned by him, she has placed her trust and her hopes of happiness in another man. . . ." (F. W. J. Hemmings, *Emile Zola*, Oxford, 1966, p. 45.) No such theory is enunciated in *Sons and Lovers*; but its presence in Lawrence's mind as a result of his reading *Germinal*, in which it figures prominently, might help to explain the only unconvincing episode in the whole novel, the handing back of Clara Dawes to her husband.

vocabulary, Lawrence's narrative manner is eminently new in the history of English fiction. Often his words are those of Midland speech rather than those of familiar literary language; we encounter, for instance, words like barkled, bursten, shapen, fridging, eddish, glistered, twitchel. And this feature of the narrative voice is further accentuated by the similes and even by the sentence construction. These are things which remind us of Lawrence's social as well as his geographical origins. And the tremendous advancement in the social range of the English novel represented by *Sons and Lovers* is brought home to us again by Lawrence's several explanations to a middle-class reading public of various phenomena of working-class life. On one occasion the remark is part of the text, as for instance when Lawrence explains that the table fork "is a modern introduction which has still scarcely reached common people"; on another it is a footnote explaining a working-class or dialect word. In such details of the narrative we can best see the effect of social change on the form and tone of fiction.

The sort of relationship which Lawrence in his capacity as narrator offers the reader is also considerably different from that of earlier novelists. It is less relaxed. Lawrence does not halt his story for chat, reminiscence or anecdote after the style of Scott, nor does he offer George Eliot's kind of lengthy moral analysis. The tone is that of a young man utterly confident of himself and of his opinions ("Sometimes life takes hold of one, carries the body along, accomplishes one's history, and yet is not real, but leaves oneself as it were slurred over") but not sufficiently at one with his readers to want to discuss anything with them. His main aim is to get on with the telling of his story. At times there is an almost breathless haste as Lawrence strives to include all the many incidents that reveal the life of the Morels during the years between Mrs. Morel's marriage and her death. For the summary narrative subsumes a multiplicity of episodes, scenes and dialogue that shows an amazing prodigality of invention and imagination. And at every stage there is the same visualisation, the same intensely seen actuality which constitutes the pre-eminent quality of the writing. Sometimes it is present in a single sentence such as the one describing the view from Paul's window when, during the period of convalescence, he would "see the fluffy horses feeding at the troughs in the field, scattering their hay on the trodden yellow snow; watch the miners troop home—small, black figures trailing slowly in gangs across the white field". Sometimes it is a matter of a completely sustained scene such as the one in which young Arthur Morel steals Beatrice Wyld's hair comb. The subject here, a joking adolescent sexuality, is not an unusual one, yet it would be hard to find the equal of this scene in any other modern novel. And it is typical of Lawrence's creative largesse that this extremely fine achievement should be peripheral to the central narrative concern. (It serves as an example of a couple in whom sexuality is not tortured in the way it is for Paul and Miriam.) In *Sons and Lovers* the narrator may be occasionally unconvincing in his interpretation of the story, but his art is already assured, finely textured and compelling.

Art is perhaps too general a term. For Lawrence's achievement as a novelist is scarcely homogeneous. Each of his major novels constitutes a distinct and particular kind of fiction, just as each stage in Paul Morel's career as a painter entails a distinct kind of painting. *Sons and Lovers* is as different from *The White Peacock* as it is from *The Rainbow*. In order to define this singularity one can only resort to the notion of realism. It is a difficult term but one which Lawrence himself as a critic readily employed and one which is indispensible to a description of Lawrence's development as a novelist. With reference to *Sons and Lovers*, the term helps to stress an accuracy in the presentation of the chosen social and geographical milieu which strikes us as documentary. Lawrence's precise and energetic description of the life of a late Victorian mining town is, after all, what makes *Sons and Lovers* one of the great documentations of English experience. Those who are at all acquainted with the old colliery towns of the Midlands will have no hesitation in recommending this novel to future social historians as the work which more than any other in fiction or non-fiction gives the true style, the detailed human reality of this type of life. Just to list some of the passages which describe the life of Bestwood will be enough to suggest the comprehensiveness and the accuracy of Lawrence's report. There are scenes which show the co-operation of mining families when a child is born, the frustration of short time, the role of the minister, the anticipation and the pleasure of a Bank Holiday, the fear and anxiety when pit accidents occur, the elegiac drama of death and funeral arrangements in the collier's small house and the system of "paying out" in the butty's house on a Friday night. And along with this documentary quality of the book, there is in the registering of the small as well as the large entities of experience an accuracy of seeing which, despite Lawrence's own later use of the word as a pejorative term, we are prompted to call photographic. Yet neither of these adjectives is able to suggest the true quality, the true realism of the novel. For this is a matter of the alertness, the creative quickness, of the narrative eye, which allows the phenomenal world of miner's home, colliery, farm, countryside and industrial landscape to figure in their actual fullness and complexity of interaction, free from all authorial predisposition.

Yet even within *Sons and Lovers* Lawrence's next mode of fictional art is developing. On occasion in the second part of the novel (in which the writing is generally less poised than in the first) Lawrence tries to present another notion of reality. He attempts to go beyond the world of character, milieu and simple appearances and to render, as did Paul Morel in his picture of the pine trees, a reality held to be anterior to phenomena. This reality is construed as the underlying process of life, which may be perceived only in certain moments of mystical or intuitive awareness. Here is the description of such a moment as Paul Morel stares down upon Nottingham from the parapet of the castle wall:

> He was brooding now, staring out over the country from under sullen brows. The little, interesting diversity of shapes had vanished from the scene; all that remained was a vast, dark matrix of sorrow and tragedy, the same in all the houses and the river-flats and the people and the birds; they were only shapen differently. And now that the forms seemed to have melted away, there remained the mass from which all the landscape was composed, a dark mass of struggle and pain. The factory, the girls, his mother, the large, uplifted church, the thicket of the town, merged into one atmosphere—dark, brooding, and sorrowful, every bit.

Other insights into that which is beyond the common reality come to Paul at moments of sexual consummation. Through his relationship with Clara Dawes Paul experiences a sense of "the tremendous living flood which carried them". "It was as if they had been blind agents of a great force." "They had met, and included in their meeting the thrust of the manifold grass stems, the cry of the peewit, the wheel of the stars." Such passages can be seen to mark the first rudimentary stage in that phase of Lawrence's art which produced *The Rainbow*. This novel, begun after Lawrence and Frieda had eloped to Italy, subsumes but also surpasses the art of *Sons and Lovers*. It attempts to render process more penetratingly than the simple phenomenal and historical terms of *Sons and Lovers* allow. In moving beyond these two staples of realism Lawrence achieves in *The Rainbow* a new and completely original mode of visual writing.

TWO
THE VISION OF
"THE RAINBOW"

I like the wide world of centuries and vast ages—mammoth worlds beyond our day, and mankind so wonderful in his distances; his history that has no beginning yet always the pomp and the magnificence of human splendour unfolding through the earth's changing periods. Floods and fire and convulsions and ice-arrest intervene between the great glamorous civilisations of mankind. But nothing will ever quench humanity and human potentiality to evolve something magnificent out of a renewed chaos.

I do not believe in evolution, but in the strangeness and rainbow-change of ever-renewed creative civilisations.

FANTASIA OF THE UNCONSCIOUS

3
BEYOND REALISM

THE final draft of the manuscript of *Sons and Lovers* was completed in the flat overlooking Lake Garda and was despatched to the publishers in November 1912. Some four months later Lawrence was well into a new work. In a letter he told Edward Garnett, "I've written rather more than half of a most fascinating (to me) novel. But nobody will ever dare to publish it. I feel I could knock my head against the wall. Yet I love and adore this new book. . . . But there, you see, it's my latest. It is all analytical—quite unlike *Sons and Lovers*, not a bit visualised."[17] Critics have habitually assumed that these words refer to *The Sisters*, the work which after several redactions was broken into two parts: *The Rainbow*, completed and published in 1915, and *Women in Love*, virtually completed in 1916 but not published until 1920. However it seems to me that Keith Sagar is altogether correct in arguing that Lawrence is here talking about *The Insurrection of Miss Houghton*.[18] (This novel was begun at the same time as *The Sisters* but abandoned when *The Sisters* came to monopolise Lawrence's creative energies. The unfinished manuscript was left in Germany during the war years and was revised, completed and published under the

[17] *Letters*, p. 193.
[18] Keith Sagar, *The Art of D. H. Lawrence* (Cambridge, 1966), pp. 36–8.

title *The Lost Girl* in 1920.) Certainly, it is difficult to find coherence in Lawrence's distinction between the "analytical" and the "visualised", if the former cannot be understood to apply to the story of Alvina Houghton. For although there are some very pronounced differences between the visual writing in *Sons and Lovers* and in *The Rainbow*, these two novels are essentially similar to each other and different from *The Lost Girl* by virtue of their highly pictorial qualities. In *The Lost Girl* the visual depiction of character and milieu has none of the same opulence and pre-eminence. In this novel the reality that is presented is primarily the reality of the character's attitudes and aspirations as they are filtered through an ironic, sometimes mocking, narrative consciousness. We respond not so much to a representation of a particular area of the phenomenal world as to the author's insight, satire and distanced poise.

The fact that it was a "visualised" rather than an "analytical" novel that emerged as Lawrence's enduring concern from among the several new ventures in fiction proposed and undertaken in the early months of 1913 tells us something of importance about Lawrence's development as a novelist. It suggests that he was not yet ready or able to write "analytically" of his own early environment. This still formed his only subject.[19] And as a novelist he continued to stand in a close living relationship to it and to grant its actuality in all its remembered richness of colour, texture and detail. The kind of distance and detachment necessary for a sustained novel length

[19] During this period of uncertainty about what to do next which followed the completion of *Sons and Lovers* Lawrence also planned and began a novel about Robert Burns as well as *The Sisters* and *The Insurrection of Miss Houghton*. Even this work was to be set in Lawrence's native milieu. He told a correspondent, "It is to be a life of Robert Burns—but I think I shall make him live near home as a Derbyshire man and shall fictionalise the circumstances. I think I can do him almost like an autobiography." *Letters*, pp. 167, 168.

"analysis" of his native place would not be demonstrated until *The Lost Girl* was completed nearly a decade later. The terms "analytical" and "visualised" apply only to matters of authorial stance, attitude and perception. These are the terms in which *The Rainbow* and *The Lost Girl* differ so strikingly, even though in subject matter they actually show many similarities. Each novel gives an account of the same period and area of English provincial life. Each has for heroine a young woman who demands a greater intensity of life than can be easily allowed by the actual environment. Alvina Houghton and Ursula Brangwen are both tempted to betray their aspirations, both are educated by unsatisfactory love relationships and both eventually make their escape. In rudimentary theme and situation the two books relate not only to each other but also to a well established tradition of fiction. The young, unmarried woman as representative of the suffering of the human spirit in the consolidation of the bourgeois and petit bourgeois hegemony is one of the characteristic subjects of the nineteenth-century realistic novel. And as Lawrence's letters demonstrate, he was well read in this kind of fiction. This is not to suggest that Lawrence is merely following on in this tradition. Indeed each of these novels is in its own way an implicit if not explicit criticism of realism as a way of construing reality. The analytical novel, *The Lost Girl*, dissociates itself from realism by virtue of its elements of satire and, occasionally, of parody. Lawrence's visual novel *The Rainbow* constitutes a similar act of dissent but by quite different means. It endows a realistic story with a texture, movement and elevatedness that induce us, as I want to show later, to resort to the notion of epic.

One instigation to the writing of what was to become *The Lost Girl* seems to have been Arnold Bennett's *Anna of the Five Towns* which Lawrence read in Gargnano in the autumn of 1912. To A. W. McLeod, a fellow teacher at Croydon who had sent him the book he wrote:

I have read *Anna of the Five Towns* today, because it is stormy weather. For five months I have scarcely seen a word of English print, and to read it makes me feel fearfully queer. I don't know where I am. I am so used to the people going by outside, talking or singing some foreign language, always Italian now: but today, to be in Hanley, and to read almost my own dialect, makes me feel quite ill. I hate England and its hopelessness. I hate Bennett's resignation. Tragedy ought really to be a great kick at misery. But *Anna of the Five Towns* seems like an acceptance—so does all the modern stuff since Flaubert. I hate it. I want to wash again quickly, wash off England, the oldness and grubbiness and despair.[20]

But Lawrence's knowledge of realism was not derived exclusively from British realists such as Bennett or George Moore, whom he had also read. Long before he encountered *Anna of the Five Towns*, Lawrence had read and been greatly impressed by *Eugénie Grandet*, the Balzac novel to which Bennett's book is obviously much indebted. In a letter of 1908 he wrote of this novel with an enthusiasm that is unmatched in his literary criticism, formal or informal, of later years.

I consider the book as perfect a novel as I have ever read. It is wonderfully concentrated; there is nothing superfluous, nothing out of place. The book has that wonderful feeling of inevitableness which is characteristic of the best French novels. It is rather astonishing that we, the cold English, should have to go to the fleshy French for levelheaded, fair unrelenting realism. Can you find a grain of sentimentality in *Eugénie*? Can you find a touch of melodrama, or caricature, or flippancy? It is all in tremendous earnestness, more serious than all the profundities of German thinkers, more affecting than all English bathos. It makes me drop my head and sit silent. Balzac can lay bare the living body of the great Life better than anybody in the world. He doesn't hesitate at the last covering; he

[20] *Letters*, p. 150.

doesn't point out the absurdities of the intricate innumer-
able wrappings and accessories of the body of Life; he goes
straight to the flesh; and, unlike de Maupassant or Zola, he
doesn't inevitably light on a wound, or a festering sore.
Balzac is magnificent and supreme; . . .[21]

The compelling relevance, so often expressed in Lawrence's early letters, of the novels of the nineteenth-
century French realists is not hard to understand. There
are so many respects in which the works of these authors
correspond with Lawrence's early life as we know it from
the memoirs and from his own autobiographical fictions.
There is the same concern with the constrictedness of
remote provincial society, the same criticism of the cult of
money and of the emotional crippling of man by the
commercial and industrial system. In Lawrence's early
fictions as in much of the work of Stendhal, Balzac and
Flaubert an important theme is the lag in consciousness,
culture and manners between the provinces and the
capital. And there is also in Lawrence a concern with
history and the generations which is more conspicuously
a characteristic of the French nineteenth-century novel
than of the English.[22] The tone of the great French

[21] *Letters*, pp. 35, 36.
[22] All this is not to deny the fact or the primacy of Lawrence's
indebtedness to the English tradition. His attention to George Eliot
and Hardy are well known. Nevertheless, like other writers of the
period, Lawrence brought to his art an ever developing awareness of
foreign traditions. He translated several works of Italian fiction into
English and took a serious critical interest in French, German and
Russian writers as well as those of England and America. Chronologically, his interest in nineteenth-century French literature came
early and it extended to poetry as well as to fiction. (Baudelaire
figures prominently in Jessie Chambers's memoir and in *Sons and
Lovers* itself and provides an important concept in *Women in Love*.
Lawrence's volume of poems *Look! We Have Come Through* seems to
have borrowed several individual titles and themes as well as the
notion of the designed poetic sequence from *Les Fleurs du Mal*.) It
is also interesting to note that to an Edwardian *literatus* such as
Edward Garnett the young Lawrence seemed "half a Frenchman
and one-eighth a Cockney". *Letters*, p. 273.

realists must also have seemed eminently intelligible and serviceable to Lawrence. It is noteworthy that in his commendation of *Eugénie Grandet* he is particularly concerned to stress the absence of sentimentality, melodrama, caricature and flippancy and to praise its "earnestness" as something "more affecting than all English bathos". It is conceivable that this is the manner which helped sustain the precision, confidence and detachment of the authorial tone in *Sons and Lovers*. In so drastically extending the social range of the English novel Lawrence must needs forsake the familiar entente between the Victorian novelist and reader. And in the undeviating "seriousness" of the French realists, who from Balzac to Zola were always more exploratory in subject matter and more uncompromising in tone than their English contemporaries, Lawrence must have perceived something that helped validate his own tonal innovations.

But the most important effect of the French realists (and here again Balzac seems likely to have been the most important individual influence) was to confirm Lawrence's fictional epistemology. The making of Lawrence as a novelist between *The White Peacock* and *Sons and Lovers* is the maturing of a realist. In the later book the determining epistemological assumption is that the issues of human experience are only to be understood in their true and full reality when made apparent in terms of the portrayal (and the metaphor is significant because realism is pre-eminently a representation of things seen)[23]

---

[23] As a recent historian of French realism reminds us, the word "realism" was originally applied not to fiction but to painting. "It was 'the landscape painter of humanity', as Gustave Courbet was known to his admirers, who first proclaimed himself a realist—or rather, accepted the epithet thrust upon him. When the Salons objected to his literal treatment of peasants and labourers and the middle classes, he retorted by issuing manifestoes in the name of realism. When the Paris exposition of 1844 refused to hang his pictures, he erected his own Pavillon du Réalisme and began to

of the total material environment within which they are enacted. After *Sons and Lovers* Lawrence became more and more critical of realism, but it can be shown that he never completely abandoned its assumptions or its categories.

An early instance of Lawrence's dissatisfaction with realism is his consistent satirising of its conventions in *The Lost Girl*.[24] The most flagrant example of this is, of course, the casual introduction into the mundane world of Woodhouse of the wholly extraordinary Natcha-Kee-Tawaras. But there is also much essentially literary criticism in the many authorial comments. When Alvina refuses her first suitor and goes to Islington to begin an independent career as a maternity nurse, Lawrence wearies of the banality of the situation of "the new woman" and denies us further description: "Surely enough books have been written about heroines in similar circumstances. There is no need to go into the details of Alvina's six months in Islington." On another occasion Lawrence cannot conceal his general boredom with ordinary people or with novels about them:

> Now so far, the story of Alvina is commonplace enough. It is more or less the story of thousands of girls. . . . And if we were dealing with an ordinary girl we should have to carry on mildly and dully down the long years of employment; or, at the best, marriage with some dull schoolteacher or office-clerk.

---

publicise the movement on an international scale." Harry Levin, *The Gates of Horn, A Study of Five French Realists* (New York, 1963), p. 68.

[24] The use of quotations from *The Lost Girl* to support contentions concerning *The Insurrection of Miss Houghton* can scarcely be justified. Nevertheless, there does appear to have been some similarity of tone. In the early summer of 1913 Frieda Lawrence described the earlier and hitherto unrecovered manuscript as "improper" and "witty too". *Letters*, p. 208.

But we protest that Alvina is not ordinary. . . .
There have been enough stories about ordinary
people. . . . We detest ordinary people. . . . Every
individual should, by nature, have his extraordinary
points. But nowadays you may look for them with a microscope, they are so worn-down by the regular machine-
friction of our average and mechanical days.

At first sight it may seem difficult to reconcile these
remarks with the admiration for Balzac's "level-headed,
fair unrelenting realism" in the letter about *Eugénie
Grandet*. But the discrepancy is easily explained both by
the deterioration of the tradition of realism between
Balzac's day and Lawrence's and, more interestingly, by
the growth of Lawrence's dissatisfaction with realism
after *Sons and Lovers*. Lawrence came to question this convention because of its inadequacy as a means of express-
ing his deepest concerns. The subject matter of nineteenth-
century realism centred upon and was pretty well
restricted to the life of the bourgeois and petit bourgeois.
And its aesthetic effect was restricted to the gamut of
emotion which could be felt for those living in such an
ambience. The characteristic feelings afforded and
elicited by this phase of fiction were compassion for those
such as Eugénie Grandet, Gervaise Macquart or Anna
Tellwright for whom life is but a loss of any kind of rich
and memorable experience, and anger, horror, indigna-
tion or perhaps merely irony at the characters or the impersonal forces or environment that are responsible for
their victimisation. To a certain extent these generalisa-
tions hold true for *Sons and Lovers*, but it is also obvious that
there is a great deal both in the subject and in the effect
of this novel which they cannot account for. Already in
this first major work Lawrence is employing the methods
of realism to present and to interpret a range of feeling
far beyond what we ordinarily understand and expect
from this type of fiction. Lawrence himself formulated the

issue very clearly in some comments he made on Flaubert in an essay on Giovanni Verga:

> The trouble with realism—and Verga was a realist—is that the writer, when he is a truly exceptional man like Flaubert or like Verga, tries to read his own sense of tragedy into people much smaller than himself. I think it is a final criticism against *Madame Bovary* that people such as Emma Bovary and her husband Charles simply are too insignificant to carry the full weight of Gustave Flaubert's sense of tragedy. Emma and Charles Bovary are a couple of little people. Gustave Flaubert is not a little person. But, because he is a realist and does not believe in "heroes", Flaubert insists on pouring his own deep and bitter tragic consciousness into the little skins of the country doctor and his uneasy wife. The result is a discrepancy. *Madame Bovary* is a great book and a very wonderful picture of life. But we cannot help resenting the fact that the great tragic soul of Gustave Flaubert is, so to speak, given only the rather commonplace bodies of Emma and Charles Bovary. There's a misfit.[25]

The misfit which Lawrence perceived in Flaubert's book is a continuing and an intensifying problem in modern fiction. The unsuitability of modern society as a means of objectifying the deepest concerns of the novelist accounts both for the degeneration of the great nineteenth-century tradition of realism and the propensity of modern novelists to revert in fiction to lyricism, myth and disembodied "ideas". The meaning of this disjunction between the novelist and society has been interestingly formulated by Georg Lukacs. In *Studies in European Realism* he comments on the deterioration of the realistic tradition after Balzac:

> The great writers of our age were all engaged in a heroic struggle against the banality, aridity and emptiness of the prosaic nature of *bourgeois* life. The formal side of the struggle against this banality and insipidity of life is the

[25] *Phoenix, The Posthumous Papers of D. H. Lawrence* (London, 1936), p. 226.

dramatic pointing of plot and incident. In Balzac, who depicts passions at their highest intensity, this is achieved by conceiving the typical as the extreme expression of certain strands in the skein of life. Only by means of such mighty dramatic explosions can a dynamic world of profound, rich and manyhued poetry emerge from the sordid prose of *bourgeois* life. The naturalists overcame this "romanticism" and by so doing, lowered literary creation to the level of the "average", of the banality of everyday life. In naturalism capitalist prose triumphed over the poetry of life.[26]

A few pages later Lukacs returns to this point and develops his ideas about it:

> The great novelists have ever fought a heroic battle to overcome, in the sphere of art, that coldness and harshness in *bourgeois* existence and in the relationships of men with each other and with nature, which opposes such a rigid resistance to poetic presentation. But the poet can overcome this resistance only by seeking out the surviving live elements of these relationships in reality itself, by culling from his own rich and real experience and expressing in concentrated form the moments in which such still living tendencies manifest themselves as relationships between individuals. For the mechanical and "finished" character of the capitalist world, described by Hegel and so often repeated after him, is, it is true, an existing and growing evolutionary tendency in capitalism, but it must never be forgotten that it is still only a tendency, that society is objectively never "finished", fulfilled, dead, petrified reality.[27]

As we know, Lawrence had no great interest in Marxism. Nevertheless, there is much in the spirit and even in the vocabulary of these remarks to remind us of Lawrence's own attitudes both to life and to the novel. And Lukacs's distinction between the average and the typical character is one which will prove extremely useful in discussing

[26] Georg Lukacs, *Studies in European Realism* (London, 1950), pp. 148, 149.
[27] *ibid.*, pp. 155, 156.

The Rainbow.[28] For this helps to explain the conspicuous difference in the manner of creating the minor characters who populate the background of that novel and the half dozen main characters who are, or at least struggle to be, its heroes. The average, as understood by Lukacs, is the familiar, predictable and thus unliving norm. The typical is drawn from what is alive in society and sometimes (and this is the case in *The Rainbow*) is "based on the mere possibility of an extreme attitude, an extreme passion, an extreme fate".[29]

In *The Rainbow* Lawrence extends and renews the emotional range of the realistic novel by the use of such "typical" characters. For *The Rainbow*, despite its striking originality, is, like *The Lost Girl*, founded upon one of the characteristic designs of realism. It is a *Familienroman*, a novel of successive generations of a family. The emergence of this particular type of novel is an inevitable consequence of that preoccupation with history which is such a major characteristic of realism. In this poetic the crucial notion of milieu is construed as much in temporal as in material or social terms. Before the period of realism novelists were never precise about the setting in time of their novels. The careers of Elizabeth Bennett or Joseph Andrews are in no way dependent upon or even affected by the particulars of time. We cannot place even an approximate date upon the important moments in their lives, nor is it important that we should. But this is definitely not the case with the realistic novel. A considerable part of the meaning and effect of, say, *Le Rouge et Le Noir* or *L'Education Sentimentale* depends upon the careful situating of the action at a particular moment in history. A condition of realistic fiction is that it proposes history as one of the forces bearing on the life and consciousness

[28] Lawrence himself makes something of the same distinction in his essay "Democracy".

[29] Lukacs, *op. cit.*, p. 178.

of the individual. For instance, in Balzac's *Eugénie Grandet*, which so interested Lawrence, the very idea of the year 1827 is an important source of the irony and the compassion which form the overall effect of the book. In 1827 the young Charles Grandet, Eugénie's cousin, whom she has loved for many years, decides to marry Mademoiselle d'Aubrion, whose family claims important connections at the court of Charles X. "He was dazzled by the prosperity of the Restoration court—the regime had been a little shaky at the time he left—and impressed by the success of the aristocratic principle. He resolved to do everything in his power to attain the high position his rapacious mother-in-law had pointed out to him."[30] The pathos lies in the fact that Charles should be committing his life and hopes (and also sacrificing Eugénie) to a search for the favour of a regime which, as the date tells us, has only three more years to last before being destroyed and replaced by the July Monarchy of Louis Philippe. The world to which the realists directed their attention was their native nineteenth century and its unending social and political change. They recognised history as a defining condition of life and, on occasion, as one of the victimisers making for a denial of hope and fulfilment.

One of the literary devices developed by the realists as a result of their commitment to the notion of history was the novel sequence, the *roman fleuve*. A series of continuous or chronologically related novels is the means by which the novelist is best able fully to render particular characters and relationships while still connecting them with the larger sweep of the historical process. A kindred device is the *retour des personnages*, which can help to suggest social density as well as historical extent. This technique was first employed by Balzac in his *Comédie humaine*, that vast association of novels and stories which attempts to

[30] Balzac, *Eugénie Grandet*, translated by Henry Reed (New York, 1964), p. 192.

relate the history of French experience from the Consulate to the July Monarchy. And it has been taken up by other fictional historians such as Zola, Proust, Galsworthy and Faulkner. Lawrence's own decision to divide the story of the Brangwens (and to resort to a *retour des personnages* in *Women in Love*) also demonstrates the virtual indispensability of such punctuation in any full and extended account of the course of history. The family novel is able to show the movement of history in very particular terms. In tracing the course and interaction of the generations of a family, it provides a metaphor for the course of society as a whole or at least for the class which, given the metonymies inherent in most societies, embodies that which is most dynamic and consequential in the society. This is what we have in Thomas Mann's *Buddenbrooks*, a novel which Lawrence read and wrote about in 1913[31] and which appears very probably to have suggested to him at least the rudimentary design of *The Rainbow*.

For all that *Buddenbrooks* is, as Erich Heller has remarked, "a story about people who live in a world philosophically interpreted by Schopenhauer",[32] it is also, in the words of the same critic, "a consistently realist or, for what the term is worth, naturalist novel, unthinkable without the example of the great masters of the genre, . . ."[33] Heller goes on to say, citing a phrase from Thomas Mann himself: "Thus the 'first and only naturalist novel' in German literature is also a philosophical novel. And as the philosophy derives from Schopenhauer, so the two cosmic antagonists in Schopenhauer's thought—the World-as-Will and the World as the human mind which, forming the true idea of the

---

[31] *Phoenix*, "German Books: Thomas Mann", pp. 308–13.
[32] Erich Heller, *Thomas Mann, The Ironic German* (New York, 1961), p. 28.
[33] *ibid*, p. 32.

57

Will-World, comes to deny it—appear in the guise of life and spirit."[34] There are two ways in which these observations bear very interestingly upon *The Rainbow*. First, Lawrence's book resembles Mann's in that it is both a work of realism and at the same time an extension of realism as a method of representing and interpreting experience. Second, Mann's thematic antinomies are to some extent shared by Lawrence. For the story of the Brangwens is also the story of the interaction of spirit and life, of self-consciousness and vital dynamic. The difference is that for Lawrence the latter term is not laden with the same Schopenhauerian and pejorative connotations and that the former does not elicit any of Mann's ambivalence. *The Rainbow* is the tracing through four generations of a tradition of life and "will" that still makes for present possibility. *Buddenbrooks* (its subtitle is *der Verfall einer Familie*) is the story of the progressive degeneration of a family and at the same time of the degeneration of what was for Thomas Mann an admirable phase of German culture. The novel is the story of four generations of a prominent burgher family in one of the Hanseatic cities. At the beginning of the book the family is at the zenith of its confidence and prosperity. Subsequently, however, each generation suffers an increasing diminution of Schopenhauerian *Wille*. Vital and spontaneous confidence becomes more and more debilitated by the susceptibility of the family to idea and consciousness. By the end of the novel the family is approaching extinction and its commercial, social and cultural position has been taken over by others. Thomas Mann's attitude to this process is one of carefully constructed and sedulously maintained irony. The contamination of will by idea is seen to be inevitable and yet the calm, unshrinking representation of the inevitable has to be reconciled, through irony, with Mann's patent

[34] *ibid*, p. 37.

regret at the passing of the Buddenbrooks. For both in themselves and as metaphors of a certain phase of German life and culture they represent something infinitely finer than the Hagenströms who replace them. The Buddenbrooks are *Bürger* and as such possess a social and cultural distinction far beyond the grasp of the Hagenströms, who are irremediably bourgeois. The particular stage in the continuing dualism of will and idea which sees the passing of the *Bürger* and the emergence of the bourgeois constitutes the turning point in Thomas Mann's fictional account of the nineteenth century in Germany.

Thomas Mann's attitude of ironic pessimism in *Buddenbrooks* contrasts strongly with the singularly creative and synthesising power of Lawrence's vision in *The Rainbow*. Nevertheless, the congruity of the two novels in both subject and design is extremely striking. So too is the common preoccupation with the nature of civilisation, culture, decadence, art and self-realisation in the nineteenth century. Occasionally particulars from one novel can help to point out an illuminating correspondence in the other. Thus the continuing relationship over the generations between the Buddenbrooks and the Hagenströms reminds us of the continuing involvement of the Brangwens with the Skrebenskys, which is also fraught with important thematic implications concerning class and culture. To establish these similarities between *Buddenbrooks* and *The Rainbow* is also to establish the essential point that *The Rainbow* is first and foremost a historical novel. An inadequate insistence on this preliminary category has prevented much of the published discussion of *The Rainbow* from properly illuminating the rich texture of this great book. The story of the Brangwens is Lawrence's metaphor for the most significant stirring of life in Victorian England. History, which in *Sons and Lovers* was resorted to implicitly as a conceptual explanation of the dilemma of the (recognisably autobiographical) hero, is in *The Rainbow* given full representation as a condition of life.

The story begins about 1840 when a colliery canal is cut across the meadows of the Marsh farm on the Derby-Notts. border where the Brangwens have lived for more than two centuries. With this sudden invasion of their remote and static order of life the Brangwen yeomen slowly begin to undergo an evolution and an enhancement of consciousness. At least those who have the capacity and the courage do. Of the four sons and two daughters who comprise the first generation that is presented to us only Tom Brangwen, the youngest, is capable of the vital daring and courage which enable him to go beyond the narrow and obscure world of Cossethay. He does this principally by marrying the refugee Polish lady, Lydia Lensky. But Lawrence also describes Tom's brothers and sisters, who fail to achieve this progress beyond familiar parochial experience. In part these descriptions help to do justice to the social complexity of the advance of the Brangwen family. That a gentleman farmer such as Tom should have a brother who is a coarse, drunken butcher and a sister who is married to a collier is a probability of English social life, even if it runs counter to our tendency to think (especially with regard to nineteenth-century England) in terms of rigid class segregation. Class is certainly an important theme in the Brangwen books, but from the outset Lawrence insists upon its true complexity and also demonstrates that the Brangwen development cannot be understood in class terms alone. The mention of Tom's brothers and sisters also contributes to the epic effect of the novel. The Brangwens are represented as a family, but there is also a sense in which we are aware of them as a tribe that is in progress towards some promised land of heightened life. In this sense, Tom Brangwen is the leader and hero of his generation. At the start Lawrence wishes to underscore the difference between the ordinary, historically familiar characters (what Lukacs calls "average" characters) and the heroes, who go beyond the known and predictable forms to achieve a new and advanced state of being. These are the growing points of the family, the tribe and the culture.

In the next generation "the curious enveloping Brangwen intimacy, so warm, so close, so stifling" is further mitigated by the marriage of the most singular member of the family to a partner who is even more detached and self-confident, more distinctively an individual. The story now takes up the stormy marriage of Tom's Polish stepdaughter, Anna Lensky, (very much the alien and the aristocrat despite her upbringing at Cossethay) and his nephew, Will Brangwen. At this stage, the consciousness of the family is sufficiently developed for issues of life to be formulated in terms of religion and of art. In the subsequent generation, of which Ursula Brangwen is the heroine, the intellectual and social sophistication is greater still. Ursula attends university, becomes a teacher and in *Women in Love* comes to know the whole social range of England, from her native mining country to the London Bohemia and the gathering places of the industrial and traditional aristocracies.

The history of the Brangwen family may be seen as a late and microcosmic re-enactment of the underlying principle of history as Lawrence defines it in his "Study of Thomas Hardy", the long essay which he wrote when at work on the final redaction of *The Rainbow*.[35] In one of his many lengthy digressions from Hardy, Lawrence

---

[35] Lawrence was at work on "Study of Thomas Hardy" in December 1914 (*Letters*, p. 298). *The Rainbow* was completed on 2 March 1915.

offers this view of the nature of the historical process:

> It seems as though one of the conditions of life is, that life
> shall continually and progressively differentiate itself,
> almost as though this differentiation were a Purpose. Life
> starts crude and unspecified, a great Mass. And it proceeds
> to evolve out of that mass ever more distinct and definite
> particular forms, an ever-multiplying number of separate
> species and orders, as if it were working always to the
> production of the infinite number of perfect individuals,
> the individual so thorough that he should have nothing in
> common with any other individual.[36]

Later on Lawrence applies this theory to the course of
European history. The Middle Ages, he maintains, were
the epoch of an unindividualised, undifferentiated
humanity—or to use Lawrence's own terms, a period
governed by the female principle, or by a devotion to the
flesh. (Clearly, all these terms are very close to the notion
of blood-intimacy employed in the opening pages of *The
Rainbow*.) The characteristic expression of the Middle
Ages, Lawrence continues, "was the collective, stupend-
ous, emotional gesture of the Cathedrals, where a blind,
collective impulse rose into concrete form". It was an art
"that admits the existence of no other form, but is
conclusive, propounding in its sum the One Being of All".
Lawrence then proceeds to argue that even in the
cathedrals there was evidence of a stirring of the spirit
against the flesh, of the male against the female principle:
"There was, however, in the Cathedrals, already the
denial of the Monism which the Whole uttered. All the
little figures, the gargoyles, the imps, the human faces,
whilst subordinated within the Great Conclusion of the
Whole, still, from their obscurity, jeered their mockery of
the Absolute, and declared for multiplicity, polygeny."[37]
The Renaissance, Lawrence suggests, constituted a proper

[36] *Phoenix*, p. 431.
[37] *Phoenix*, p. 454.

balancing of the individual and the collective and of the flesh and the spirit. With the "addition of male influence", "medieval art became complete Renaissance art", "there was the union and fusion of the male and female spirits, creating a perfect expression for the time being".[38] Lawrence then traces various phases of the Renaissance as they are revealed in Italian painting. He writes at some length of Botticelli, Correggio, Raphael and Michelangelo, all the time gradually advancing the argument that during and after the Renaissance the medieval consciousness becomes more and more over-born by the male principle of abstraction and individual-ism: "Which conception reached its fullest in Turner's pictures, which were utterly bodiless; and also in the great scientists or thinkers of the last generation, even Darwin and Spencer and Huxley."[39]

The directing purpose of this finely managed paren-thetical essay in the history and criticism of art ranging from Raphael's "Madonna degli Ansidei" to Boccioni's "Development of a Bottle Through Space" is to explain the character and sources of what Lawrence perceived as modern decadence, the propensity to respond and to perceive too much in terms of spiritual and intellectual abstractions and of solipsistic individualism. The Brang-wen family is still anterior to this decadence. They are caught up in a stage of process which in Lawrence's

[38] *Phoenix*, p. 485.
[39] From the several references to Herbert Spencer in Lawrence's writing, it seems that he had some knowledge of the work of this now unread philosopher. To suggest that Spencer's rigid systematising had any great effect on Lawrence would be absurd. Nevertheless, the rudiments of Lawrence's view of history seem to be the same as those of Spencer, who once wrote: "From the earliest traceable cosmical changes down to the latest results of civilisation, we shall find that the transformation of the homogeneous into the hetero-geneous is that in which progress essentially consists." Herbert Spencer, *Essays; Scientific, Political and Speculative* (London, 1891), vol. I, p. 10.

cyclical view of history corresponds to that existing before
the Renaissance balance. They are the last element of
English society to emerge from an age old stasis and un-
consciousness and to undergo the historical process. And
as such they are very much an apocalyptic group. They
represent England's last opportunity to evolve an alternative in being, relationship and culture to the course of
decadence upon which the preceding phases in the evolution of English consciousness, the aristocracy and the
middle class, are inescapably set. There can be no doubt
that Lawrence intended Ursula, the most sophisticated
of the Brangwens, to illustrate the emergence into full
consciousness of the lower strata of English society, and
that their emergence also represents the last possibility
for the country's salvation and renaissance. Part of
Ursula's function is to free Birkin from his involvement
with Hermione and the whole world of decadent Whig
culture represented by Breadalby, which we recognise as
a thinly camouflaged Garsington, the country seat of
Bloomsbury. On one occasion when Ursula is with
Birkin and Hermione, Lawrence comments:

> Ursula felt that she was an outsider. The very tea-cups and
> the old silver was a bond between Hermione and Birkin.
> It seemed to belong to an old, past world which they had
> inhabited together, and in which Ursula was a foreigner.
> She was almost a parvenue in their old cultured milieu.
> Her convention was not their convention, their standards
> were not her standards. But theirs were established, they
> had the sanction and the grace of age. He and she to-
> gether, Hermione and Birkin, were people of the same old
> tradition, the same withered deadening culture. And she,
> Ursula, was an intruder.[40]

Hermione makes the same point even more clearly. She
tells Ursula,

[40] *Women in Love* (New York, 1950), p. 342.

"But I think you are vital and young—it isn't a question of years, or even of experience—it is almost a question of race. Rupert is race-old, he comes of an old race—and you seem to me so young, you come of a young, inexperienced race."[41]

The further implication of the novel is that it is the Brangwens' comparative lack of history which makes Ursula the means of Birkin's release from the historical doom of his longer established class culture. "But the passion of gratitude with which he received her . . . he, who was so nearly dead, who was so near to being gone with the rest of his race down the slope of mechanical death, could never be understood by her."[42] "She was so new, so wonder-clear, so undimmed. And he was so old, so steeped in heavy memories."[43]

In considering Lawrence's treatment of the emergence into consciousness of the submerged and inarticulate elements of English society, I find myself going beyond *The Rainbow* and considering its continuation in *Women in Love*. To a great extent such a relating of the books is natural and inevitable. For though each novel has its coherent meaning in isolation, there are also many ways in which the two constitute a unity. Understandably the historical themes are least disrupted by the division of the volumes. In both books there is the continuing concern with the development of the forms and implications of industrialisation. Gerald Crich's reorganisation of his mines is but the last chapter of a story that begins in the opening pages of *The Rainbow*. A similar continuity is to be found in Lawrence's account of the progress of women into confidence and initiative. The freedom of Ursula and Gudrun is but the historical extension of that of their grandmother Lydia Lensky, the first "emancipée" of

[41] *ibid*, p. 338.
[42] *ibid*, p. 423.
[43] *ibid*, p. 422.

the novel. Other large historical concerns maintained throughout both books are Lawrence's tactful suggestion of the character and of the decay of Victorian Christianity and also of the consequent recourse to education and the establishment of Education as an institution.

But aside from the treatment of these major developments in Victorian society, there is a further sense in which the story of the Brangwens is the story of late nineteenth-century England. Like *Buddenbrooks* it presents and interprets the particulars and specifics of history as well as its larger movements. The moment the Brangwens start to transcend their ancient parochial consciousness they become involved with characters who are, in greater or lesser degrees of complexity, socio-historical. Some of the minor characters are introduced into the novel in order to concede the familiar historical reference points of the period. Thus Lensky, with his dedication to doctrines of liberalism and national independence serves to establish the phase in the modern history of Europe during which the Brangwens begin their development. Alfred Brangwen embodies the suffering and estrangement of the first generation to be translated from the farm to the industrial routine. The final inheritors of the Marsh farm, Ursula's Uncle Fred and his wife Laura ("She had been to Salisbury Training College, knew folk-songs and morris-dancing.") represent the studied cult of the rural which begins once the other and more vital elements in Brangwen and English life have moved from the country to the city or, more accurately, to suburbia. Winifred Inger and Maggie Schofield suggest (and for Ursula exemplify) different stages and possibilities in woman's early movement towards freedom.

I cite these few examples merely to emphasise Lawrence's determination to maintain a detailed historical perspective. In the economy of the novel these characters are minor ones—though as character creations they are invested with a life that makes them more than mere historical ciphers. The major characters are endowed with far greater complexity. They do more than elicit and confirm our established notions about Victorian people. An example of particular interest is Anton Skrebensky, Ursula's lover and suitor. Skrebensky is of an aristocratic line which is both literally and metaphorically alien to the Brangwens. His father, an emigré Polish baron, is an old acquaintance of Lydia Lensky, whose daughter Anna visits him when Anton is a small boy. Anna is very conscious of the difference between the Brangwen closeness and intimacy and the way of the Skrebenskys:

> It was queer, the stiff, aristocratic manner of the father with the child, the distance in the relationship, the classic fatherhood on the one hand, the filial subordination on the other. They played together, in their different degrees very separate, two different beings, differing as it were in rank rather than in relationship.

When we next encounter Anton Skrebensky he is a young army officer coming to pay court to Ursula. Paradoxically, when Ursula speaks up for the value and function of aristocracy, Skrebensky displays uneasiness and a lack of confidence about his background:

> He always felt that by rights he belonged to the ruling aristocracy. Yet to hear her speak for his class pained him with a curious, painful pleasure. He felt he was acquiescing in something illegal, taking to himself some wrong, reprehensible advantage.

Skrebensky's guilt at his own nature is explained by his susceptibility to the utilitarian view of life:

> The good of the greatest number was all that mattered. That which was the greatest good for them all, collectively, was the greatest good for the individual. And so, every man must give himself to support the state, and so labour for the greatest good of all. One might make improvements in the state, perhaps, but always with a view to preserving it intact.

This uneasy conjunction in Skrebensky of aristocratic feeling and liberal thought is Lawrence's unobtrusive, and yet for the novel as a whole richly suggestive, way of revealing the major realignment in Victorian social and political life. But Skrebensky signifies even more than this. Lawrence also shows how Skrebensky's uneasy Whig-liberal outlook is further conditioned by his imperial experience. The first serious disagreement between Ursula and Skrebensky concerns the Mahdi and Khartoum. And the life which Skrebensky offers with his proposal of marriage is that of a British officer's wife in India. But Ursula is quick to see imperial life as a pastiche of true aristocracy:

> She could see him so well out there, in India—one of the governing class, superimposed upon an old civilisation, lord and master of a clumsier civilisation than his own. It was his choice. He would become again an aristocrat, invested with authority and responsibility, having a great helpless populace beneath him. . . . But that was not her road.

A major phase in Skrebensky's life and one that significantly punctuates his relationship with Ursula is his service against the Boers in South Africa. Again Ursula's attitude is unenthusiastic: "Ursula watched the newspapers, vaguely, concerning the war in South Africa. They made her miserable, and she tried to have as little to do with them as possible." The long series of adversely judged imperial associations in Skrebensky's life is more than coincidental. They are crucial to an understanding of his character and his failure. Skrebensky's true nature is compromised by his inability to resist the influence of Bentham, but it is even more gravely affected by that later phase of liberal opinion which we are accustomed to associate with the name of Joseph Chamberlain.

The rendering of the major characters in *The Rainbow* is of a texture that does more than provide an invitation to this kind of historical diagramming. The centre of the novel, the story of Will Brangwen, the representative of the second and, so to speak, pivotal generation of the family, is a memorably creative achievement of historical imagination. It is an empathetic representation of a crucial tension in Victorian consciousness. Lawrence's full and extensive portrayal of Will's emotional life is also by implication a critique of the attitudes and influence of Ruskin; for Will Brangwen is the Ruskinite of Cossethay. And in his representation and critique of the range and quality of feeling informing Ruskinite attitudes to architecture, culture and society, Lawrence is assessing the effect of a critic of Victorian life who for such as the emergent Brangwens was *the* critic. The Ruskinite tradition and influence is also shown to go beyond this second generation. Will and Anna name their first child Ursula, we are told, "because of the picture of the saint". And there is every reason to suppose that the picture in question is Carpaccio's "The Dream of St. Ursula", which had such a profound effect upon Ruskin. In *Fors Clavigera* Ruskin frequently writes of Carpaccio's picture and in the seventy-first letter he commends St. Ursula as a patronal figure to the members of his St. George's Company in their dedication to the reclamation of English life. The correspondence is of interest in our understanding of Ursula Brangwen and her tradition as a force for the regeneration of England. It also underlines the influence of Ruskinism as a mode of visualisation and of social and aesthetic feeling upon the second and third generations of the Brangwens.

4
THE TRADITION OF RUSKIN

A PRELIMINARY and far less ambitious study of Ruskin's influence upon nineteenth-century English life is the early short story "Goose Fair", which is a kind of preparatory essay upon one of the major themes of *The Rainbow*. The overall effect of the story is largely composed of contrasts. The first paragraph reads something like the opening of a fairy story; it describes a tired and miserable goose-girl driving her flock of birds to market through the city streets. But in the very next paragraph Lawrence makes it clear that the world of romance is only vestigial. The story may be of the age-old festival of Goose Fair, but it is set in the industrial Nottingham of the 1870s where all is determined by trade and where life and business and prosperity are depressed in the aftermath of the Franco-Prussian War. In the second section of the story the narrator establishes a further contrast by switching the story from the poor goose-girl in the shabby streets to a more prosperous part of Nottingham and to Lois Buxton, the daughter of a wealthy lace manufacturer. We learn that the other, less successful, factory owners of the area are suspected of purposely setting their premises on fire in order to make money from the insurance. And Lois is anxious about the whereabouts that night of her suitor, Will Selby, whose father's business is in difficulty. Lois waits up late to see if he will return and passes the time by reading Ruskin's *Sesame and Lilies*. The following morning she learns that a factory has in fact been set ablaze during the night and immediately she sets out with her maid to look for Will Selby. They find him and learn that he has had no part in the arson. Abetted by Lois's brother, he has confined his activities to teasing and bullying the poor goose-girl.

This discovery, at once anticlimatic and thoroughly contemptible, sharply illuminates the indictment of the provincial middle class which is a major point of the story. Far from being involved in the drama of the burning factory, these two gallants of Nottingham have done nothing more than indulge their brutal loutishness. For Lawrence there is a certain human drama involved in the rise and fall of trade (Will Selby's father is a self-made man), but there is something both comic and despicable in the ugly provinciality and vacuousness of these young men born into an established middle-class prosperity. Father and son together form a contrast between the middle-class mind in its pristine aspect of creative enterprise and its subsequent aspect of bored and vulgar complacency. But if Lawrence's criticism of the middle class here seems to have something in common with a characteristic Ruskinian emphasis, there is yet a further contrast in the story which constitutes a clear criticism of Ruskin's proposed alternatives to such barbarism. This involves Lois herself, who figures in the story as a representative of education and sensibility. At the same time, however, there is a lack of authenticity in Lois's culture. She betrays a certain pretentiousness, a certain propensity for attitudinising. On one occasion we read of her laying her hand on her lover's arm "in the true fashion of romance"; on another we are given an example of the style of her thought: "She felt an intense longing at this uncanny hour to slough the body's trammelled uneasiness and to issue at once into the new bright warmth

of the far Dawn where a lover waited transfigured; . . ."
But the precise point of Lawrence's criticism of Lois becomes fully clear only at the end of the story when we
learn of her attitude to Will's behaviour. When she had
thought him guilty of a crime against Trade, her attitude
had been unambiguous: "She knew it was over between
them." But his ugly treatment of the goose-girl elicits no
such firmness from Lois: "She was far from forgiving
him, but she was still farther from letting him go."
Clearly Lois's cultivation of the manners of romance and
of Ruskinite sensibility has nothing more than a surface
effect upon her. She and Will belong together: "Curiously
enough, they walked side by side as if they belonged to
each other." In the last resort Lois is implicated in the
same moral vulgarity, the same brutal uncouthness. It is
fitting that in such a milieu Ruskin's book should be seen
at the last in a position of comic indignity. While the
factory is burning Lois runs upstairs to find her mother
"dressed, but all unbuttoned again, lying back in the
chair in her daughter's room, suffering from palpitations
of the heart, with *Sesame and Lilies* crushed beneath her".
One effect of this incident is to make the story appear as
an ironic riposte to "Of Kings' Treasuries", the first
essay in Ruskin's book, which argues the importance of
books in personal and national life. More pervasively, the
story of Lois is a comment upon Ruskin's exalted notion
of the queenly office of women in "Of Queens' Gardens",
the second of the three essays that make up *Sesame and
Lilies*.

On the evidence of this early short story it is clear that
Lawrence was under no illusion about the incongruity of
Ruskin's exhortations and the Victorian actuality. Nevertheless, Lawrence grew to maturity at a time when
Ruskin was still regarded as a major writer and though
his attitude to Ruskin was always critical, it was never
altogether dismissive. In his early letters the references

are often joking; "*all* Ruskinites are not fools," he tells Blanche Jennings in a letter of October, 1908,[44] but goes on to add: "The deep damnation of self-righteousness sticks tight to every creed, to every 'ism' and every 'ite'; but it lies thick all over the Ruskinite, like painted feathers on a skinny peacock."[45] Some months earlier Lawrence had remarked to the same correspondent: "Had I been rich, I should have been something Ruskinian (—blessed poverty!)."[46] The dissociation is made plain enough, yet even the comic suggestion of a possible identification with Ruskin is of interest. For it reminds us of Lawrence's famous letter to Edward Garnett about *Sons and Lovers* in which he compares the situation of Paul Morel, reminiscent as it is of Lawrence's own, with that of Ruskin. Lawrence told his friend and publisher: "It's the tragedy of thousands of young men in England— . . . I think is was Ruskin's, and men like him."[47]

This indirect comparison between Lawrence's experience and that of Ruskin helps to explain the fine fictional achievement represented by the characterisation of Will Brangwen. Ruskinism, we sense, was more than a mere set of ideas to Lawrence; it was rather a particular range of emotional reverberation which he had known both in himself and in others.[48] And this accounts for the full and detailed empathy in the realisation of Will. There is one further respect in which Will undergoes the same kind of early experience that affected Paul Morel and Lawrence himself: "Sometimes, he talked of his father, whom he

[44] *Letters*, p. 29.
[45] *Letters*, p. 30.
[46] *Letters*, p. 13.
[47] *Letters*, p. 161.
[48] There is a good account of the many similarities between Will Brangwen and Alfred Burrows, the father of Lawrence's one time fiancée Louie Burrows, in the introduction to James T. Boulton's edition of Lawrence's letters to Louie entitled *Lawrence in Love* (Nottingham, 1968).

hated with a hatred that was burningly close to love, of his mother, whom he loved, with a love that was keenly close to hatred, or to revolt." This is not, of course, to suggest that Will Brangwen's emotional history can be interpreted exclusively or even primarily in terms of early oedipal experience. In the economy of the novel this point is but a hint and there is no encouragement to apply to Will the kind of psychological explanations which critics have applied to Paul Morel and which, incidentally, Lawrence was to apply to Ruskin when in *Fantasia of the Unconscious* he claimed that "when Mrs. Ruskin said that John Ruskin should have married his mother she spoke the truth".[49] Will Brangwen's nature is far too intricate to be explained so simply. Nevertheless, within the continuity of Lawrence's fictional canon, Will more than anyone else strikes us as Paul Morel's successor in Lawrence's further examination of the peculiarly hazardous situation of the late nineteenth-century artist. Furthermore, as with Paul Morel, Will Brangwen's career as a painter and carver is shaped by his particular range and resources of feeling. And these, the implication runs, are conditioned and exemplified by the artist's relations with woman as mother, lover and wife. With Paul Morel the first two categories predominate, with Will Brangwen the two latter. Will Brangwen represents a more mature and extended account of the artist's situation. In his case Lawrence's grasp of the issue has gone far beyond the recognisably personal concern of *Sons and Lovers*; he is now able to objectify the artist in more complete socio-historical terms. But common to the description of both artists is the suggestion of the continuity between sexuality, feeling, perception and the art that is created. All such terms are but different ways of describing the fundamental emotional texture that Lawrence's narrative assumes as the reality of the

[49] *Fantasia of the Unconscious* (New York, 1960), pp. 153, 154.

74

individual life and which deters us from thinking of the people in the book as characters in the sense of being made what they are by social situation, aptitudes, beliefs, humours. It was to this very important distinction that Lawrence was referring when in his famous letter to Edward Garnett about *The Rainbow* he maintained that "that which is physic—non-human, in humanity, is more interesting to me than the old-fashioned human element —which causes one to conceive a character in a certain moral scheme and make him consistent".[50] It is not easy to find one single and concise critical term to suggest the particular apprehension of reality which Lawrence proceeds to develop at considerable length in this letter. But I think it will be none too great a distortion to refer to it as the timbre of an individual life, in the sense of the resonance that is at once physical and emotional and which precedes and determines the other more easily isolated attributes of an individual's nature. The term Ruskinian means just such a timbre and one of which Will Brangwen, the Nottingham lace designer and draughtsman, is a vivid if somewhat provincial example.

The story of Will Brangwen, from our first knowledge of it in *The Rainbow* to the last mention of it in *Women in Love*, is intimately involved with the church. The first episode to involve Will is that in which as a youth he pays his first visit to the Marsh Farm and escorts the eighteen year old Anna to morning service. (Anna's giggling fit, brought on by the sound of Will saying the responses and by his ringing tenor voice as he sings the hymns, remains in the mind as a most conspicuously successful narrative achievement, conveying as it does both the shock and the deep comedy of the first dawning of an adolescent sexual consciousness.) Will Brangwen's passion for the church is aesthetic as well as devotional:

---

[50] *Letters*, p. 281.

He was interested in churches, in church architecture. The influence of Ruskin had stimulated him to a pleasure in the medieval forms. His talk was fragmentary, he was only half articulate. But listening to him, as he spoke of church after church, of nave and chancel and transept, of rood-screen and font, of hatchet-carving and moulding and tracery, speaking always with close passion of particular things, particular places, there gathered in her heart a pregnant hush of churches, a mystery, a ponderous significance of bowed stone, a dim-coloured light through which something took place obscurely, passing into darkness: a high, delighted framework of the mystic screen, and beyond, in the furthest beyond, the altar. It was a very real experience. She was carried away. And the land seemed to be covered with a vast, mystic church, reserved in gloom, thrilled with an unknown Presence.

This simultaneously religious and aesthetic passion in Will is of the same depth and intensity as his feeling for Anna. His love for the church and his love for his bride are the two ways in which he searches out that rhapsodic exhilaration of feeling which his nature craves. And, as Lawrence suggests in a metaphor that further emphasises Will's medievalism, nothing else has any great significance for him:

> He did not attach any vital importance to his life in the drafting office, or his life among men. That was just merely the margin to the text. The verity was his connection with Anna and his connection with the Church, his real being lay in his dark emotional experience of the Infinite, of the Absolute. And the great mysterious, illuminated capitals to the text, were his feelings with the Church.

The compatibility of these two loves does not endure beyond the early days of the marriage. For although Anna Brangwen is at first ready to let herself be charmed into loving "the jewelled glass" instead of the reality of "the lilacs towering in the vivid sunshine", the spell is only short-lived. In her nature there is a haughtiness and a common sense positivism which prevent her from being easily subsumed in Will's churchly ecstasies. Above all, she is a more realised and confident individual than her husband. (This is established very quickly and economically in the descriptions of the first days of the marriage and of Will's considerable uneasiness at Anna's casual flaunting of the orthodoxies of household management and routine.) And in her subsequent mounting antagonism towards Will's love for the church there is displayed a more radical disharmony, one that counterposes the selfhood of Anna and what is termed the "soul" of Will.

It exasperated her beyond measure. She could not get out of the Church the satisfaction he got. The thought of her soul was intimately mixed up with the thought of her own self. Indeed, her soul and her own self were one and the same in her. Whereas he seemed simply to ignore the fact of his own self, almost to refute it. He had a soul—a dark, inhuman thing caring nothing for humanity. So she conceived it. And in the gloom and mystery of the Church his soul lived and ran free, like some strange, underground thing, abstract.

He was very strange to her, and, in this church spirit, in conceiving himself as a soul, he seemed to escape and run free of her. In a way, she envied it him, this dark freedom and jubilation of the soul, some strange entity in him. It fascinated her. Again she hated it. And again, she despised him, wanted to destroy it in him.

The antipathy suggested here is the origin of that great crescendo of marital frustration, anger and hatred which slowly gathers and comes to a climax in the first of the very long chapters of the novel, "Anna Victrix". Lawrence's account of the movement and rhythm of emotion in and between two people and of the changing forms of deadlock in the oppressive claustrophobia of the marriage has the same detailed accuracy that we find in the descriptions of the visible world. Lawrence's meticulous and unrelenting representation of feeling demands a special effort of attention from the reader; nevertheless, the general movement of the chapter is clear enough. As the title suggests, the ultimate victory is Anna's. Yet it is a pyrrhic victory. Like Mrs. Morel, who also sought to transform her husband into a responsible individual, Anna succeeds only in making her husband admit tacitly and resentfully her greater assurance and his essential dependence. It is true that at the last and after many years he is "born for a second time, born at last unto himself, out of the vast body of humanity". "But it was a very dumb, weak, helpless self, a crawling nursling." In principle Anna has brought about the evolution in her husband which she sought, but it has the weakness and debilitation of a growth that is prematurely forced and too much at variance with the proper laws of process. And for Anna herself, victory, or the realisation of her pre-eminence and dominance, is also a recognition of the impossibility of achieving that further development of self of which she knows she is capable. At this point the narrative focus moves beyond her. Her life can be no more than repetition. We learn only of her bearing more children. Once a possible heroine, she now becomes a minor character. Anna forces her husband Will into an inappropriate and precarious individuality, but he, by virtue of his lesser degree of identity, retards and in effect destroys her capacity for a finer and more achieved selfhood.

The meaning and the problems of full self-realisation constitute the central theme of *The Rainbow*. The issue is common to all three generations and often the experience of one generation in this matter is implicitly referred to and explained by the experience of another. For instance, the particular timbre of Will's nature and his failure in selfhood are accentuated by a comparison between an episode in the life of his uncle Tom Brangwen, the central

3 Carpaccio, "The Dream of St Ursula"   (*By courtesy of Osvaldo Bohm, Venice*)

4 Fra Angelico, "Last Judgment"

(By courtesy of Staatliche Museen Preussischer Kulturbesitz Gemäldegalerie, Berlin)

5 Mark Gertler, "Merry-Go-Round" ("Whirligig")

figure in the preceding generation, and a similar one in his own life. After the trip to Matlock during which he meets the aristocrat and his mistress, Tom becomes fascinated by the thought of worlds beyond his own very limited experience: "There was a life so different from what he knew it. What was there outside his knowledge, how much? . . . What did everything mean? Where was life, in that which he knew or all outside him?" With this sudden inkling there comes a dissatisfaction with his present form of existence.

> Then a fever of restless anger came upon him. He wanted to go away—right away. He dreamed of foreign parts. But somehow he had no contact with them. And it was a very strong root which held him to the Marsh, to his own house and land.

Eventually this tension in Tom Brangwen is released by his marriage to the emigré Polish lady who is house-keeper at the vicarage. But before this resolution occurs, Tom tries to obliterate the painfully contradictory impulses within himself by excessive drinking.

> He drank to get drunk. He gulped down the brandy, and more brandy, till his face became pale, his eyes burning. . . . Gradually the tension in him began to relax. He began to feel happy. His riveted silence was unfastened, he began to talk and babble. He was happy and at one with all the world, he was united with all flesh in a hot blood-relationship.

The spuriousness of this attempt to revert to the old blood intimacy and to evade the promptings to individualisation are explicitly condemned in an authorial comment: "But he had achieved his satisfaction by obliterating his own individuality, that which it depended on his manhood to preserve and develop."

Lawrence nowhere supplies such a concise explanation of Will Brangwen's difficulties. Yet the principle established here does have direct bearing upon Will's more complicated situation. One important instance is the first quarrel between Will and Anna, which occurs during the honeymoon. Anna tires of their first protracted experience of privacy and intimacy sooner than Will: "She was less hampered than he, so she came more quickly to her fullness, and was sooner ready to enjoy again a return to the outside world. She was going to give a tea-party." Will's uneasiness at this sudden indifference develops into a blank anger against his wife. His bleak ignoring of her comes gradually to terrify her and the mounting tension between them reaches its climax when Anna at last openly weeps at Will's hostile neglect of her. This has its effect upon Will.

> Suddenly his heart was torn with compassion for her. He became alive again, in an anguish of compassion. He could not bear to think of her tears—he could not bear it. He wanted to go to her and pour out his heart's blood to her. He wanted to give everything to her, all his blood, his life, to the last dregs, pour everything away to her. He yearned with passionate desire to offer himself to her, utterly.

The failure that is so carefully conveyed in the rhythm as well as the vocabulary of this passage is essentially of the same order as that experienced by Tom Brangwen. Will is not merely allowing free rein to an impulse of reconciliation and compassion. He is using the occasion to indulge his desire for self-abandonment. This kind of rapture is for him what alcohol once was for his uncle. It is a deeply craved release from the constriction, the consistency and the responsibility which are the conditions of an individuality and selfhood forced upon him by his marriage and by his stage in the evolution of his family line.

To suggest the continuance over the generations of this issue of selfhood is not to imply that one generation is merely repeating the experience of its predecessor. *The Rainbow* is a book of echoes both in the obvious matter of contrasting episodes and in the recurrence of phrase and motif, but the reverberations suggest change as much as continuity. For to Lawrence the movement to individuality signifies also a developing consciousness of the self as a function of time and history. Although Tom Brangwen and then his nephew Will confront the same essential issue in life, their experience of it is considerably different. They themselves are very dissimilar people. The very timbre and texture of sensuousness in each is different. Tom as a young man is "a fresh, fair young fellow with heavy limbs and head held back, mostly silent, though alert and attentive, very hearty in his greeting of everybody he knew, shy of strangers". Will at the same age is very different.

> He had town clothes and was thin, with a very curious head, black as jet, with hair like sleek, thin fur. It was a curious head: it reminded her [Anna] she knew not of what: of some animal, some mysterious animal that lived in the darkness under the leaves and never came out, but which lived vividly, swift and intense.

A kindred aspect of Will's physical and emotional nature is his peculiarly feline sexuality.

> But he had the wonderful voice, that could ring its vibration through the girl's soul, transport her into his feeling. Sometimes his voice was hot and declamatory, sometimes it had a strange, twanging, almost catlike sound, sometimes it hesitated, puzzled, sometimes there was the break of a little laugh.

His nature is beyond his uncle's understanding. "There was no getting hold of the fellow, Brangwen irritably thought. He was like a grinning young tom-cat, that came when he thought he would, and without cognizance of the other person." Furthermore, Will's consciousness is more tutored, more sophisticated than that of his uncle. Tom has a certain moral and emotional heroism that

Will lacks, but his mind and outlook are restricted to what is suggested by the notion of the yeoman farmer. Will Brangwen's range of awareness is far more extensive. He is a lace designer, a devotee of arts and crafts, a musician and eventually a teacher. When Will and his family finally move from the village to suburbia, they represent something that would have been beyond the comprehension of Tom Brangwen.

> After all, they would be, as one of their acquaintances said, among the élite of Beldover. They would represent culture. And as there was no one of higher social importance than the doctors, the colliery-managers, and the chemists, they would shine, with their Della Robbia beautiful Madonna, their lovely reliefs from Donatello, their reproductions from Botticelli. Nay, the large photographs of the Primavera and the Aphrodite and the Nativity in the dining-room, the ordinary reception-room, would make dumb the mouth of Beldover.

The increase in sophistication which Will represents is not primarily social or intellectual, but visual. In Lawrence's presentation of him there is, as we have just seen, a pronouncedly tactile, sensuous quality; and this same quality informs Will's own apprehension of the world. Most characteristically he is rendered in terms of a physical undertaking such as carving, painting, modelling, carpentry or even just gardening. Also his life and home and family are conditioned by his highly developed love of art. In this section of the novel experience is frequently specified by reference to a whole succession of painters: Greuze, Reynolds, Rubens, Giotto, Fra Lippo Lippi. And the little development there is in Will's life also finds expression in terms of a changing taste in art which, though reasonably intelligible in itself, is fully glossed by the theory of art developed in "Study of Thomas Hardy". The debility of Will's individuality, the failure of his generation to achieve full renaissance, is suggested by the enthusiasm for the work of Donatello and Della Robbia that accompanies his late flowering selfhood. At this stage, we are told, "He loved the Della Robbia and Donatello as he had loved Fra Angelico when he was a young man." Walter Pater, in his essay "Luca Della Robbia" in *The Renaissance*, claims for these sculptors of the early fifteenth century a distinct achievement "within the narrow limits which they chose to impose on their work", while at the same time clearly conceding the slightness of their work in comparison with that of the complete Renaissance artist, Michelangelo, for whom work "which was not concerned with the individual expression, with individual character and feeling, the special history of the special soul, was not worth doing at all". And it seems likely that Lawrence invokes these names in the novel in order to imply a similar contrast.[51] Will's consciousness has undergone a development, but one that must seem quaint and slight in comparison with the kind of renaissance experienced by his daughter Ursula, whose story strikes us very much as "the special history of the special soul". Will Brangwen, like the artists he comes to admire, is of his nature inescapably preliminary to the historic moment of full and balanced consciousness.[52]

The more detailed references to the art of Fra Angelico perform the same function in the novel as the references to the Tuscan sculptors. Will Brangwen's early love for Fra Angelico's painting further defines his situation in

[51] The idea of the Renaissance which is developed in "Study of Thomas Hardy" seems to owe something to Pater's book. Lawrence read Pater while he was at work on this essay and *The Rainbow*.

[52] The incapacity for full development that is suggested by the history of Will Brangwen's taste is also indicated by his performance as an artist. "In his first passion, he got a beautiful suggestion of his desire. But the pitch of concentration would not come. With a little ash in his mouth he gave up. He continued to copy, or to make designs by selecting motives from classic stuff."

terms of the categories of life and history established in *The Rainbow* and in "Study of Thomas Hardy". In fact, in one place in the latter work Lawrence distinctly associates Fra Angelico with the medieval cathedral, which is a major symbol in *The Rainbow*, as an expression of the female principle of the composite and the collective: "The Cathedrals, Fra Angelico, frighten us or [bore] us with their final annunciation of centrality and stability. We want to escape. The influence is too female for us."[53] This particular admiration of Will's is a further indication of his yearning and sympathy for the medieval, which in turn is the cultural expression of his fear of singleness and his cult of the kind of experience that may serve as a solvent of individuality.[54] But the several references to Fra Angelico in *The Rainbow* are more than ciphers that can only be understood in terms of some philosophy of history external to the novel. For Lawrence writes of particular paintings and particular responses, and his writing both subsumes and extends any bald propositions that might be excerpted from "Study of Thomas Hardy". This is the case with the differing responses of Will and Anna to Fra Angelico. For Anna, in her first pregnancy, a reproduction of the "Entry of the Blessed into Paradise" is a confirmation of her own momentary and somewhat precious sense of joyful innocence:

> This filled Anna with bliss. The beautiful, innocent way in which the Blessed held each other by the hand as they moved towards the radiance, the real, real, angelic melody, made her weep with happiness. The floweriness, the beams of light, the linking of hands, was almost too much for her, too innocent.

For Will, on the other hand, Fra Angelico has a different

[53] *Phoenix*, p. 457.
[54] It is, of course, a taste shared by Ruskin at the time he wrote the second volume of *Modern Painters*.

significance, one that involves more than particular representational elements:

> He loved the early Italian painters, but particularly Giotto and Fra Angelico and Filippo Lippi. The great compositions cast a spell over him. How many times had he turned to Raphael's "Dispute of the Sacrament" or Fra Angelico's "Last Judgment" or the beautiful, complicated renderings of the Adoration of the Magi, and always, each time, he received the same gradual fulfilment of delight. It had to do with the establishment of a whole mystical, architectural conception which used the human figure as a unit. Sometimes he had to hurry home, and go to the Fra Angelico "Last Judgment". The pathway of open graves, the huddled earth on either side, the seemly heaven arranged above, the singing progress to paradise on the one hand, the stuttering descent to hell on the other, completed and satisfied him. He did not care whether or not he believed in devils or angels. The whole conception gave him the deepest satisfaction, and he wanted nothing more.

Their different responses to Fra Angelico reveal very distinctly the contrast between Will and Anna in range of feeling.[55] Also the account of Will's response shows how his passionate interest in art is in no way founded on a concern with the representation of specific phenomena but on a fascination with the kind of form and composition that caters to his own need to see the world in terms of stasis and matrix. Will's response to the painting is of

[55] The contrast is made even sharper by the fact that Will and Anna are looking at the same picture. What Lawrence calls "The Entry of the Blessed into Paradise" is a component part of a larger composition by Fra Angelico entitled "The Last Judgment". Lawrence may be referring either to the Fra Angelico triptych "The Last Judgment" in Berlin of which "The Entry of the Blessed" is a part or to another version of "The Last Judgment" in the Museum of San Marco in Florence which also incorporates a distinct representation of the Blessed. In any case, there is no independent painting by Fra Angelico entitled "The Entry of the Blessed into Paradise". That Anna should isolate one thematic element in the work and miss the "whole mystical, architectural conception" is in keeping with the point that is being made in the novel.

exactly the same order as his response to Lincoln Cathedral. As both painting and cathedral serve to suggest, art for Will Brangwen is not a means for better understanding or appreciating reality but rather a means of experiencing the heightened consciousness that life does not ordinarily allow. The cathedral signifies a major aesthetic experience for Will. Like the episode of Ursula and the horses at the very end of the novel, the comparatively brief chapter "The Cathedral" is a recapitulation of the emotional centre of a human life. And nothing shows Will Brangwen's kinship with Ruskin better than the densely written account of his aesthetic joy in experiencing the great building. The significance that Lincoln Cathedral has for Will is very similar to that which Ruskin demanded of all great architecture when, by way of defining the principle he called "The Lamp of Power", he maintained that "the reality of its works, and the use and influence they have in the daily life of men, . . . require of it that it should express a kind of human sympathy, by a measure of darkness as great as there is in human life: and that as the great poem and great fiction generally affect us most by the majesty of their masses of shade, and cannot take hold of us if they affect a continuance of lyric sprightliness, but must be often serious, and sometimes melancholy, else they do not express the truth of this wild world of ours; so there must be, in this magnificently human art of architecture, some equivalent expression for the trouble and wrath of life, for its sorrow and its mystery. . . ."[56] Lawrence's description of Will's visit to the cathedral is a re-creation of the very spirit and feeling which we associate with *The Seven Lamps of Architecture*. At the same time, the writing also contains a criticism of Ruskinite sensibility. The following three paragraphs describing Will's response to the cathedral

[56] John Ruskin, *The Seven Lamps of Architecture* (London, 1906), pp. 152, 153.

illustrate the way in which Lawrence's art both represents
and judges a given timbre of feeling.

> Away from time, always outside of time! Between east and
> west, between dawn and sunset, the church lay like a seed in
> silence, dark before germination, silenced after death.
> Containing birth and death, potential with all the noise
> and transition of life, the cathedral remained hushed, a
> great, involved seed, whereof the flower would be radiant
> life inconceivable, but whose beginning and whose end
> were the circle of silence Spanned round with the rainbow,
> the jewelled gloom folded music upon silence, light upon
> darkness, fecundity upon death, as a seed folds leaf upon
> leaf and silence upon the root and the flower, hushing up
> the secret of all between its parts, the death out of which
> it fell, the life into which it has dropped, the immortality it
> involves, and the death it will embrace again.
> Here in the church, "before" and "after" were folded
> together, all was contained in oneness. Brangwen came
> to his consummation. Out of the doors of the womb he had
> come, putting aside the wings of the womb, and pro-
> ceeding into the light. Through daylight and day-after-day
> he had come, knowledge after knowledge, and experience
> after experience, remembering the darkness of the womb,
> having prescience of the darkness after death. Then between-
> while he had pushed open the doors of the cathedral,
> and entered the twilight of both darknesses, the hush of the
> two-fold silence, where dawn was sunset, and the begin-
> ning and the end were one.
> Here the stone leapt up from the plain of earth, leapt up
> in a manifold, clustered desire each time, up, away from
> the horizontal earth, through twilight and dusk and the
> whole range of desire, through the swerving, the declina-
> tion, ah, to the ecstasy, the touch, to the meeting and the
> consummation, the meeting, the clasp, the close embrace,
> the neutrality, the perfect, swooning consummation, the
> timeless ecstasy. There his soul remained, at the apex of the
> arch, clinched in the timeless ecstasy, consummated.

The response that is represented here is well summarised in some remarks of Wilhelm Worringer, whose
famous and influential study of Gothic art and feeling

was published some three years before *The Rainbow*. Worringer wrote of the Gothic mind:

> Distressed by actuality, debarred from naturalness, it aspires to a world above the actual, above the sensuous. It uses this tumult of sensations to lift itself out of itself. It is only in intoxication that it experiences the thrill of eternity. It is this exalted hysteria which is above all else the distinguishing mark of the Gothic phenomenon.[57]

Admittedly there is more to these three paragraphs of Lawrence's than can be suggested by any paraphrase. The verbal art with which Lawrence represents Gothic feeling is of a texture, density and richness of implication that give us vastly more than a conceptual statement. It recreates a whole complex experience. What is most immediately striking in this remarkable passage is the manoeuvrability of Lawrence as narrator. The first and the third paragraphs present an empathising re-creation of Will's consciousness as it is affected by the cathedral. The intervening paragraph reasserts the more stable perspective of the narrator, which both explains and relieves the complex intensity of the feeling described. (This is Lawrence's recurrent device in *The Rainbow* for allowing full fidelity to the particular emotional phenomenon while at the same time maintaining the necessary interpretative position.) Lawrence's responsiveness to the feeling is most clearly shown by the movement of the sentences. Thus from the opening exclamation, through the series of sinuous adverbial phrases, to the ejaculating syllable which introduces the climax that is registered in the ecstatic piling up of noun phrases, the writing gives us a very specific sense of the rhythm of Will's excitement.

[57] *Form in Gothic* (London, 1964), p. 79. Worringer's work was known in England in the years before 1915 in great part through the writings of T. E. Hulme. There is no evidence to suggest that Lawrence read Worringer but the view of the Gothic that we find in "Study of Thomas Hardy" is very similar to Worringer's.

The rhythm is further particularised by the increasing length of the sentences in the first and third paragraphs and by the effect of the sudden repetition of main verbs at the beginning of paragraph three.

The design and structure of the sentences suggest something of the quality and texture of the feeling as well as its movement. In the last sentence of the first paragraph the series of appositional accusatives at the beginning and the sequence of nouns with adjectival clauses at the end give to the sentence a sonority very reminiscent of that of the creed. The suggestion of chanting, of incantation, helps to convey something of Will's state of rapture. But the comparison suggested by the composition of the sentence can only serve to indict the quality of the feeling conveyed. Will's consciousness adopts the modulations of the creed not for the sake of its original intellectual and theological scrupulousness, but in order to elevate and poeticise what can only be described as a moment of emotional self-indulgence. And to make sure that this implicit judgment against the feeling here evoked is unambiguous, Lawrence, now very much the authoritative narrator, devotes the next paragraph to explaining how this experience of the cathedral is not primarily religious but rather caters to a particular nature and emotional condition. That there is something oppressive and even decadent in this condition is brought out some paragraphs later by Anna's rejection of this kind of experience. The brevity of the sentences describing her attitude, the insistence on simple, untextured opinion, help to ventilate the oppressive density of the language that describes Will's emotion:

> But even in the dazed swoon of the cathedral, she claimed another right. The altar was barren, its lights gone out. God burned no more in that bush. It was dead matter lying there. She claimed the right to freedom above her, higher than the roof. She had always a sense of being roofed in.

The flagrant convertibility of the spiritual and the sexual in the three paragraphs cited recalls the sensibility which we associate with the decadence. So also does the way in which the language and the feeling of the passage function as a narcotic. Phrases such as "circle of silence" and "a seed in darkness", for example, subordinate sense to sound. And others such as "coloured darkness" and "jewelled gloom" are unmistakably language mannerisms that belong to what we think of as characteristically nineties feeling. The heavy Latinity of the vocabulary which accounts for the general quality of the writing further accentuates this reference, for it exists to further sonority rather than precision. This sonority, at once sensuous and devotional, is one aspect of the desired consummation in a choice ecstasy. In stressing this quality of the three paragraphs I do not intend to suggest that they are in any way a conscious stylistic exercise on Lawrence's part. They are not pastiche but rather an empathetic re-creation of a particular phase in the history of feeling.

The term decadence has at least two reasonably clear meanings: it can refer to a phase of art in the late nineteenth century; or, more generally, it can denote certain emotional predilections and kinds of behaviour. Both senses of the word are highly relevant to the subsequent career of Will Brangwen. There is no contradiction in associating Will's consciousness with that of certain artists of the nineties while at the same time insisting on his indebtedness to Ruskin. In Will, Lawrence is showing a particular version of an emotional strain that pervades the second half of the nineteenth century, a tradition of feeling of which Ruskin is the most easily identified and the most influential founder. The tradition has been described by Graham Hough in his book *The Last Romantics*. Beginning with Ruskin, Hough traces a distinct continuity of thought and feeling in the careers of, among others, Rossetti, Walter Pater, the *fin-de-siècle* poets and W. B. Yeats. And what he says in his introduction by way of defining the common features of this company can easily accommodate Will Brangwen, the painter, sculptor and musician of Cossethay.

> What they share is a common passion for the life of the imagination, conceived as an all-embracing activity, apart from the expression of it in any one particular art. Hence a tendency to assimilate the different arts to each other, to allow their values to interpenetrate each other, forming together a realm of transcendental importance, for which a status has somehow to be found in an inhospitable world. This endeavour becomes so absorbing that it leads to a gradual severance, increasingly apparent from Ruskin onwards, of art from the interests of common life, and a constant tendency to turn art itself into the highest value, to assimilate aesthetic to religious experience.[58]

The severance of this tradition from common life is in one very conspicuous way a sexual matter. From the time of the notoriety surrounding Ruskin's marriage until the scandals of the nineties, the tradition was signalised by, and has since been associated with, a certain sexual imbalance. Admittedly, the kind of sexual decadence that Lawrence identifies in Will Brangwen is not directly comparable with, say, Ruskin's sexual malaise. But in observing Lawrence's presentation of the improprieties of feeling that inform Will's sexuality as well as his cult of the aesthetic, we discover insights about the integrity and the continuity of feeling in all areas of an individual's experience that are distinctly relevant to the Ruskinite tradition. This side of Will's nature starts to become a major subject of the novel at the beginning of the second phase of his relationship with Anna. After seven years the compromise based on a tacit acceptance of Anna's vital pre-eminence and on their commitment to parenthood starts to break down.

[58] Graham Hough, *The Last Romantics* (London, 1961), xvi.

> For years he had gone on beside her, never really encroaching upon her. Then gradually another self seemed to assert its being within him. . . . Gradually he became indifferent of responsibility. He would do what pleased him, and no more.

This new impulse in Will expresses itself in an attempt at adultery. Going alone to the Nottingham Empire one night, Will picks up "a common girl", takes her to a park and tries to seduce her. Within the overall economy of *The Rainbow* this again is something which takes on its full significance only when we register it as one of the contrasting episodes of the novel. In the first generation Tom Brangwen undergoes a somewhat similar adventure. Tom is strongly impressed when he meets his brother's mistress Mrs. Forbes. "His brother was this woman's lover! It was too amazing. Brangwen went home despising himself for his own poor way of life. He was a clod-hopper and a boor, dull, stuck in the mud." Tom's thought of a relationship with a woman other than his wife helps to aggravate the coolness that has come over the marriage by the end of two years. Yet this very suggestion of an alternative way of life helps to elicit from a deeper level of consciousness in both Tom and Lydia a realisation of their inevitable relationship. In a finely written scene there occurs an irresistible access of resurgent feeling:

> Their coming together now, after two years of married life, was much more wonderful to them than it had been before. It was the entry into another circle of existence, it was the baptism to another life, it was the complete confirmation.

But at the similar moment in the experience of the second generation there is no corresponding achievement of a new height of mutual feeling, understanding and esteem. Will and Anna do not come to any such new and exhilarating self-realisation. Will's return home after his experience with the girl precipitates merely an abandonment to sensation. "To his latent, cruel smile she replied with brilliant challenge. He expected her to keep the moral fortress. Not she! It was much too dull a part. She challenged him back with a sort of radiance, very bright and free, opposite to him." Lawrence goes on to say: "They abandoned in one motion the moral position, each was seeking gratification pure and simple." And the full implication of the word "moral" here is made clear in the subsequent lengthy descriptions of the new state of relationship between Will and Anna. The maintenance and development of the self are completely renounced in favour of an abandonment to a cult of what Lawrence calls "Absolute Beauty". This, as he also makes plain, is a form of death.

> Sometimes he felt he was going mad with a sense of Absolute Beauty, perceived by him in her through his senses. It was something too much for him. And in everything, was this same, almost sinister, terrifying beauty. But in the revelations of her body through contact with his body, was the ultimate beauty, to know which was almost death in itself, and yet for the knowledge of which he would have undergone endless torture. . . .
> This was what their love had become, a sensuality violent and extreme as death. They had no conscious intimacy, no tenderness of love. It was all the lust and the infinite, maddening intoxication of the senses, a passion of death.

The passion described here is the result of a lack of a proper polarity (to use the term proposed by Lawrence in *Women in Love*) both within Will and in his relationship with Anna. This emotional imbalance, intrinsic and extrinsic, is caused most obviously by Will's inability to engage in any moral or emotional exchange, any dialectic of growth with Anna. And this incapacity results from the lack of knowledge of, and thus the fear of, his own emotional depths. These two failings are the consequences of Will's early intimidation. Lawrence suggests that Will's love of Gothic is a way of escaping the frightening and uncharted turbulence of his feelings and desires:

> He had always, all his life, had a secret dread of Absolute Beauty. It had always been like a fetish to him, something to fear, really. For it was immoral and against mankind. So he had turned to the Gothic form, which always asserted the broken desire of mankind in its pointed arches, escaping the rolling, absolute beauty of the round arch.

This terror (also discussed by Worringer in his account of the Gothic) continues even after Will "with infinite sensual violence gave himself to the realisation of this supreme, immoral, Absolute Beauty, in the body of woman." Lawrence puts the matter in these words:

> But still the thing terrified him. Awful and threatening it was, dangerous to a degree, even whilst he gave himself to it. It was pure darkness, also. All the shameful things of the body revealed themselves to him now with a sort of sinister, tropical beauty. All the shameful, natural and unnatural acts of sensual voluptuousness which he and the woman partook of together, created together, they had their heavy beauty and their delight.

The suggestion here of unorthodox sexual practices provides the final emphasis in Lawrence's account of Will Brangwen's emotional condition. In essence, what he is describing is a nature of considerable emotional depth which, as a result of a certain restriction, builds to an intensity and a violence that prevent it from finding release, satisfaction and confirmation in a balanced relationship with the world or with a woman. The relationship with the world is replaced by the cult of Gothic feeling and the relationship with woman by a propensity to fetishistic frenzy.

The restriction which is the cause of Will's situation is essentially a historical matter. Will even more than Tom Brangwen marries above his own level of development and self-confidence. And like his father Alfred Brangwen, who reads Herbert Spencer and Browning and comes at last to cultivate a cynical stoicism, Will inherits no categories of feeling that can conduce to a true propriety of the emotions. Ruskinism, like his father's pessimism, is unable to replace the long established pieties of the Marsh farm; it is a symptom of the condition and not its remedy. The self-conscious civilisation into which the second generation of Brangwens is immigrant can offer as its orthodoxies of feeling only derivative evasions. And at this point the Brangwens themselves are not sufficiently evolved in consciousness to produce their own forms.

Often in the published discussion of *The Rainbow* one encounters the view that the second stage of Will Brangwen's marriage represents something good in that "it set another man in him free" and that "this new man turned with interest to public life, to see what part he could take in it". Will becomes interested in Education and starts a woodwork class in Cossethay. Lawrence makes no direct criticism of this venture in itself, but within the novel as a whole it figures as a very dubious achievement. "At this time Education was in the forefront as a subject of interest." The introduction of the subject in the higher case is surely significant. There is a sense in which education may be said to be a theme of *The Rainbow*, but it does not involve the institutionality and the piety intimated here. If the simple but very convincing dignity of the marriage of Tom and Lydia constitutes a judgment against that of Will and Anna, then the protracted experience of Education that dominates the life of Ursula both as pupil and as teacher is also an implicit criticism of Will's commitment and subordination of himself to Education as an institution. The new impulses in English life represented by the Brangwens fail in this second generation. At every stage that is presented to us, Will Brangwen's life is at best a compromising of the self. And

95

as he grows older he becomes negligible in a way that Tom Brangwen never does. The final judgment is Birkin's in *Women in Love*. It is concise and damning. For him, Will Brangwen "was not a coherent human being, he was a roomful of old echoes."

5
A CULTURE HEROINE

IN the third generation the vital advancement of the Brangwens is in the hands of the two eldest children, Ursula and Gudrun. Their very names serve to emphasise the parental, or at any rate the paternal, immersion in late Victorian romanticism. Ursula is named for the saint in the Carpaccio painting which so strongly affected Ruskin. (Lawrence himself in the essay "Making Pictures" recalls the pleasure of making a copy of "a Carpaccio picture in Venice".)[59] And it seems possible that Gudrun's name was prompted by that of a major character in one of William Morris's verse romances.[60] Of the two sisters Gudrun is the one who continues Will Brangwen's dedication to art. In *The Rainbow* we read of her "attending the Art School at Nottingham", "working particularly at sculpture", and "making little models in clay, of

[59] *Phoenix II, Uncollected, Unpublished and Other Prose Works by D. H. Lawrence*, ed. Warren Roberts and Harry T. Moore (London, 1968), p. 606.

[60] It could come either from "The Lovers of Gudrun" in *The Earthly Paradise* or from *The Story of Sigurd the Volsung and the Fall of the Niblungs*. This latter seems a more likely source. As in the former, the narrative focuses on a Gudrun who is fated to destruction and on a quartet of central characters; but here, with the succession of social and familial hegemonies, there is also something of the same sense of saga that we get in the Brangwen books. Possibly the frequent metaphorising of Gerald Crich as a Niblung in *Women in Love* was also suggested by this work. Certainly the name Loerke derives from this tradition of narrative.

children or of animals". And in the opening chapter of
Women in Love Gudrun has "just come back from London,
where she had spent several years, working at an art-
school, as a student, and living a studio life". Yet Gudrun's career as an artist, though in a sense more serious
and unquestionably more professional than her father's,
is not accorded in terms of the economy of the two novels
the same centrality, the same detailed assessment that
his was. In *The Rainbow* Gudrun is only a minor character,
and within the antiphonal ordering of *Women in Love*
her career comes to represent quite unambiguously a
form of destruction and of life denial. Indeed one thematic function of Gudrun's art as it is characterised
in the two novels is to raise the issue of the extent to
which in the twentieth century the term "art" has come
to be both restrictive and pejorative. Lawrence's criticism of the modern orthodoxy in art as represented by
Gudrun and by Loerke is a central theme of *Women
In Love*. Yet the full implication of Gudrun's commitment to art is only fully intelligible when placed against
the lengthy account of Ursula's education in feeling
and selfhood which is the pre-eminent theme of the
second half of *The Rainbow*.

The first major difficulty in Ursula's progress and one
that entails an important contrast with Gudrun is her
unavoidable repudiation of her father. This decision,
which is shown in all its slow and gradual maturation
during Ursula's girlhood, is one of the consequences of the
marital discord between Will and Anna. In his uneasiness
with his wife Will turns to his eldest daughter for affection
and companionship and demands of her an adulthood
which it is beyond her age and powers to sustain. The
most vivid scenes of Ursula's childhood portray her agon-
ising sense of failure towards her father and his often unreasonable and excessive anger against her. Furthermore,
Will attempts to use the child as a means of testing and

confirming his own very suspect confidence. He challenges her to feats of emotional endurance and at the same time tries to implicate her in the enormities of sensation which these involve and which serve him as a release. At the fair he challenges her to go higher and higher with him in the swingboats and makes her ill; and on swimming expeditions he frightens the child by recklessly diving into the water with her on his back. On one of these occasions they come very close to death. These efforts to provoke the child into a communion of sensation, and also into submission, come to an end when Will enters into the second phase of relationship with his wife. But for Ursula's life the damage is already done. The staple rhythm of Will's relationship with his daughter is already established. Intense and excessive demands followed by bitter and unreasonable hostility at her failure to fulfil them continue to mark his conduct towards her. "And very early she learned to harden her soul in resistance and denial of all that was outside her, harden herself upon her own being."

An important point about this third Brangwen generation is that its best representative is not, as with the earlier generations, a man, but a woman. Obviously this can be seen to represent that emergence of female independence and initiative which is such a familiar feature of the history of the period. But Lawrence is not merely confirming a phenomenon or rehearsing a known "issue" as, say, H. G. Wells does in *Ann Veronica*. His concern is rather to render that displacement in the old orthodoxies of feeling between man and woman which prefigures the phenomenon and the issue. It is interesting to note that Lawrence's account of the origins of woman's quest for independence begins with a relationship between a father and a daughter, not one between lovers or between husband and wife. Ursula, who is the first of the Brangwen women to be preoccupied with "this one desire to take her place in the world", is not motivated initially by the unsatisfactoriness of her relationship with Skrebensky. Her ambition comes primarily from her uncertainty with regard to her father and her home. Something of the dis-affection between father and daughter is suggested in the following brief passage of dialogue in which Ursula first broaches her determination to go out to work:

"Go out to work, what for?"
His voice was so strong, and ready, and vibrant. It irritated her.
"I want some other life than this."
A flash of strong rage arrested all his blood for a moment.
"Some other life?" he repeated. "Why, what other life do you want?"
She hesitated.
"Something else besides housework and hanging about. And I want to earn something."
Her curious, brutal hardness of speech, and the fierce invincibility of her youth, which ignored him, made him also harden with anger.
"And how do you think *you're* going to earn anything?" he asked.
"I can become a teacher—I'm qualified by my matric."
He wished her matric. in hell.
"And how much are you qualified to earn by your matric.?" he asked, jeering.
"Fifty pounds a year," she said.
He was silent, his power taken out of his hand.

Ursula only starts to feel fully at ease in herself on the day she receives her first salary as a teacher and senses "Whitehall far beyond her as her ultimate home". Significantly her new position and role afford her new notions of fatherhood. "In the government, she knew which minister had supreme control over Education, and it seemed to her that, in some way, he was connected with her, as her father was connected with her."
In what was the first and still is the best full critical

account of *The Rainbow*, F. R. Leavis says of Lawrence, "As a recorder of essential English history he is a great successor to George Eliot."[61] And in developing this notion of the essential, he goes on to say a few pages later:

> Lawrence . . . feels with a peculiar responsiveness the paradox of a continuity that is at the same time discontinuity: lives are separate, but life is continuous—it continues in the fresh start by the separate life in each generation. No work, I think, has presented this perception as an imaginatively realised truth more compellingly than *The Rainbow*, or given more subtly in related particular lives the complex movement, or pattern in time, of succeeding (and co-existent) generations.[62]

This complex movement of the generations is what gives full meaning to the first great tendency in Ursula's life. A standard of comparison for her difficult feeling for her father is there in the story of Anna's relationship with Tom Brangwen. Here too there is considerable strain. We recall the magnificent scene in which Tom tries to put the child to bed only to find himself involved in what is, as Lawrence suggests with a delicate accuracy, not only a simple conflict between parent and child but also a more complex dialectic of male and female will. Another instance is Tom's jealousy and regret at the prospect of Anna's marriage and departure from home. "He remembered the soft, warm weight of the little girl on his arm, round his neck. Now she would say he was finished. She was going away, to deny him, to leave an unendurable emptiness in him, a void that he could not bear. Almost he hated her." But the resentments between them are always contained and accommodated by the countervailing affection which exists on both sides. Even

[61] F. R. Leavis, *D. H. Lawrence Novelist* (Harmondsworth, 1964), p. 110.
[62] *ibid.*, p. 125.

after she is married, Tom Brangwen continues to stand for Anna as a figure of strength and stature. But with Will Brangwen the emphasis in the dialectic runs the other way. He fulfils no such role for his daughter, any more than he does for his wife. The failure of Will, and by implication of the developing English life of the time, to achieve a proper coherence has its familial as well as its sexual and marital consequences.

The element of falsification in Will's feeling about women and about his daughter in particular is shown in his attempt from the moment of her birth to associate her with Ruskin's cherished image of St. Ursula. In certain respects, it is true, the legend of the saint and the story of Lawrence's heroine have something in common. Each is in some sense a pilgrim, each is motivated by a dream of a higher level of being, each is resolutely uncynical. Lawrence's character also strikes us sometimes as a figure of possibility rather than of actuality in the same way that, as Ruskin himself suggested, Carpaccio's St. Ursula does. Nevertheless, because of the sensitive robustness of her way of living and feeling, the Ursula whom Lawrence portrays can only seem a criticism of the Carpaccio image cherished alike by Ruskin and by Will Brangwen. To read of Ursula Brangwen and then to look at the Carpaccio painting or to read Ruskin's lengthy descriptions of it in *Fors Clavigera* is to become especially alert to the extent to which the Carpaccio, for all the charm of its spaciousness and peacefulness is marked by a spirituality that is to some extent precious and sentimental. The youthfulness of the Carpaccio figure reminds us of Ursula's achieved and mature womanhood; its physical immaturity underscores her adult sexuality. The virginal somnolence of the Carpaccio also contrasts with Ursula's sensitive expectancy. And the epicene angel in the painting differs strongly from the image of the "Sons of God [who] saw the daughters of men that they were fair" which is ever the vision of promise for Ursula.[63]

The associations accompanying Will Brangwen's choice of name for his first child demonstrate again his propensity to sentimentalise and thus to evade the reality of womanhood.[64] The feeling about women that is present in this painting, or at least in the Ruskinian view of it, is as self-indulgent, evasive and irrelevant as that expressed in *Sesame and Lilies*. In his formal notions and professions of feeling as well as in his everyday relationship with his daughter, Will Brangwen is constrained to a serious emotional falsification which expresses itself at times in sentimentality and at times in a brutal harshness. Ironically Will Brangwen's second child, Gudrun, conforms more to the icons of femininity referred to in his naming of the first. Gudrun "with her sleepy, half-languid girlishness that looked so soft, and yet was balanced and inalterable underneath" is more recognisably Ursuline. And her attitude to her father is more fond and submissive than Ursula's: "She was happy at home, Ursula was not." She assists her father in the handicraft school, and from him, presumably, she derives her own ambition to become an artist. Also, the very limitedness of her art reminds us of the slightness of Will's creative achievement. And her perpetuation of the notion of irreconcilable division between art and life shows her continuing intellectual affiliation with her father. Her contributions to the discussions about art with Loerke at the end of *Women In Love* also demonstrate the extent to which this old aestheticism may inform even the most ostentatious modernism.

Ursula comes to reject the tradition of feeling expressed in the art and the taste of her father and sister. Her whole

[63] For a more explicit Lawrentian assessment of a Carpaccio painting see the poem "St. Mark" in *Birds, Beasts and Flowers*. Its subject is one of Carpaccio's later works, "The Lion of St. Mark".

[64] This is further suggested by his inability to complete his carving, "The Creation of Eve".

career, in fact, constitutes a quest to experience life in such a way as to know a fuller and less constricted range of feeling. The title of the novel, which emblematises this quest, only starts to take on its full significance when we relate it to the other major emblem of the novel, the Gothic arch, to which it stands as a contrast. The rainbow is less restrictive; it encompasses more and it suggests an infinitely greater range of colour and texture. It serves to convey the new freedom and enrichment of consciousness which Ursula and her generation desire. Of course, the Gothic arch continues to have some influence upon Ursula's life. It is inevitably a part of her experience just as it is a part of received English townscape. Nevertheless for Ursula it is a dead form; it is in no way genuinely correspondent to an inner state as it was for her father. It is merely an item of design, and one with repressive connotations. Thus the Gothic architecture of the school where Ursula first teaches is ugly to her for more than casual or aesthetic reasons: "She entered the arched doorway of the porch. The whole place seemed to have a threatening expression, imitating the church's architecture, for the purpose of domineering, like a gesture of vulgar authority." The university is even more superannuated; it is merely something to patronise as a "rather pretty, plaything, Gothic form". And at the last Ursula comes to despise it as she despises the kind of education that is offered: "But the whole thing seemed sham, spurious; spurious Gothic arches, spurious peace, spurious Latinity, spurious dignity of France, spurious naïveté of Chaucer." The contour of feeling which is so central to her father's nature is increasingly a matter of indifference to Ursula. And rejecting the Gothic arch, she endeavours to explore and to define a new contour of feeling, the rainbow.

Yet despite this very clear-cut distinction, the course of Ursula's life is significantly affected by her father's

passionate interest in the visual arts. The following two
paragraphs convey something of the positive as well as the
negative aspects of Ursula's complex inheritance. They
illustrate her early exposure to the paintings which her
father admires as well as her propensity to reject the
paternal icons and her fascination with the larger world
of nature.

> Ursula, accustomed to these pictures from her childhood,
> hunted out their detail. She adored Fra Angelico's flowers
> and light and angels, she liked the demons and enjoyed
> the hell. But the representation of the encircled God,
> surrounded by all the angels on high, suddenly bored her.
> The figure of the Most High bored her, and roused her
> resentment. Was this the culmination and the meaning
> of it all, this draped, null figure? The angels were so lovely,
> and the light so beautiful. And only for this, to surround
> such a banality for God!
>
> She was dissatisfied, but not fit as yet to criticise. There
> was yet so much to wonder over. Winter came, pine
> branches were torn down in the snow, the green pine
> needles looked rich upon the ground. There was the
> wonderful, starry, straight track of a pheasant's footsteps
> across the snow imprinted so clear; there was the lobbing
> mark of the rabbit, two holes abreast, two holes following
> behind; the hare shoved deeper shafts, slanting, and his two
> hind feet came down together and made one large pit; the
> cat podded little holes, and birds made a lacy pattern.

The consecutiveness of these paragraphs illustrates
with rare clarity the particular nature of Ursula's perception. The dialectic of tutored vision and actuality that
is intimated here constitutes the central issue underlying
and informing the long and carefully related story of
Ursula's progress to maturity. Here is another example
from her childhood in which distinctly Pre-Raphaelite
images of the self collide with a more mundane actuality.

> Ursula was just coming to the stage when Andersen and
> Grimm were being left behind for the "Idylls of the King"
> and romantic love-stories.

"Elaine the fair, Elaine the lovable,
Elaine the lily maid of Astolat,
High in her chamber in a tower to the east
Guarded the sacred shield of Launcelot."

How she loved it! How she leaned in her bedroom window with her black, rough hair on her shoulders, and her warm face all rapt, and gazed across at the churchyard and the little church, which was a turretted castle, whence Launcelot would ride just now, would wave to her as he rode by, his scarlet cloak passing behind the dark yew-trees and between the open space: whilst she, ah, she, would remain the lonely maid high up and isolated in the tower, polishing the terrible shield, weaving it a covering with a true device, and waiting, waiting, always remote and high.

At which point there would be a faint scuffle on the stairs, a light-pitched whispering outside the door, and a creaking of the latch: then Billy, excited, whispering:

"It's locked—it's locked."

Then the knocking, kicking at the door with childish knees, and the urgent, childish:

"Ursula—our Ursula? Ursula? Eh, our Ursula?"

No reply.

"Ursula! Eh—our Ursula?" the name was shouted now. Still no answer.

"Mother, she won't answer," came the yell. "She's dead."

There are many examples of this type of juxtaposition in Lawrence's descriptions of Ursula's childhood. Her early life is in fact a series of colourful visions of herself. She is now "the only daughter of the old lord, . . . gifted with magic", now the Lady Ursula "seated on horseback in a green riding habit". Always in her life there is this evolving tension between the envisioned and the actual. Nowhere is it more richly suggested than in the lengthy account of the contrast between the Sunday world and the weekday world, which is also the first point at which we see Ursula's situation being related to and integrated into the condition of English culture. Amusing though it may be at times, this central tension in Ursula's experience is not something which Lawrence simply dismisses as part of the comedy or the pathos of youth. It is a dualism which in its most evolved and mature form constitutes the leading theme of the second half of the book.

Once the description of Ursula's childhood is completed, the narrative presents five relatively distinct episodes in her life. There is the first and very youthful stage of her relationship with Anton Skrebensky; then come three experiences of Education: first the relationship with her teacher Miss Inger, secondly the experience of being a teacher herself and thirdly the student period at college in Nottingham. The final episode begins with Skrebensky's return from Africa and Ursula's renewal of her foredoomed relationship with him. And in all five stages the central and continuing theme is the division in Ursula's perception between, to use Lawrence's own terms, the ordinary and the heroic. Speaking again of Verga and realism, Lawrence wrote:

> Ordinary people don't have much sense of heroic effort in life; and by the heroic effort we mean that instinctive fighting for more life to come into being, which is a basic impulse in more men than we like to admit; women too. Or it used to be. The discrediting of the heroic effort has almost extinguished that effort in the young, hence the appalling "flatness" of their lives. . . . Life without the heroic effort, and without *belief* in the subtle, life-long validity of the heroic impulse, is just stale, flat and unprofitable. As the great realistic novels will show you.[65]

The achievement and consolidation of Ursula's identity is a matter of new formulations and new resolutions, in the course of the five experiences we have mentioned, of the same essential dialectic that Lawrence has in mind here.

[65] "Introduction to *Mastro-don Gesualdo* by Giovanni Verga", *Phoenix II*, p. 282.

And in each case, this issue of alternative epistemologies presents itself at its most irreducible in visual terms.

The climax of the first phase of Ursula's relationship with Skrebensky occurs at the corn-dance, that memorably specified scene which contains Ursula's first awakening to sexual desire. Lawrence describes the harvest dance, the strange moonlit countryside (which objectifies the sudden new emotion that makes Ursula a stranger to herself) and also the desperate bankruptcy of the willed self-assertion with which Skrebensky seeks to confront the situation. Skrebensky's fear of Ursula's strange intensity is to some extent shared by the girl herself: "She was afraid of what she was." And after the diffusion of the situation as a result of Skrebensky's sexual retreat, we become aware of the characteristic dichotomy as Ursula begins "to come to herself". "Gradually a sort of daytime consciousness came back to her." "Gradually she realised that the night was common and ordinary, that the great, blistering, transcendent night did not really exist." Skrebensky's crucial failure is that he is unable to confirm and sustain a relationship through which the world can be perceived in its full density and texture. His is more that "daytime consciousness" which perceives in what are thought of as "real" and "ordinary" terms. This early scene in Ursula's progress makes it unnecessary to refer to Lawrence's discursive prose in order to understand how for him the words "real" and "ordinary" have less to do with the objects to which they may be applied than with the emotional condition, the emotional timbre of the perceiver.

The dawning realisation that comes to Ursula at this highly important moment in her education is also confirmed by her experience of Education in its institutional sense. Her chief discovery in her comparatively protracted academic education is that in herself she possesses greater powers of vital advancement than even the teacher who has the strongest intellectual and emotional effect upon her. Ursula's relationship with Winifred Inger follows immediately upon the departure of Skrebensky and reveals to her another radical failure of properly sensuous feeling. Miss Inger's initial attraction for Ursula is essentially visual. That which settles Ursula's love for her is the sight of her teacher swimming: "Miss Inger came out, dressed in a rust-red tunic like a Greek girl's, tied round the waist, and a red silk handkerchief round her head. How lovely she looked! Her knees were so white and strong and proud, and she was firm-bodied as Diana." But the overtly lesbian infatuation that ensues is soon dissipated by Ursula's fuller perception both of a physical ugliness in Winifred Inger and of the vital failure which the ugliness exemplifies: "And sometimes she thought Winifred was ugly, clayey. Her female hips seemed big and earthy, her ankles and her arms were too thick. She wanted some fine intensity, instead of this heavy cleaving of moist clay, that cleaves because it has no life of its own." It is a measure of Ursula's poise that she has so much influence in bringing about the marriage of her uncle Tom Brangwen to Winifred. The marriage is appropriate, for Tom and Winifred have the same essential nature. Each is sensuous, but only statically and self-indulgently. Neither is in any way capable of growth and development in sensuousness. Both are complacent and bourgeois and this helps to explain their signal in-difference to the ugly townscape of the place where Tom is the colliery manager. Landscape and townscape form highly important reference points in Ursula's mind and experience. And Wiggiston is among the most important. It is the first example in *The Rainbow* of the horrors of industrialisation. And Ursula is deeply appalled by the sight of "human bodies and lives subjected in slavery to that symmetric monster of the colliery". Significantly, Winifred, like Tom, is unmoved by her surroundings and unsusceptible to Ursula's alternative vision; she merely remains (and the literary reference is of interest) "superior to the Zolaesque tragedy". ,

This same contrast between a complacent acceptance and a creative denial of an emotionally debilitating reality continues to inform Ursula's life when she herself becomes a teacher. The period at Brinsley Street school is the experience in Ursula's life which receives the longest treatment. This is because it constitutes the most important phase in her development. Characteristically she begins her career with some very detailed, highly coloured and extremely romantic visual images in her mind. Each of her applications for her first teaching position evokes something of a picture postcard vision. This, for instance, is how she visualises Gillingham:

> Gillingham was such a lovely name, and Kent was the Garden of England. So that, in Gillingham, an old, old village by the hopfields, where the sun shone softly, she came out of school in the afternoon into the shadow of the plane-trees by the gate, and turned down the sleepy road towards the cottage where cornflowers poked their blue heads through an old wooden fence, and phlox stood built up of blossom beside the path.
> A delicate, silver-haired lady rose with delicate, ivory hands uplifted as Ursula entered the room, and,
> "Oh, my dear, what do you think!"
> "What is it, Mrs Wetherall?"
> Frederick had come home.

The "gorgeous dreams" which Lawrence gently derides here are soon set aside by the unpleasant reality of Brinsley Street School in nearby industrial Ilkeston. Similarly Ursula's intention to enjoy a close relationship with her pupils, to be "so personal" as a teacher and to "give all her great stores of wealth to her children" is dissipated in her distressing experiences of the classroom. She quickly and painfully learns the need to put herself out of account and to treat the children as a collectivity that must be manipulated by power and will.

> She was here in this hard, stark reality—*reality*. . . . This was the reality, and Cossethay, her beloved, beautiful, well-known Cossethay, which was as herself unto her, that was minor reality. . . . She had brought her feelings and her generosity to where neither generosity nor emotion were wanted.

But to regard the chapter "The Man's World" as simply an account of the dissipation of callow dreams and of the growth of a more realistic outlook on Ursula's part would be a falsification of what we are in fact offered. Ursula comes to understand "the system" and she learns to operate it, but she never accepts the rightness of it. Her youthful romanticism disappears but she never capitulates to orthodox contemporary notions of an inevitably inhuman reality. Tacitly she still protests on behalf of a more enriching and less constricting perception of the world. The old dichotomy of her life persists; though now it expresses itself in a more tutored, more experienced and more adult way. The significance of Ursula's experience as a teacher is put by Lawrence in these sentences: "Her real, individual self drew together and became more coherent during these two years of teaching, during the struggle against the odds of class teaching. It was always a prison to her, the school. But it was a prison where her wild, chaotic soul became hard and independent."

Again at the university Ursula is enmeshed within a system and yet at the same time is able to make a forceful reservation in favour of the possibility of a mode of perception that justifies her assessment of the university as "a little side-show to the factories of the town", a place where "the religious virtue of knowledge was become a flunkey to the god of material success". The state of

feeling and thought which is responsible for "the perma-
nent sub-stratum of ugliness under everything" is
revealed to Ursula in a conversation she has with Dr.
Frankstone, "a woman doctor of physics in the college".
Dr. Frankstone (the connotations of the name are more
immediately familiar in its German form) questions
whether life is anything more than "a complexity of
physical and chemical activities, of the same order as the
activities we already know in science". And Ursula herself, watching a cell under her microscope, wonders:
"What then was its will? If it was a conjunction of forces,
physical and chemical, what held these forces unified, and
for what purpose were they unified?" The answer to
these questions comes to her as a moment of understanding which repudiates the Schopenhauerian notion of will,
just as it repudiates bourgeois notions of mechanism:

> Suddenly she had passed away into an intensely-gleaming
> light of knowledge. She could not understand what it all
> was. She only knew that it was not limited mechanical
> energy, nor mere purpose of self-preservation and self-
> assertion. It was a consummation, a being infinite. Self
> was a oneness with the infinite.

It is significant that this realisation should come to
Ursula on the very same day that Skrebensky re-enters
her life. For the realisation is a conscious and conceptual
confirmation of the element in Ursula's nature which
accounts for the fundamentally irreconcilable difference
between her and Skrebensky which is the subject of the
last fifty pages of the book. Despite their efforts to establish an enduring relationship, the incompatibility is incorrigible, as Ursula herself recognises in the first
moments of their reunion: "She knew, vaguely, in the
first minute, that they were enemies come together in a
truce. Every movement and word of his was alien to her
being." Admittedly this new relationship brings Ursula
an experience of physical passion which in comparison

with the first is both adult and, in restrictedly sexual terms, confirming. But beyond this, Skrebensky has little to offer. He lacks that openness to the revitalising forces beyond the self which Ursula in the laboratory formulates to herself somewhat haltingly as the infinite, the forces that Lawrence himself suggests more fully in the poem "Song of a Man Who Has Come Through" and which *The Rainbow* as a whole (and particularly in scenes such as the one in which the first Tom Brangwen awaits the birth of his son) dramatises so memorably. Skrebensky is capable of no such experience: "He aroused no fruitful fecundity in her. He seemed added up, finished. She knew him all round, not on any side did he lead into the unknown." He is no more than a physical lover to her and in consequence becomes at the last, and this is the most painful judgment of all, merely "an incubus upon her".

Ultimately Skrebensky flees from this humiliation. And as on a somewhat similar occasion years before, Ursula grows fearful of what she now considers the excessiveness of her demands and expectations of life. Objectified as the fear of pregnancy, this new and radical uncertainty leads her to write a letter to Skrebensky in India asking to be taken back as his wife. Her former visions and demands of experience she now dismisses as "fantasies". This momentary panic undoubtedly represents the nadir of Ursula's emotional history. But it is also the prelude to that final consolidation of her selfhood which is a donnée of *Women In Love*. Ursula's recovery and reintegration of herself are mimed in the great finale to the novel represented by the episode of the horses. There are essentially three stages in this famous passage of the book. In the first the carefully described landscape is a counterpart of Ursula's original nature: "It was very splendid, free and chaotic." During the second stage, in which the horses appear and start to harrass her, Ursula feels frightened by her extendedness, her sudden sense of her distance from home and the familiar. This of course reproduces the same feeling that on two important occasions Skrebensky had elicited in her. (It is also noteworthy that Skrebensky is a horseman.) Ursula's fear about her situation builds to a climax, but she eventually manages to escape from the field where the horses are. At this point the fear abates; the horses no longer present a challenge. "They were almost pathetic now." In overcoming and refuting this fear, which is essentially a fear of her own isolate way of feeling and living (and one that is aggravated by the menace of the herd mentality of one such as Skrebensky), she achieves an ultimate and irreducible realisation of self: "She was in some way like the stone at the bottom of the river, inviolable and unalterable, no matter what storm raged in her body. . . . Under all her illness, persisted a deep, inalterable knowledge."

Ursula's final, difficult act of adherence to the alternative vision which more than anything else constitutes the peculiar Brangwen capacity for life is what is recorded in the closing paragraphs of the novel which describe Ursula's enduring vision of the rainbow. Many critics have seen this conclusion as abrupt and stylistically inconsistent with what has gone before. And the criticism must, I think, be allowed to stand. Plainly Lawrence was sufficiently anxious to finish this novel which had been with him for so many years that he was prepared to "tack on" an ending. Nevertheless the imperfection is not all that great. The landscape described here contrasts significantly with that in the very first paragraph of the book and thus helps to illuminate the very real if not obvious unity of the work. And given the dense complexity of the experiences just described, a clear-cut thematic emphasis such as this coda provides helps to underscore the pattern and the meaning of the novel. This last paragraph restates the central dualism of Ursula's life, the essentially visual distinction between on the one hand the seen world of damaged landscape and on the other the insistently envisioned world of a new covenant and a new order that recalls Blake's English Jerusalem.[66]

Ursula's final vision is only one of many elements in *The Rainbow* which demonstrate that the mode of visualisation signified by the notion of nineteenth-century realism was not the only mode of seeing to offer itself to Lawrence. Another strong feature in his imagination relates to that tradition of vision established in England by Blake and sustained during the Victorian period, though tenuously and less impressively, by painter-poets such as Ruskin and Rossetti. One important condition of Lawrence's genius was that it grew to maturity during one of those rare periods in which the visual arts in England attained a European significance. The writings of Ruskin and the works of the Pre-Raphaelites, of William Morris, of Voysey and of Mackintosh constitute a tradition which, until its sudden and inexplicable demise at the end of the Edwardian age, had a profound effect throughout Europe.[67] And that Lawrence with his strong albeit secondary interest in the visual arts was sensitively aware of both the aesthetic and the cultural implications of this tradition is shown by the very themes and characterisations in *The Rainbow*. It also seems likely that Lawrence's experience of this late Victorian art helped to second the pronouncedly visual emphasis in his own fictional style in the same way that it conditioned the minds and the lives of Will and Gudrun and Ursula Brangwen. As in the life of his heroine, so in Lawrence's actual writing in this

[66] The same reference is made more explicitly in *Women in Love*. To Birkin, Beldover on its hill "looked like Jerusalem to his fancy", p. 290.

[67] A good account of this tradition and its influence is contained in Nikolaus Pevsner's *Pioneers of Modern Design* (Harmondsworth, 1960). Further relevant information is provided in the second volume of the same author's *Studies in Art, Architecture and Design* (London, 1968).

novel, the drab, limited outlook of realism is modified and enlarged by a pictorial vision that introduces a new, simultaneously moral and visual quality into his fictional art. This quality is one of the factors which accounts for the epic character of *The Rainbow*.

6

"THE RAINBOW" AND EPIC

THE RAINBOW is epic not because it adheres closely to the conditions of an established literary form but rather by virtue of the kind of epistemology, the vision, which informs and directs the writing. It would be possible, certainly, to argue that this novel contains many of the thematic constituents usually deemed necessary to epic. *The Rainbow* treats of a turning point in history, it focuses upon individuals who are basically representative of a larger humanity, it shows how in each generation the hero descends into some underground of suffering and returns to discover some sense of the "eternal", it treats of journeying, of conflict and of relations between the human and something which is apprehended as the suprahuman. But that which E. M. W. Tillyard once sought to define as "the epic spirit"[68] and which asserts itself so powerfully in *The Rainbow* involves far more than an inventory of attributes. Initially it is a matter of the scale on which human life is perceived and of the significance with which it is endowed. Formal attributes are but secondary.

This is not to suggest that the epic qualities in *The Rainbow* are in some way uniquely expressive and without precedent or pattern in the literature of the past. The

[68] E. M. W. Tillyard, *The Epic Strain in the English Novel* (London, 1958), pp. 14–17.

term epic applies not only to the great narrative poems of Greece and Rome but also to the historical books of the Old Testament. And the Bible was a very significant factor in Lawrence's early intellectual life.[69] In one of his essays Lawrence identifies this element in the Bible and compares it favourably with Homer.

> Modern research has been able to put the Bible back into its living connections, and it is splendid: no longer the Jewish-moral book and a stick to beat an immoral dog, but a fascinating account of the adventure of the Jewish—or Hebrew or Israelite nation, among the great old civilised nations of the past, Egypt, Assyria, Babylon, and Persia: then on into the Hellenic world, the Seleucids, and the Romans, Pompey and Anthony. Reading the Bible in a new translation, with modern notes and comments, is more fascinating than reading Homer, for the adventure goes even deeper into time and into the soul, and continues through the centuries, and moves from Egypt to Ur and to Nineveh, from Sheba to Tarshish and Athens and Rome. It is the very quick of ancient history.[70]

The contrast between Biblical and classical epic is of relevance for the themes as well as the form of *The Rainbow*. In the opening pages of the novel classical epic is immediately associated with the life and culture of the established social and political hegemony, which is represented by the Hardys at nearby Shelly Hall. By the end of the book the most advanced Brangwen consciousness will have surpassed the old order;[71] but at the

[69] In *Apocalypse* Lawrence wrote: "From earliest years right into manhood, like any other nonconformist child I had the Bible poured every day into my helpless consciousness, till there came almost a saturation point. Long before one could think or even vaguely understand his Bible language, these 'portions' of the Bible were *douched* over the mind and consciousness, till they became soaked in, they became an influence which affected all the processes of emotion and thought." *Apocalypse* (New York, 1966), p. 3.

[70] *Phoenix*, p. 302.

[71] A book that made a strong impression on Lawrence during the period he was writing *The Rainbow* was Jane Harrison's *Ancient*

beginning of the novel the Brangwen women stand in awe of the glamorous world of the Hall.

> The lady of the Hall was the living dream of their lives, her life was the epic that inspired their lives. In her they lived imaginatively, and in gossiping of her husband who drank, of her scandalous brother, of Lord William Bentley her friend, member of Parliament for the division, they had their own Odyssey enacting itself, Penelope and Ulysses before them, and Circe and the swine and the endless web.

Lawrence's use of the word epic here initiates a contrast between two phases of history and between two class cultures which will continue as a significant theme in the story of the Brangwens until the end of *Women in Love*. Brangwen culture and consciousness is different from that of the old rural gentry and aristocracy. They do not see themselves, nor are they seen by Lawrence, in terms that are conditioned by the literature and culture of Greece and Rome. Their story, their consciousness, their development is made what it is above all by a habit of reference, a range of feeling and a form of wisdom that are drawn from the English Bible. They embody a vernacular culture which at last emerges to replace a devitalised classical gentility. And what is true of the characters is also true of the narrator. The epic story of *The Rainbow*

Art and Ritual. (*Letters*, pp. 234, 249, 250.) Besides catering to Lawrence's continuing concern with the relation between art and religion, this book would also have offered some confirmation for Lawrence's sense of the epic scale involved in the story of the migration and cultural emergence of the Brangwens. Towards the end of her book, Jane Harrison has much to say about the nature of the heroic. And her basic theory would hold true for *The Rainbow* and *Women in Love*: "In a word, the heroic spirit, as seen in heroic poetry, is the outcome of a society cut loose from its roots, of a time of migrations, of the shifting of populations. . . . Such conditions, such a contrast of new and old, of settled splendour beset by unbridled adventure, go to the making of a heroic age, . . ." Jane Harrison, *Ancient Art and Ritual* (London, 1913), pp. 161, 162.

is one of the great literary artefacts of the verbal culture of English Protestantism and any attempt to characterise the literary art of the novel must begin with this proposition.

The qualities of Biblical epic in *The Rainbow* inform its structure, characterisation and narrative style. The basic story, which is of the passing of agrarian England and the coming of industrialisation, is expressly associated with the story of Noah and the flood as related in the sixth chapter of Genesis. The opening of *The Rainbow*, which describes the incipient dissolution of the old life of blood intimacy, constitutes something of a parallel with God's early prophecy to Noah that "the end of all flesh is come before me". And of course it is a great flood which destroys Tom Brangwen and the old Brangwen way of life which he represents. When the canal constructed by the colliery owners bursts its banks and floods the farm, the intimation is that, as with Noah, one epoch has ended and a new dispensation is about to begin. In the book of Genesis God promises the rainbow, the bow in the cloud, as the sign of a new, postdiluvian covenant. In Lawrence's book, the rainbow, serving both as title and as major symbol, also represents a new covenant, the new principle for reconciling the here and the beyond, the momentary and the eternal, which the succeeding generations of Brangwens aspire so ardently to discover. The correspondences between *The Rainbow* and the Genesis story are not as numerous, as detailed or as prolonged as those between James Joyce's *Ulysses* and its Homeric counterpart. *The Rainbow* has the same narrative climax and the same central image as the Old Testament story. Lawrence also refers frequently to Noah and on one occasion in the eleventh chapter quotes some eight verses from Genesis. Yet the overall effect is not, as with Joyce, of a sedulously maintained narrative mechanism but rather of a rich and extended simile that helps to establish the quality and the dignity of the Brangwen enterprise. Lawrence is not at all interested in the ironic juxtaposing of the past and present to the disadvantage and discredit of the latter. Rather he is concerned to allow to what is alive and courageous in the present and in recent times the same worth and stature which it is customary to attribute to "the great past".

References to the Bible also figure prominently in the depiction of character and the rendering of consciousness. This is because the life of the Derbyshire yeoman family is imbued with the same rich scriptural knowledge that Lawrence's was. For them, reflection, analogy and aspiration, in so far as these become explicit, most readily find expression in Biblical terms. Historically the Brangwens are antecedent to the world of "the media" and popular songs and commercial jingles, and socially they are apart from the world in which consciousness is organised around Latin tags or Greek concepts. For the Brangwens it is the Bible which supplies the words and images and analogies to embody feeling. Thus at a crucial juncture in the development of her marriage Anna Brangwen comes suddenly to despise her husband for undertaking somewhat rhetorically the role of master in his own house. The words that immediately come to her mind both as an expression and as a validation of her calm scorn are a paraphrase of some verses in the seventeenth chapter of the first book of Samuel.

> "Thou comest to me with a sword and a spear and a shield, but I come to thee in the name of the Lord:— for the battle is the Lord's, and he will give you into our hands."
>
> Her heart rang to the words She walked in her pride. And her battle was her own Lord's, her husband was delivered over.

Even for Anna's daughter Ursula, whose links with Christian culture grow ever more tenuous, the Bible

continues as a strongly formative influence upon consciousness. Above all, the desire for vitalising and exalting
experience which dominates her life from early adulthood
takes its special formulation from a passage in the Bible.
The words are from Genesis:

> "The Sons of God saw the daughters of men that they were
> fair: and they took them wives of all which they chose.
> "And the Lord said, My spirit shall not always strive
> with Man, for that he also is flesh; yet his days shall be an
> hundred and twenty years.
> "There were giants in the earth in those days; and also
> after that, when the Sons of God came in unto the
> daughters of men, and they bare children unto them, the
> same became mighty men which were of old, men of re-
> nown."

Over this Ursula was stirred as by a call from far off.

In thus revealing the active presence of the Bible in the
thought and feeling of his characters Lawrence is not just
evoking a certain phase of English social history. More
importantly, he is suggesting how the figures and the
language of the Bible represent a stature and a heroic
quality against which the Brangwens tacitly assess their
own experience.

In the same way that there is something unusual in
terms of twentieth-century fiction in the epic properties
with which Lawrence endows his characters, there is
something equally remarkable in the narrative voice
which describes and presents them. In *The Rainbow* the
impression given is no longer that of the brisk, business-
like, competent and utterly confident story-teller of the
previous novel. Like *Sons and Lovers*, *The Rainbow* is
packed with incident, yet in this later novel narrative
movement is no longer the pre-eminent concern of the
story-teller. There is a new propensity to decelerate the
narrative progress in order to dwell on, to characterise
further and often to celebrate, experience as undergone
by a particular consciousness. We may say that there is

more of conscious and intended poetry in *The Rainbow* than in *Sons and Lovers*. In vocabulary alone it is demonstrably richer, more varied, more complicated, more daring than its predecessor. And although there is the familiar accuracy about simple human and material realities and the same fine rendering of dialect and dialogue (one thinks, to take one amusing instance, of Tom Brangwen's exchanges with Tilly), there is also a completely new and arresting elevation of tone. This forms the major development in fictional art represented by the book. In great part the new tone is a matter of the metaphors used. And these show the narrator's adherence to the same cultural tradition as his characters. Sometimes the metaphors allude to the heroes of the Old Testament; they invoke figures as diverse as Abraham, Moses, Balaam, Samuel, David, Saul and Micah. Sometimes, as in the case of "the Pisgah mount" and "the pillar of fire and the pillar of cloud", they recall specific Biblical incidents. And on occasion the reference involves more than a phrase or two. Ursula's thrilled excitement after her first meeting with Skrebensky is put very effectively in a single sentence of authorial comment: "Once three angels stood in Abraham's doorway, and greeted him, and stayed and ate with him, leaving his household enriched forever when they went."

In addition to these allusions to Biblical epic, another feature of the heroic style of *The Rainbow* is the composition and ordering of the sentences. For there are many in which the verbal design recalls the manner of the Old Testament historians as known to us in the Jacobean version of the Bible. Right at the beginning of the book the description of the old Brangwen world of blood intimacy establishes a distinctly psalmic tone in the writing:

> So much warmth and generating and pain and death did
> they know in their blood, earth and sky and beast and

green plants, so much exchange and interchange they had
with these, that they lived full and surcharged, their
senses full fed, their faces always turned to the heat of the
blood, staring into the sun, dazed with looking towards the
source of generation, unable to turn round.

The manner that is established in these opening pages
recurs throughout the novel. Sometimes it is a matter of
vocabulary and modulation: "He and she, one flesh, out
of which life must be put forth. The rent was not in his
body, but it was of his body. On her the blows fell, but
the quiver ran through to him, to his last fibre." Sometimes it is a recourse to the characteristic idiom of the
King James version: "And he bent down and kissed her
on the lips. And the dawn blazed in them, their new life
came to pass, it was beyond all conceiving good, it was so
good, that it was almost like a passing-away, a trespass."
Sometimes one single word is enough to sustain the sense
of significance that this style implies: "Will Brangwen
worked at his wood-carving. It was a passion, a passion
for him to have the chisel under his grip. Verily the
passion of his heart lifted the fine bit of steel."

The full significance of these examples is not intrinsic
but dependent on a larger context in the novel. And
taken outside this context they can at best indicate only
something of the Biblical quality in the writing. This
difficulty occurs in all criticism and especially in the
criticism of fiction. But it is all the more intense here on
account of Lawrence's use of increment and repetition in
his writing. And the difficulty is even greater when one
attempts to consider certain other features of the style.
Lawrence's secularisation of Christian terminology, for
instance, seems to me to be particularly effective. But to
cite some sentences in which this device is used is not to
convey any real sense of its success: "His heart was
tormented within him, he did not try to smile. The time
of his trial and his admittance, his Gethsemane and his

Triumphal Entry in one, had come now." This statement concerning Tom Brangwen's first radical confrontation with his wife comes not only at the end of a carefully documented scene but also as the concluding and clinching sentence in a detailed description of the growth of an emotion. In their actual context the sentences I have cited constitute a certain crescendo which they cannot do in isolated quotation. Another feature of the writing which is difficult to illustrate with quotations (and which, incidentally, critics have sometimes found unacceptable) is the description of feeling in terms of physical metaphors. For example, in his description of the Brangwens moving into their new house in Beldover Lawrence writes: "There the hard rush floor-covering made the ground light, reflecting light upon the bottom of their hearts; ... " And on one occasion during the searing conflict between Will and Anna we are told that "All the blood in his body went black and powerful and corrosive as he heard her." And on another, "His heart was scalded, his brain hurt in his head, he went away, out of the house." In isolation these sentences may seem, word for word, to be strained and excessive. But in the actual text this physical representation of an emotion is what lends authenticity and intelligibility to the dense complexes of feeling which it is one of the prime purposes of Lawrence's art to elucidate. Indeed, this mode of suggesting non-cerebral states of consciousness may even be regarded as one of the innovating achievements of this novel in representing the reality of human experience. Certainly some of the epic effect of the novel derives from the immediacy of emotions which Lawrence achieves in great part by depicting the physicality of the feelings and consciousness of his characters.

The influence of the Bible on prose is likely to be as problematical as that of Shakespeare on poetry, but Lawrence completely avoids the two great perils of this influence. Nowhere does his writing seek to achieve some easy poetic effect through pastiche. Nor does it draw on the Bible in order to arrogate to itself some high significance and thereby degenerate into pretentiousness. Essentially Lawrence's recourse to this tradition in literary culture is justified by two patent conditions in his situation as a writer. First of all, he understands and shares the Biblical culture of his characters. In thinking about the major issues of experience, he has the same vocabulary, imagery, references and analogies as the four leading figures of the book. As we have seen in the passage describing Will Brangwen's response to the cathedral, this profoundly responsive empathy ultimately has its limits. In the final instance it must be subordinate to the narrator's need and responsibility to consider, assess and judge. Nevertheless, there is here a rich cultural continuousness between the narrator and his characters such as there will not be again in any of Lawrence's subsequent novels. And this is the chief source of the psychological, social and cultural density of this novel. *The Rainbow* describes a particular phase in the history of a protestant yeoman family, and at the same time it also gives the voice of a protestant consciousness of our own century. The voice is secularised, non-ideological, humane. But its dominant metaphors of death and rebirth and its final celebration of hope and faith clearly reveal its ancestry. This essentially religious perspective on the part of the narrator is the second justification for the style of the novel. The characteristics of the writing are not consciously imported or in some pejorative sense of the word, literary. The singular verbal categories and syntax of *The Rainbow* derive ultimately from the heroic scale of perception within which Lawrence learned to apprehend the significance of the individual human life and the exalted aim of the larger human progress.

The important change in narrative scale that occurs

between *Sons and Lovers* and *The Rainbow* has a very pronounced effect upon the intensely accurate reproduction
of the visible world which is such a central and continuing
feature of Lawrence's art. The development is incremental
rather than radical. In the same way that *Sons and Lovers*
continues some of the visual elements of *The White
Peacock* and at the same time introduces new ones, so *The
Rainbow*, while revealing many of the qualities familiar to
us from its predecessor, also introduces a wholly new
kind of visual writing. What the two novels have in
common is a vivid and careful evocation of a given social
milieu in the realistic mode. That which constitutes the
distinctly new accretion to Lawrence's visual art in *The
Rainbow* is its pictorial quality.

The development of the visual into the pictorial is in its
smallest manifestation a matter of single sentences. Anna,
for instance, occasionally sees her husband in terms of the
Angelico figures with which they are both so well
acquainted. This, for instance, is one definition of a
particular stage of his sexual attraction for her:

> And ever and again he appeared to her as the dread flame
> of power. Sometimes, when he stood in the doorway, his
> face lit up, he seemed like an Annunciation to her, her
> heart beat fast. . . . She was subject to him as to the Angel
> of the Presence. She waited upon him and heard his will,
> and she trembled in his service.

And at another moment Will Brangwen visualises himself
in distinctly Blakean terms:

> Then as if his soul had six wings of bliss he stood absorbed
> in praise, feeling the radiance from the Almighty beat
> through him like a pulse, as he stood in the upright flame
> of praise, transmitting the pulse of Creation.

One effect of such small and local examples of pictorial
style is to alert us to the larger, more central and more
sustained passages that also show the influence of painting

upon the prose of *The Rainbow*. These are scenes which both reproduce an intelligible visual reality and at the same time, by virtue of the way they are written, patterned and organised, have attached to them a further set of implications and meanings. In the scenes which I am thinking of Lawrence is completely faithful to the seen actuality and can in no way be said to be employing symbols. It is just that along with this fidelity to phenomena there is in the writing an accentuation, a heightening, a pictorial quality and organisation that disposes us to think of them less as scenes than as tableaux, or perhaps even as icons.

Five major examples of the kind of passage I have in mind are these: the mother and child configuration which Lydia and Anna unwittingly compose for Tom Brangwen in the first chapter; Will and Anna bringing in the sheaves in the fourth chapter; Anna's dance of exaltation over her husband in "Anna Victrix"; the moonlight dance of Ursula and Skrebensky in "First Love", and the account of Ursula and the horses in the concluding pages. To this list one might add Ursula's vision in the concluding paragraphs of the novel. For although it is shorter and less rich in content than the others and though it has a distinctly rhetorical quality for the sake of the emphasis necessary to the conclusion, it does nevertheless possess the two main pictorial characteristics of the other passages listed; namely the representation of a visual actuality and the conditioning of the representation by reference to an established and familiar configuration, in this case that of sky and landscape and of the earth redeemed. The writing is pictorial in that it resorts to known forms in order to give pattern and meaning to the representation of a visual subject. That Lawrence himself was alive to the pictorial qualities of this concluding passage is suggested by the fact that on the day he completed *The Rainbow* he was prompted to attempt a drawing of the image that it evokes.[72]

This, like the five other major icons in *The Rainbow*, expresses and encapsulates a quintessential moment in the history of the Brangwens. By concentrating on these passages alone it would be possible to give a very full account of the development of the novel. And that Lawrence does in fact intend to retard the movement of our reading and to induce us to dwell on these configurations is made evident by the relation of each to its immediate context. Within the narrative continuum, every one of these passages constitutes a sudden deceleration, a heavy emphasis, an insistence that the reader observe something closely and with care.

One term for the reality that is presented in *The Rainbow* is rhythm. We are made to feel the rhythms of an individual nature, the rhythms of sexual relationship, the rhythms of growth into awareness and the rhythms of a whole culture. And in the iconographic passages which comprise the quintessential stages in the familial evolution, rhythm is always conveyed in primarily visual terms. A comparison between the first and last icons, between Tom Brangwen's vision of mother and child and Ursula's vision of the horses, shows how the rhythms of life in England have become more rapid, intense and even frenetic over the three generations.

In his art criticism in "Study of Thomas Hardy" Lawrence's two major concepts are stability and movement. All the many paintings and sculptures which he there considers are shown to have a preponderance of one or the other. The development of movement is for Lawrence the crucial feature in the history of medieval art. And the balancing of movement and stability is

[72] The sketch was enclosed in a letter sent to Viola Meynell on 2 March 1915 announcing the completion of *The Rainbow*. It is reproduced in Harry T. Moore's *The Intelligent Heart* (Harmondsworth, 1960), p. 244.

what is signified by the great cultural achievement of the Renaissance. Lawrence suggests that we can see its "highest utterance perhaps in Botticelli, as in his *Nativity of the Saviour*, in our National Gallery. Still there is the architectural composition, but what an outburst of movement from the source of motion."[73] And in the icons of *The Rainbow* we see the development of a similar dialectic. At first gradually and then ever more rapidly, stability is dissipated by movement. The first icon, in itself and in its social and cultural implications, represents virtually a complete stasis. The next four depict scenes of dancing in each of which the movement is ever more accelerated and (in the last two, at least) increasingly strained and desperate. And in the penultimate icon of Ursula and the horses, which precedes the concluding vision of equalisation and renaissance, movement threatens to break free from all stabilising order and to become a destructive stampede.

The considerable length of the dance passages prohibits their quotation and makes difficult any extensive or detailed comment upon them. All one can do is to establish that each exists, that each constitutes a discrete entity and that each can be denominated, as in my list, by a phrase that might just as easily serve as the title of a painting. One can also establish certain features common to the visual character of all of them. In each the location of the light source is of special importance. In its use of light this fragment from the description of Ursula's dance with Skrebensky gives a fine visual representation of a significant moment of tension in Ursula's life:

> They went towards the stackyard. There he saw, with something like terror, the great new stacks of corn glistening and gleaming transfigured, silvery and present under the night-blue sky, throwing dark, substantial shadows, but themselves majestic and dimly present. She, like glim-

[73] *Phoenix*, p. 455.

mering gossamer, seemed to burn among them, as they rose like cold fires to the silvery-bluish air. All was intangible, a burning of cold, glimmering, whitish-steely fires. He was afraid of the great moon-conflagration of the cornstacks rising above him. His heart grew smaller, it began to fuse like a bead. He knew he would die.

She stood for some moments out in the overwhelming luminosity of the moon. She seemed a beam of gleaming power.

Furthermore, the writing in the iconographical passages registers light as an atmospheric quality as well as an item of contrast. This is the opening paragraph in the representation of Will and Anna bringing in the sheaves. The almost exclusively visual vocabulary is of a very delicate specification.

Corn harvest came on. One evening they walked out through the farm buildings at nightfall. A large gold moon hung heavily to the grey horizon, trees hovered tall, standing back in the dusk, waiting. Anna and the young man went on noiselessly by the hedge, along where the farm-carts had made dark ruts in the grass. They came through a gate into a wide open field where still much light seemed to spread against their faces. In the under-shadow the sheaves lay on the ground where the reapers had left them, many sheaves like bodies prostrate in shadowy bulk; others were riding hazily in shocks, like ships in the haze of moonlight and of dusk, further off.

Light and darkness contribute significantly to the pre-eminent rhythmic quality of all five passages. But of even greater importance is the careful detailing of foreground movement in each one. Here is Lawrence's close observation and careful reproduction of the irreconcilable motion of Will and Anna as they gather the sheaves:

They stooped, grasped the wet, soft hair of the corn, lifted the heavy bundles, and returned. She was always first. She set down her sheaves, making a pent house with those others. He was coming shadowy across the stubble, carrying his bundles. She turned away, hearing only the sharp hiss of his mingling corn. She walked between the moon and his shadowy figure.

She took her new two sheaves and walked towards him, as he rose from stooping over the earth. He was coming out of the near distance. She set down her sheaves to make a new stook. They were unsure. Her hands fluttered. Yet she broke away, and turned to the moon, which laid bare her bosom, so she felt as if her bosom were heaving and panting with moonlight. And he had to put up her two sheaves, which had fallen down. He worked in silence. The rhythm of the work carried him away again, as she was coming near.

This kind of piecemeal anthologising is unfortunately the only way in which one can suggest how primarily visual vocabulary and essentially pictorial design determine the organisation of these icons of dancing. However, one example of this kind of writing which it is possible to quote in full is Lawrence's representation of Lydia and Anna as they are seen by Tom Brangwen on the night he goes to make his proposal of marriage. It is the first pictorial entity in the book and the smallest. It comprises no more than half a dozen paragraphs.

There was a light streaming on to the bushes at the back from the kitchen window. He began to hesitate. How could he do this? Looking through the window, he saw her seated in the rocking-chair with the child, already in its night-dress, sitting on her knee. The fair head with its wild, fierce hair was drooping towards the fire-warmth, which reflected on the bright cheeks and clear skin of the child, who seemed to be musing, almost like a grown-up person. The mother's face was dark and still, and he saw, with a pang, that she was away back in the life that had been. The child's hair gleamed like spun glass, her face was illuminated till it seemed like wax lit up from the inside. The wind boomed strongly. Mother and child sat motionless, silent, the child staring with vacant dark eyes into the fire, the mother looking into space. The little girl was almost asleep. It was her will which kept her eyes so wide.

Suddenly she looked round, troubled, as the wind shook

the house, and Brangwen saw the small lips move. The mother began to rock, he heard the slight crunch of the rockers of the chair. Then he heard the low, mono- tonous murmur of a song in a foreign language. Then a great burst of wind, the mother seemed to have drifted away, the child's eyes were black and dilated. Brangwen looked up at the clouds which packed in great, alarming haste across the dark sky.

Then there came the child's high, complaining, yet imperative voice:

"Don't sing that stuff, mother; I don't want to hear it."

The singing died away.

"You will go to bed," said the mother.

He saw the clinging protest of the child, the unmoved far-awayness of the mother, the clinging, grasping effort of the child. Then suddenly the clear childish challenge:

"I want you to tell me a story."

The wind blew, the story began, the child nestled against the mother, Brangwen waited outside, suspended, looking at the wild waving of the trees in the wind and the gathering darkness. He had his fate to follow, he lingered here at the threshold.

The child crouched distinct and motionless, curled in against her mother, the eyes dark and unblinking among the keen wisps of hair, like a curled-up animal asleep but for the eyes. The mother sat as if in shadow, the story went on as if by itself. Bragwen stood outside seeing the night fall. He did not notice the passage of time. The hand that held the daffodils was fixed and cold.

In the actual context in *The Rainbow* the painterly qualities of this passage are further emphasised by the fact that it is preceded and succeeded by an altogether different kind of writing, namely dialogue. The taciturn uneasiness that informs Tom's words to Tilly and to the neighbour as he sets out for the vicarage and then the tense resolution that is expressed in his awkwardly direct proposal to Lydia are punctuated and summarised by this major image. The pictorial qualities are there both in small items and in the overall design. Part of the effect depends on a detail such as the simile which describes the child's face as "illuminated till it seemed like wax lit up from the inside"; another part derives from our recognition that the image entails distinct connotations and comparisons by virtue of being a mother and child configuration. The larger thematic significance of Lawrence's version of this traditional image is basically a matter of two major contrasts. The first involves a juxtaposition of the turbulent evening sky and weather with the close stillness of the figures in the lighted interior. As our eye is directed around a picture by the syntax of its design, so Lawrence's writing continually moves our attention back and forth from the dark violent exterior where the clouds "packed in great, alarming haste across the dark sky" and where "the wind boomed strongly", to the quiet lamp-lit kitchen in the vicarage in which "mother and child sat motionless, silent, the child staring with vacant dark eyes into the fire. . . ." This central item of contrast serves as an objectification of Tom Brangwen's own state. The violent skyscape is a textural counterpart of his own turbulent and sometimes terrifying freedom. The quiet and strangely alien interior is a version of the stabilising relationship which he has now, virtually unconsciously, determined upon. It also caters to the old Brangwen propensity, so strong in him, to refer and assign to woman, in however grumbling and quarrelsome a way, an ultimate moral authority and responsibility. Thus in utilising the madonna theme Lawrence is employing a motif which, besides alluding to a familiar item in the general western tradition of feeling, also has a special significance in Brangwen experience.

The second major item in the composition is the organisation of the light. The source is established in the opening sentence and the direction and effect of the light are continually insisted upon until the very end. The light illuminates the face of the child; the fire-warmth "reflected on the bright cheeks and clear skin of the child . . ." The mother is in shadow and thus less distinct. "The mother's face was dark and still . . ." "The mother sat as if in shadow . . ." The implications of this very firm distinction are several. It emphasises the strangeness, the mystery, of Lydia for Tom, which will later be described as "a curious strain on him, a suffering, like a fate". And yet, paradoxically, the ensemble is at the same time comforting and reassuring, an object of love and reverence. The icon is especially effective at suggesting the contradictoriness and the complexity of apparently simple feeling. One further point involved in the compositional pre-eminence of the child is that approach for Tom is difficult and daunting. Marriage for him is no facile commitment made in some moment of spurious glamour. Marriage is a whole way of life which involves not only the pain of commitment to the intimidating unknown represented by the woman, but also the often defeatingly difficult demands of fatherhood. The bright presence of the child in the picture is not only a beautiful if unexpected focal point, it is also an intimation, borne out in later chapters, of the deeper demands and often harrowing complications involved in Tom Brangwen's marriage to the Polish lady. The icon is both an expression and a resolution of contrasting feelings. That Lawrence can so successfully present this in the form of a traditional religious image without the slightest suspicion of sentimentality is an index of the authenticity and intensity of emotion involved. The great tableaux of *The Rainbow*, like the other epic features which we have considered, demonstrate what is (for a twentieth-century novelist especially) a most unusual insight into and respect for the heroic capacities of human feeling.

Without the great iconographic passages *The Rainbow* would be deprived of a major part of its power. The effects which are achieved in it are clearly beyond the powers of dialogue, of mere description or of summary narrative. They are even beyond the kind of carefully managed scene creation that is familiar to us from the vividly realistic fiction represented by *Sons and Lovers*. What Lawrence needed in order to do justice to his perception were principles of emphasis, design and significance that could give to these passages the heightening and the salience they required. And it was this that Lawrence drew from his extensive knowledge of painting. The point needs to be insisted upon. For Lawrence, in *The Rainbow*, brings to the novel qualities that cannot be accounted for by literary tradition alone. And in so far as it is possible or worth while to pursue the provenance of such an achievement, it can be said that his vision was sustained and enhanced by his rich visual culture. *The Rainbow* is in great part about the awakening of the visual sense in Victorian England, and Lawrence as author of the novel is himself an important instance of the process. It was this tradition of visual sensibility more than anything in the recent history of fiction which made possible and sustained this prodigious work of epic.

THREE
THE TENSION IN
"WOMEN IN LOVE"

Another very fine tomb is the Tomb of the Baron, with its frieze of single figures, dark on a light background going round the walls. There are horses and men, all in dark silhouette, and very fascinating in drawing. These archaic horses are so perfectly satisfying *as* horses: so far more horse-like, to the soul, than those of Rosa Bonheur or Rubens or even Velazquez, though he comes nearer to these; so that one asks oneself, what, after all, is the horsiness of a horse? What is it that man sees, when he looks at a horse?—what is it, that will never be put into words? For a man who sees, sees not as a camera does when it takes a snapshot, not even as a cinema-camera, taking its succession of instantaneous snaps; but in a curious rolling flood of vision, in which the image itself seethes and rolls; and only the mind *picks out* certain factors which *shall* represent the image seen. That is why a camera is so unsatisfactory: its eye is flat, it is related only to a negative thing inside the box: whereas inside our living box there is a decided positive.

ETRUSCAN PLACES

7

A VISUAL EDUCATION

T HE RAINBOW was completed early in March 1915 and
published at the end of the following September. On
3 November police officers seized a thousand copies of the
book from the publishers and printers. Ten days later at
Bow Street Magistrates' Court an order for the destruction
of the books was made on grounds of obscenity. The
prosecution of *The Rainbow* constitutes the first damaging episode of Lawrence's career. Nevertheless, the bitter
setback did not deter him from continuing his work of
converting the unused part of the manuscript of *The
Sisters* into a sequel to *The Rainbow*. The letters
suggest that he began this work sometime in April 1916
while he and Frieda were living in a cottage near Zennor
in Cornwall. And on 9 July of that year Lawrence was
able to announce to Catherine Carswell: "I have
finished my novel and am going to try to type it."[74] The
letters of the next six months or so occasionally suggest
the difficulties encountered by Pinker, Lawrence's
literary agent, in trying to place the manuscript. Lawrence
even speculates on the possibility of obtaining the aid of a
patron: "I was wondering if it would be wise to try to get
some well-known and important person to take the novel
under his protection; that is, if I could dedicate it with a
proper inscription, in the eighteenth century fashion, to

[74] *Letters*, p. 461.

some patron whose name would be likely to save it from the yelping of the small newspaper curs."[75] But by January of 1917 Lawrence is reconciled to the idea that *Women in Love* "will not find a publisher in England at all". As he remarks to the same correspondent, "Everybody refuses to publish the novel. It will not get done over here."[76] And this view was borne out by events. The suppression of *The Rainbow* made English publishers extremely reluctant to handle any of Lawrence's work. And in the end it was a New York publisher who undertook to publish *Women in Love*. The novel appeared in a limited edition in 1920.

There is evidence to indicate that the book brought out by Seltzer is somewhat different from that which Lawrence offered to the English publishers in the later months of 1917. As yet we have insufficient knowledge for a full description of the several stages of the composition of *Women in Love*. Nevertheless it seems that Lawrence was still making additions to the manuscript as late as 1919.[77] The fact that *Women in Love* is of, if not (as Lawrence insists in his foreword) explicitly about, the period of the Great War helps to explain the great difference in subject and feeling between this book and its predecessor. The book is in part a representation of the deterioration in the quality of English life which Lawrence, like so many others, saw as a major consequence of the Great War. And the mood of the novel is very likely a product of the painful experiences which the war entailed for Lawrence personally: the banning of *The Rainbow*, his difficulty in

[75] *Letters*, p. 494.
[76] *Letters*, p. 498.
[77] Ursula's reference in the concluding pages of the novel to the Kaiser's "Ich hab' es nicht gewollt" is one very obvious piece of evidence to show that Lawrence worked on the book after 1917. An interesting discussion of the history of the composition of *Women in Love* appeared in the correspondence columns of the *Times Literary Supplement* in the autumn of 1969.

publishing even small items, his deportation from Cornwall under the vague suspicion of spying for the Germans.
But at the same time that the writing in *Women in Love* is
palpably affected by personal suffering and by a sense of
social dislocation, it is also profoundly conditioned by
another major experience for Lawrence, his introduction
to modern painting and sculpture. This experience
explains Lawrence's altogether new treatment of the
artist and of works of art in *Women in Love*. It also accounts
for the radical development in Lawrence's fictional art
that this novel represents. It is no over-simplification to
say that while the narrative art of *The Rainbow* accords
with the Victorian concern with Quattrocento and
Renaissance painting (which the novel employs both as
metaphor and as subject), the new narrative manner of
Women in Love is conditioned by Lawrence's exposure during the war years to the theory and practice of what is
understood as specifically and distinctively "modern" art.

A brief resumé of the development of Lawrence's visual
imagination up to the time of the composition of *Women
in Love* will help to define this crucial new experience and
to establish some terminology which will be useful in discussing *Women in Love*. The main facts of Lawrence's early
visual education are elements in his early novels and can
be easily inferred from them. The Eastwood he grew up
in, though a mining village, was surrounded by attractive
countryside. And though Lawrence learned to perceive
and to appreciate the colliery, it was the as yet unspoiled
Notts. and Derby border country which first engaged his
eye. About a year before he died Lawrence wrote an
essay entitled "Nottingham and the Mining Countryside"
in which he reveals a still very vivid memory of the locality
he had left nearly twenty years before.

It is hilly country, looking west to Crich and towards Matlock, sixteen miles away, and east and north-east towards Mansfield and the Sherwood Forest district. To me it seemed, and still seems, an extremely beautiful country-side, just between the red sandstone and the oak-trees of Nottingham, and the cold limestone, the ash-trees, the stone fences of Derbyshire. To me, as a child and a young man, it was still the old England of the forest and agricultural past; there were no motor-cars, the mines were, in a sense, an accident in the landscape, and Robin Hood and his merry men were not very far away.[78]

As the early novels and stories show, Lawrence was intimately acquainted with this countryside, its seasons, fauna and animal life. He was also extremely well versed in local history, topography and architecture. And the two great medieval buildings of the region made a pro-found impression upon his imagination. In his corre-spondence, as in all his early novels, Lawrence reveals the fascination held for him by the great romanesque arches of the Norman minster at Southwell and by the Gothic arches and carving of the early English cathedral at Lincoln. That Lawrence grew up in close acquaintance with buildings which are such magnificent examples of their kind and which constitute such a striking and reveal-ing contrast in architectural styles is perhaps one explana-tion of the confident feeling for medieval art and culture in "Study of Thomas Hardy" and *The Rainbow*.

But the landscape of the East Midlands was not the sole item in the education and development of Lawrence's early vision. Another factor was his lifelong interest in painting. This again, is something which is amply evidenced by the novels. In *The White Peacock* alone Lawrence alludes to Blake, Millais, Burne-Jones, Girtin, David Cox, Watts and Beardsley as well as to a host of lesser artists. But Lawrence's interest in painting was more intense than the kind which just sustains allusions. He was

[78] *Phoenix*, p. 133.

not content merely to look at and to appreciate art. He also gained a deeper understanding of pictures from his careful attempts at making copies. Such copying was an activity to which Lawrence returned throughout his life but he pursued it with particular intensity during his early years. He describes his method in the essay "Making Pictures".

> I learnt to paint from copying other pictures—usually reproductions, sometimes even photographs. When I was a boy, how I concentrated over it! Copying some perfectly worthless scene reproduction in some magazine. I worked with almost dry water-colour, stroke by stroke, covering half a square-inch at a time, each square-inch perfect and completed, proceeding in a kind of mosaic advance, with no idea at all of laying on a broad wash. Hours and hours of intense concentration, inch by inch progress, in a method entirely wrong—and yet those copies of mine managed, when they were finished, to have a certain something that delighted me: a certain glow of life, which was beauty to me. A picture lives with the life you put into it. If you put no *life* into it—no thrill, no concentration of delight or exaltation of visual discovery—then the picture is dead, like so many canvases, no matter how much thorough and scientific work is put into it.[79]

In the same essay Lawrence goes on to mention the pictures that especially interested him as a copyist. He also gives some account of what he regards as the chief value of the art of copying. The following sentences do much to trace the development of the visual imagination which works so strongly in the design and the writing of *The Rainbow*.

> I can never be sufficiently grateful for the series of English water-colour painters, published by the *Studio* in eight parts, when I was a youth. I had only six of the eight parts, but they were invaluable to me. I copied them with the greatest joy, and found some of them extremely difficult.

[79] *Phoenix II*, p. 604.

Surely I put as much labour into copying from those water-colour reproductions as most modern art students put into all their years of study. And I had enormous profit from it. I not only acquired a considerable technical skill in handling water-colour—let any man try copying the English water-colour artists, from Paul Sandby and Peter de Wint and Girtin, up to Frank Brangwyn and the impressionists like Brabazon, and he will see how much skill he requires—but also I developed my visionary awareness. And I believe one can only develop one's visionary awareness by close contact with the vision itself: that is, by knowing pictures, real vision pictures, and by dwelling on them, and really dwelling in them. It is a great delight, to dwell in a picture.[80]

A further stage in the education of Lawrence's extraordinarily sensitive perception occurs with his first experience of Italy.[81] Following their elopement, Lawrence and Frieda went to Italy in September 1912 and, except for a visit to England in the summer of 1913, continued to live there until 1914. The outbreak of war in that year frustrated their firm intention of returning. Yet these two years were of crucial importance to Lawrence's development as an artist. This importance is revealed in *Twilight in Italy*, the volume which contains Lawrence's essays on his experiences in Italy at this time. The book is more than the collection of travel pieces that it is ordinarily thought to be. It is a well organised and fully unified book about a phase in the development of the author's

[80] *Phoenix II*, p. 605.
[81] There is a case for regarding Lawrence's years as a teacher in Croydon as a distinct phase of simultaneously visual and aesthetic experience. The realistic description of poverty in some of the chapters of *The White Peacock* and in certain parts of *The Trespasser* seem to have been confirmed not only by Lawrence's personal experiences of the metropolis but also by the work of the French realist painter Bastien-Lepage which so impressed Lawrence at the Royal Academy in 1909. (*Letters*, pp. 51, 52.) But even if the case is admitted, the Croydon years are not as important to this aspect of Lawrence's development as his years in Eastwood and in Italy.

social, cultural and historical awareness. The book is rich in descriptions of milieu, character and incident, but the central and guiding concern is Lawrence's desire to realise some notion of Italian life (that is to say, of the life of the North Italian peasantry among whom he lived), both in itself and as a contrast to the altogether different life style of the Northern European countries and of England in particular. The volume is a work of intellectual speculation as well as a record of experiences. Lawrence's attempt to formulate here his sense of the difference between his own way of feeling and that of the Italians around Lake Garda is the experiential origin of the concepts of "light" and "dark" which ever after figure so prominently in what is sometimes thought of as Lawrence's "philosophy".

The essays that make up *Twilight in Italy* were written during Lawrence's stay in Italy and published originally as articles. They were rewritten so as to form a book during 1915. In other words, *Twilight in Italy* was completed very close to the time that Lawrence was finishing *The Rainbow*, and it is as much a source book for the novel as "Study of Thomas Hardy". There are several important features of the novel which can be seen to derive from Lawrence's experience of Italian life. Most obviously, the description of the life of the Alpine peasantry in the first chapter is in substance, and to some extent even in phrasing, similar to the evocation of blood intimacy in the early pages of *The Rainbow*. Some of the characters in the two books also show resemblances. In the chapter entitled "San Gaudenzio", Maria, who "in her soul, jeered at the church and at religion" and who "wanted the human society as the absolute, without religious abstractions", is strongly reminiscent of Anna Brangwen. And the Signore in the charming and amusing essay "The Lemon Gardens", who is described as "the last shrivelled representative of his race" and as "an ardent, aristocratic

145

monkey", recalls the aristocratic stranger whom Tom Brangwen meets at the inn at Matlock. At one point in *The Rainbow* Ursula and Skrebensky stay at an Italian hotel in London, and Italy is very much with them:

> She woke in the morning to a sound of water dashed on a courtyard, to sunlight streaming through a lattice. She thought she was in a foreign country. . . .
> Vaguely, in a sort of silver light, she wandered at large and at ease. The bonds of the world were broken. This world of England had vanished away. She heard a voice in the yard below calling:
> "O Giovann'—O'—O'—O'—Giovann'—!"
> And she knew she was in a new country, in a new life.

Twilight in Italy shows how much Italy was with the Lawrence who wrote *The Rainbow*. Indeed the effect of Italy upon Lawrence is one of the important causes of the striking development in his fiction between *Sons and Lovers* and *The Rainbow*. In Italy Lawrence had his first protracted experience of another nation and another culture. This not only initiated his enduring interest in Italian art and literature—much of Lawrence's activity as a translator was devoted to Italian fiction—it also supplied him with a new and distanced perspective upon his own country and society. And this is the likely explanation of the important shift of focus from a single hero in *Sons and Lovers* to a whole culture and its processes in *The Rainbow*.

The specifically visual impact of Italy upon Lawrence is another very important and distinct item in the development of his art. In *The Lost Girl* one of the great experiences for the heroine, Alvina, is the contrast between the depressing townscape of her native Woodhouse and the to her almost painful visual richness of the Italian landscape. Lawrence's writing also makes this a great effect for the reader. The darkness of life in industrial England, which is established as, at its most living, a matter of attitudes, humours and ironies, is displaced by a sudden onset of light, colour and texture. And one feels that Lawrence in recording such a transition is reproducing a memorable personal experience. Certainly to read the letters that Lawrence wrote from Italy during the years 1912–14 is to see how for him Italy represented a startlingly new range of possibilities in landscape, atmosphere and human form and movement. Here, for instance, is a paragraph from a letter to a former colleague at Croydon, in which Lawrence describes one of the ceremonies in the church of a nearby coastal village. This passage shows how peasant ceremony and ritual served to confirm that sense of the significant moment or action which is such an important part of what I have called Lawrence's pictorial imagination. The visual style here points forward unmistakably to that of *The Rainbow*.

We went on Good Friday eve to see the procession of Jesus to the tomb. The houses in Tellaro are stuck about on the rocks in a tiny opening. It was a still night with a great moon, but the village was deep in shadow, only the moonlight shining out at sea. And on all the window-sills were rows of candles trembling on the still air, long rows in the square, big windows, very golden in the blue dark shadow under a lighted sky. Then the procession came out of church, the lads running in front clapping wooden clappers, like those they scare birds with at home. Such a din of clappers. And the noise means the grinding of the bones of Judas. Then came the procession—a white bier with drawn curtains, carried high on the shoulders of men dressed all in white, with white cloths on their heads—a weird chanting noise broken by the noise of the sea, and candles fluttering as the white figures moved, and two great, gilt rococo lanterns carried above. Then, with all the clatter and the broken mournful chanting and the hoarse wash of the sea, they began to climb the steep staircase between the high, dark houses, a white, ghostly winding procession, with the dark-dressed villagers crowding behind. It was gone in a minute. And it made a fearful impression on me. It is the *mystery* that does it—it is Death itself, robbed of its horrors, and only Fear and Wonder going humbly behind.[82]

As well as providing new and powerfully stimulating objects of perception, Italy also introduced Lawrence to some totally unfamiliar yet extremely interesting categories of perception. Here Lawrence first became acquainted with modernism; he encountered it in the form of futurism, the stridently assertive aesthetic which had in recent years so agitated the intellectual life of the country. On 2 June 1914 Lawrence wrote to McLeod: "I have been interested in the futurists. I got a book of their poetry —a very fat book too—and a book of pictures—and I read Marinetti's and Paolo Buzzi's manifestations and essays and Soffici's essays on cubism and futurism. It interests me very much."[83] A letter written three days later shows how the principles of futurism (with which Lawrence was by no means fully in sympathy) served to illuminate and define something of his own evolving perception. Above all, they helped to formulate his tendency to break free from established fictional concepts, "the old forms and sentimentalities", such as ego, character and appearance in order to represent that more compelling and less trivial reality which in his description of the ceremony at Tellaro he calls "the mystery" and which in these letters on futurism he terms at one point "the non-human in humanity" and at another "the inhuman will". The desire, which Lawrence formulates here, to free perception from all preconceived idea and feeling and to realise phenomena, animate and inanimate, without the mediation of sentiment is that which relates his undertaking as a mature novelist to what we think of

[82] *Letters*, pp. 271, 272.
[83] *Letters*, p. 279. The two books mentioned may be more precisely identified as *I poeti futuristi con una proclama di F. T. Marinetti e uno studio sol verso libero di Paolo Buzzi* which was edited by F. T. Marinetti and published in Milan in 1912 and *Cubismo et futurismo* by Soffici, which was published in Florence in 1914.

as a, indeed *the*, characteristically modern insistence. (The most concise of the many similar intentions that one might cite is the programme of the Imagist poets.) But it is of considerable significance that a book of futurist pictures as well as a statement of futurist theory should have been so relevant to Lawrence's concerns. In moving beyond the realism of *Sons and Lovers* Lawrence was not to abandon but rather strongly to develop his essentially visual prose art. *The Rainbow* and *Women in Love* are two stages of this development. Each in its own distinct way shows how visual writing, like futurist painting, can represent what was not traditionally considered to be visual, namely rhythm, movement and dynamic, which from now on serve more and more as Lawrence's initial categorisations of life itself. They are in "the laugh of the woman" just as they are in "the binding of the molecules of steel or their action in heat".

These last letters from Italy provide a very important preface to the next stage in the rapid development of Lawrence's visual awareness. With his return to England in the summer of 1914 and his entrée into Bloomsbury, Lawrence first became acquainted in more than a theoretical way with the modernist revolution in the visual arts. The kind of painting that we think of as modern was introduced and promoted in England by members of the Bloomsbury group. In November of 1910 Roger Fry organised an exhibition entitled "Manet and the Post-Impressionists" and this is generally recognised as constituting the first, if somewhat belated, entry of modern painting into English life. Some four years later, when Lawrence was entering upon his short-lived and always tentative stay in Bloomsbury circles, the interest of its members in painting and sculpture was still primary and intense. As a historian of the group has noted:

Interest in the creation and appreciation of paintings became a dominant characteristic of Bloomsbury. Lytton

Strachey and Clive Bell, who had championed the visual arts at Cambridge and had aroused Keynes's lively interest, retained their enthusiasm. Clive Bell wrote on art and became a well-known critic. Vanessa Bell and Duncan Grant painted together. . . . There was scarcely anyone in the group who did not have a lively interest in the visual arts; and the leader in this interest was Roger Fry.[84]

The development of Bloomsbury is a matter of relatively clear-cut phases. It is customary to date the origins of the group some ten years before Lawrence was introduced to it. In 1904 Sir Leslie Stephen died and his two daughters, Virginia and Vanessa, set up a new household in Gordon Square, Bloomsbury. Here their brother Thoby brought his university friends from Cambridge. Among them were Clive Bell, Leonard Woolf, Maynard Keynes and Lytton Strachey. This original group was soon supplemented by Roger Fry, Duncan Grant and E. M. Forster. During the Edwardian years Bloomsbury achievement was restricted (except for Fry's important exhibitions) to discussion and to the tacit consolidation of a collective identity. Only during the years around the end of the first World War did its members begin to complete and to publish their individual work. In 1918 there appeared Keynes's *The Economic Consequences of the Peace* and Virginia Woolf's novel, *Night and Day*, and in 1920 Roger Fry's *Vision and Design*.

Each of these books was to initiate a considerable fame and influence for its author and together they provide a good account of what Bloombsury represents in English cultural history. That which provoked criticism, scorn and mockery from Pound and Wyndham Lewis as well as from Lawrence himself is fully mainfest here. Although these books show how Bloomsbury rebelled against what it regarded as the repressive Philistinism of the Victorian age, they also reveal the lack of weight, robustness and

[84] J. K. Johnstone, *The Bloomsbury Group* (London, 1954), p. 11.

real radicalism in the Bloomsbury intellect. It seems altogether appropriate that the major work of the finest Bloomsbury intelligence should have been Keynes's *The General Theory of Employment, Interest and Money*. For this famous work, which is radical only in the sense that it proposes a new diagnosis of the ills of capitalism and new measures for the preservation of the status quo, typifies the way in which Bloomsbury was interested in the new and the original only in so far as these helped to adorn and sustain (or at the most merely modify) an old elitist order in society and feeling. In every field of thought and expression Bloomsbury appears limited and barren in comparison with the authentic innovators of this century. Virginia Woolf is far less of a pioneer in the techniques of fiction than James Joyce, whose work she disliked yet at the same time imitated. Duncan Grant cannot be compared with the great modern painters of Paris and Munich who were his models. And as proponents of the modern in art, neither Clive Bell nor Roger Fry have the centrality of Apollinaire or Kandinsky or Klee. In general, Bloomsbury writing is the work not of original talents but, to use a term applied by Lawrence to one of the characters in *Women in Love*, of *Kulturträger*. H. G. Wells's description of the Bloomsbury set as "genteel Whigs" still seems accurate and helps to explain why the membership should have found it difficult to be intellectually and socially hospitable to more truly innovating and energising talents such as Pound and Lawrence.

Lawrence's entry into Bloomsbury circles began at the very end of 1914 when he met Lady Ottoline Morrell whose country house at Garsington was the rural gathering place for Bloomsbury. (Her husband Philip Morrell was a Liberal M.P. and a pacifist spokesman in Parliament during the war years.) Through Lady Ottoline, Lawrence met Clive Bell and also Bertrand Russell, who in early March 1915, invited him to Cambridge where he met Maynard Keynes. At this time Lawrence's attitude to Bloomsbury was essentially friendly if somewhat uncertain. "I rather liked Clive Bell—not deeply," he told Ottoline Morrell.[85] And towards E. M. Forster, whom he also met in 1915, he took a similarly divided though warmer attitude. At this time Lawrence was hoping for a worthwhile collaboration with Bertrand Russell in a public campaign to end the war and institute a programme of social renewal in England. Russell was at best a distant and peripheral adherent of Bloomsbury. Nevertheless Lawrence's profound dissatisfaction with Russell was in great part the same as he was to experience with regard to Bloomsbury in general and to that whole range of sensibility nurtured in Cambridge by the thought of G. E. Moore and the ethos of the society known as "the Apostles". What Lawrence deplored was the curtailment of feeling which he saw as the cause and the condition of a particular kind of cerebration. The long and important letter which he wrote to Russell on 12 February 1915 makes this very point. In part it is an account of Forster, in part it is an appeal to Russell. In general it can be regarded as Lawrence's first diagnosis of the deficiencies of Bloomsbury culture. Lawrence here deplores the containment of life within a fixed set of ideas that are but the formulations of known and past experiences:

> There comes a point when the shell, the form of life, is a prison to the life. Then the life must either concentrate on breaking the shell, or it must turn round, turn in upon itself, and try infinite variations of a known reaction upon itself. . . . Or, the best thing such a life can do, that knows it is confined, is to set-to to arrange and assort all the facts and knowledge of the contained life.[86]

Lawrence regards Forster's liberal ideas as belonging to such an experiential vacuum. They are thus irrelevant to

[85] *Letters*, p. 380.
[86] *Letters*, p. 320.

the repairing of the distortions of feeling in the individual and in society: "Forster knows, as every thinking man now knows, that all his thinking and his passion for humanity amounts to no more than trying to soothe with poetry a man raging with pain which can be cured."[87] Forster's and (the implication is clear enough) Russell's "social passion" and "love for humanity" are in effect evasions of the real and radical effort that is needed. And for Lawrence this entails the experience of self-realisation which comes from the experience of the self in relation to that which is unknown and therefore unideational, "the unexplored, the woman, the whatever-it-is I am up against".[88] The great failure of the "ordinary Englishman of the educated class" is that he is incapable of this kind of adventurousness, that is to say, of the openness and responsiveness to the uncategorised which are the virtues most commended by all distinctively modern aesthetics. The retreat from relationship with the unknown and thus from growth itself is Lawrence's main complaint against Bloomsbury. It is at the centre of all his subsequent and often more angrily worded criticisms of the intellectual, emotional and sexual insufficiencies of the group.

The intellectual dissociation intimated in this as in other letters of the time was soon followed by the first stage of the social breach. This involved some of the younger members of Bloomsbury. As Quentin Bell has noted, "Already before the war the older members were joined by a rather younger generation, notably David Garnett and Francis Birrell: both of these are, as one may say, 'marginal'."[89] And it was with these that Lawrence was to have the bitter quarrel that set in train his estrangement from Bloomsbury. David Garnett was the son of Edward Garnett, Lawrence's early publisher and literary

[87] *Letters*, pp. 317, 318.
[88] *Letters*, p. 319.
[89] Quentin Bell, *Bloomsbury* (London, 1968), p. 15.

mentor, and had been a friend of Lawrence's for several years. It seems likely that the assimilation of David Garnett by Bloomsbury was especially painful to Lawrence. In any case a visit in the spring of 1915 was to fill him with dislike and disgust. In a letter he wrote: ". . . David Garnett and Francis Birrell turned up the other day—Saturday. I like David, but Birrell I have come to detest. These horrible little frowsty people, men lovers of men, they give me such a sense of corruption, almost putrescence, that I dream of beetles. It is abominable."[90] And in another letter dealing with this same visit Lawrence expressed further criticisms that were just as severe as his strictures upon the particular homosexual ethos of Bloomsbury. They reveal a specific social instance of the vital deficiency that Lawrence had described to Russell:

> To hear these young people talking really fills me with black fury: they talk endlessly, but endlessly—and never, never a good or real thing said. Their attitude is so irreverent and blatant. They are cased each in a hard little shell of his own, and out of this they talk words. There is never for one second any outgoing of feeling, and no reverence, not a crumb or grain of reverence. I cannot stand it. I *will not* have people like this—I had rather be alone.[91]

After this important incident the links between Lawrence and Bloomsbury continued one by one to disappear. A year later his association with Russell ceased and shortly after that his friendship with Lady Ottoline also came to an end. Henceforth Lawrence was to have no further significant contact with Bloomsbury.

It is easy to see how the story of the Brangwen sisters in *Women in Love* is in many ways founded upon Lawrence's own short-lived relationship with Bloomsbury. Breadalby is plainly modelled upon Garsington and, as Harry T. Moore has shown in his biography of Lawrence, many

[90] *Letters*, p. 333.
[91] *Letters*, p. 332.

of the characters in the novel constitute easily recognisable portraits. And although it would be misleading to insist on *Women in Love* as a *roman à clef*, the novel is in one very important respect a representation of the condition of England at a particular moment in which the word Bloomsbury is the inevitable and indispensable term for the most advanced intellectual consciousness. It is also in great part about the range and idea of modern art that was made available to Lawrence in Bloomsbury circles during the years 1914–16. To equate characters in the book with actual members of Bloomsbury is to risk (and to little profit) some dubious equivalences; but to recognise the distinctively Bloomsbury talk, thought, and enthusiasms in sculpture and painting is to be aware of a major critical concern of the novel.

Of the several painters associated with Bloomsbury Duncan Grant was the one whom Lawrence came to know first. In the second volume of his autobiography David Garnett describes how in January 1915 he accompanied Lawrence on a visit to Grant's studio:

> Ottoline had talked to Lawrence about Duncan's pictures and, as Lawrence asked to see some of them, Duncan invited him and Frieda and E. M. Forster to tea in his studio the following afternoon. . . . We all sat in silence as Duncan brought out one picture after another. Then Lawrence rose to his feet—a bad sign—and walking up and down the studio, began to explain to Duncan what was wrong with his painting. It was not simply that the pictures themselves were bad—hopelessly bad—but they were worthless because Duncan was full of the wrong ideas. He was barking up the wrong tree and would have to learn to approach his subjects in a completely different frame of mind if he wanted ever to become an artist.
>
> Soon after Lawrence's first words, Morgan made some gentle remark about catching the train to Weybridge and faded out of the studio. Lawrence warmed to his subject and went on speaking with absolute frankness, having decided it was better to open Duncan's eyes and tell him

the truth. . . . Finally, in despair, Duncan brought out a long band of green cotton on two rollers. I stood and held one roller vertically and unwound while, standing a couple of yards away, Duncan wound up the other, and a series of supposedly related, abstract shapes was displayed before our disgusted visitors. That was the worst of all.[92]

Garnett's description of this incident constitutes a somewhat comic vignette. Lawrence gave his own more serious and more considered assessment of Grant and his work in a letter to Lady Ottoline Morrell soon after the visit. He criticised Grant's "silly experiments in the futuristic line, with bits of colour on a moving paper" and went on to proclaim that rejection of abstract art which he was never to modify: "But one cannot build a complete abstraction, or absolute, out of a number of small abstractions, or absolutes. Therefore one cannot make a picture out of geometric figures. . . . Painting is *not* architecture. . . . The architecture comes in in painting, only with the suggestion of some whole, some conception which conveys in its own manner the whole universe."[93] This notion of "the whole universe" here stands for that largeness of concern which was for Lawrence inherent in all serious art. Modern, experimental and theoretical art seemed all too often slight and trivial. Towards the end of his life Lawrence wrote:

I have lived enough among painters and around studios to have had all the theories—and how contradictory they are —rammed down my throat. . . . The modern theories of art make real pictures impossible. You only get these expositions, critical ventures in paint, and fantastic negations. And the bit of fantasy that may lie in the negation— as in a Dufy or a Chirico—is just the bit that has escaped theory and perhaps saves the picture. Theorize, theorize all you like—but when you start to paint, shut your theoretic eyes and go for it with instinct and intuition.[94]

[92] David Garnett, *The Flowers of the Forest* (London, 1955), pp. 34, 35.
[93] *Letters*, p. 308.   [94] *Phoenix II*, p. 603.

What Lawrence most deplores here is the lack of passional involvement with phenomena which results in an aestheticism that is experimental but essentially trivial.[95]

In the work of Mark Gertler, another Bloomsbury painter, Lawrence showed much greater interest. Indeed of Gertler's "Whirligig" (which considerably resembles Loerke's factory frieze in *Women in Love*) Lawrence wrote: ". . . it is the best *modern* picture I have seen: I think it is great and true." He goes on: "I won't say what I, as a man of words and ideas, read in the pictures. But I *do* think that in this combination of blaze, and violent mechanised rotation and complete involution, and ghastly, utterly mindless human intensity of sensational extremity, you have made a real and ultimate revelation." But although Lawrence accords to Gertler's work a seriousness and significance that he could not discover in Grant's, though he recognises in it the presence of authentic feeling such as he could not find in the work of the older painter, he is nevertheless dismayed by the actual nature of the feeling, the "violent maelstrom of destruction and horror", "the violent and lurid processes of inner decomposition" which the painting expresses. The last phrase cited is reminiscent of words used to describe Loerke in *Women in Love*. An although no exact equation of the two characters is possible, the kind of corruption of feeling which Lawrence so frequently ascribed to Bloomsbury is the same as that which marks Loerke and his art. Loerke is not a recognisable member of Bloomsbury, but his aesthetic and his thought, and the

[95] This contempt for modern painting persists throughout Lawrence's life. Criticising a friend's drawings in 1929, Lawrence made an unfavourable comparison between them and the work of Blake and then went on to offer this sweeping judgment: "It is modern and all things modern are merely shallow." (*Letters*, p. 1204) For a more complete account of Lawrence's rejection of the modern see Knud Merrild, *A Poet and Two Painters, A Memoir of D. H. Lawrence* (London, 1938), pp. 218–25.

emotional condition to which these attest, suggest the characteristic modernist ethos of the group. Loerke's views, for instance, are strikingly coincident with the set of ideas denoted by the term "significant form" that was first propounded by Clive Bell and subsequently developed by Roger Fry. In "An Essay in Aesthetics", which was reprinted in *Vision and Design* but which was first published as early as 1909, Fry sets out the basic theory. First he distinguishes between what he calls actual life and the imaginative life. He proceeds to argue that it is to the latter alone that art caters: "Morality, then, appreciates emotion by the standard of resultant action. Art appreciates emotion in and for itself."[96] Fry distinguishes his aesthetic position from that of Tolstoy who (like Lawrence, we may add) "values the emotions aroused by art entirely for their reaction upon actual life. . . ." Fry goes on to say, in words that remind us strongly of Loerke's defence of his statuette against Ursula's criticisms: "We must therefore give up the attempt to judge the work of art by its reaction upon life, and consider it as an expression of emotions regarded as ends in themselves."[97] This kind of aestheticism and self-consciousness was absolutely unacceptable to Lawrence. His actual critique of Fry's doctrine is to be found in one of his later essays, "Introduction to These Paintings", where he devotes several pages to a mocking comparison of Fry's aesthetic categories and the language of religious revivalists: "Oh, purify yourselves, ye who would know the aesthetic ecstasy, and be lifted up to the 'white peaks of artistic inspiration'. Purify yourselves of all base hankering for a tale that is told, and of all low lust for likenesses. Purify yourselves, and know the one supreme way, the way of Significant Form."[98] Deploring the

[96] *Vision and Design* (Harmondsworth, 1961), p. 31.
[97] *ibid*, p. 32.
[98] *Phoenix*, p. 565.

self-indulgence that so easily attaches to the symbols emphasised by the Christian revivalists, Lawrence goes on to make his point against Fry with a more serious emphasis. The paragraph can easily stand as a statement of the judgment against Loerke in *Women in Love*.

> And I find myself equally mystified by the cant phrases like Significant Form and Pure Form. They are as mysterious to me as the Cross and the Blood of the Lamb. They are just the magic jargon of invocation, nothing else. If you want to invoke an aesthetic ecstasy, stand in front of a Matisse and whisper fervently under your breath: "Significant Form! Significant Form!"—and it will come. It sounds to me like a form of masturbation, an attempt to make the body react to some cerebral formula.[99]

Cognate with the theory of significant form was Bloomsbury's interest in primitive art. In Fry's *Vision and Design*, for instance, there is an essay entitled "Negro Sculpture" and several others on the art of non-European peoples. And Bloomsbury and its adherents were collectors of African art. It was in the flat of Philip Heseltine (who, like Lady Ottoline Morrell, regarded *Women in Love* as a *roman à clef* and threatened a legal suit over the representation of himself as Halliday) that Lawrence first saw statues from West Africa. The interest in this kind of art was not, of course, original to Bloomsbury. As early as 1907 it had figured as a prominent influence and item in the cubist art initiated by Picasso and his associates in Paris. And it seems very probable that this particular Bloomsbury taste derived, through the mediation of Fry, directly from that historic moment of creativity. In Lawrence's novel the African statuary that is so carefully described establishes the modish taste which is a part of a particular social milieu. It also constitutes a highly important, if unobtrusive, approach to the concern with primitivism, emotional wholeness and the relation

[99] *Phoenix*, p. 567.

between thought and feeling which is such a central
theme of the novel. One recalls, for instance, Birkin's
quarrel with Hermione in the chapter entitled "Class-
room", in which Hermione calls in question the whole
notion of education.

> "When we have knowledge, don't we lose everything but
> knowledge?" she asked pathetically. "If I know about the
> flower, don't I lose the flower and have only the know-
> ledge? Aren't we exchanging the substance for the shadow,
> aren't we forfeiting life for this dead quantity of know-
> ledge? And what does it mean to me, after all? What does
> all this knowledge mean to me? It means nothing."
> "You are merely making words," he said; "knowledge
> means everything to you. Even your animalism, you want
> it in your head. You don't want to *be* an animal, you want
> to observe your own animal functions, to get a mental
> thrill out of them. It is all purely secondary—and more
> decadent than the most hide-bound intellectualism."

The dramatic context of this conversation makes it
evident that Birkin is not solely concerned to deny the
validity of the point that Hermione is raising. He is also
criticising her involvement with words and ideas that are
irremediably compromised, and all the more so, we may
suppose, for being received by Hermione from Birkin
himself. In the society and the time presented in *Women
in Love*, the primitive has already become a modish
concept entailing only facile emotion. Birkin alone of all
the characters in the novel actually experiences the
African statue and the feeling behind it. Hermione is just
indolently wording the issue which it is Birkin's urgent
desire to try to resolve. His course in the novel is experientially and theoretically to achieve a directing intelligence that is fully vitalised or, to put it another way, an
undebilitated vitality that is adult and humane by virtue
of being intelligent. Birkin's progress involves a climactic
realisation of the negro statue, which, within the novel as

in the intellectual life of the time, constitutes a characteristic and familiar icon of feeling.

Both Brangwen books have as a major and continuing
theme the significance of art. The change in the form of
the issue between the two books is, like so much else in
them, a matter of history. In *The Rainbow* the issue is
raised by the manner of Will's interest in art and in the
Arts and Crafts movement. In *Women in Love* the theme is
resumed by the representation of a kind of modernism
known in England during the years of the Great War.
The new subject matter in *Women in Love* accompanies,
and at least in part occasions, a major and radical
revision of Lawrence's fictional art. To understand this
new concern with art and the artist, it is necessary to say
something in general of the new manner of narrative
through which these central concerns are mediated.

8

A DANCE OF OPPOSITES

I<small>N</small> *The Rainbow* certain chapters run to fifty or sixty pages. In *Women in Love* the length of the average chapter is little more than a dozen pages. This dissimilarity in punctuation is an expression of a radical and highly important difference between the books. For Lawrence, we see, is now no longer concerned with the long extents of time that are the subjects of his previous major novels. *The Rainbow* covers some six or seven decades, *Sons and Lovers* and *The White Peacock* three or four, but the action of *Women in Love* takes less than one year. The story of the two love relationships begins in spring and ends in winter.[100]

The conspicuously reduced duration of *Women in Love* is also accompanied by an end of that energetic and urgent continuousness which is such a prominent feature in the narrative of the earlier novels. Here in *Women in Love* Lawrence has two stories to tell. And the narrative continually moves to and fro between the Ursula–Birkin relationship and that of Gudrun and Gerald. The result is that successive chapters (for instance, "Excurse" and

[100] The way in which this particular movement in time helps to suggest the disastrous failure of the relationship between Gudrun and Gerald Crich and the incomplete success of Ursula and Rupert Birkin is underscored by the geographic movement of the novel, which also seems to have more than literal significance. The story moves from an English spring to an Alpine winter.

"Death and Love") constitute a contrast rather than a continuity. The overall effect of the novel is not one of process and movement, but rather one of a pattern of contrasts that compose a moment of psychological, social, historical and, to use a word urged in the novel itself, evolutionary tension. The novel is a matter of balance rather than sequence. On occasion the course of the narrative is strikingly elliptical. For example, in the nineteenth chapter Birkin makes a panicky and ill-judged proposal of marriage to Ursula. Three chapters later, without any suggestion of reconciliation between them and without any account of the disappearance of Birkin's "blithe drift of rage" against her, it is suddenly announced that Birkin is to entertain Ursula to tea. And there are whole chapters whose particular location in the novel is dictated less by chronological propriety than by Lawrence's desire to stress or amplify the nature of a character or a relationship. The novel is a pattern of stresses, and not that long and rhythmic sequence which constitutes each of the preceding novels.

This thoroughgoing change in Lawrence's art must in turn be seen as a manifestation of a startling alteration in his fictional concerns. In *Women in Love*, for the first time in his career as a novelist, Lawrence abandons his old, longstanding concern with the notion and experience of process. Process is no longer the prime category of vital, moral or aesthetic apprehension. The representation of social and cultural process which we identified in Lawrence's first novel *The White Peacock* and which we saw developed in a more informed and textured way in *Sons and Lovers* and in *The Rainbow* is suddenly no longer the centre of Lawrence's concerns as a novelist. The explanation of this momentous change is that in his role as narrator of the story of the Brangwens Lawrence has surrendered his earlier optimistic feelings concerning the future course of man and civilisation. The confident view of the future of England that was taken by Ursula at the end of *The Rainbow* and that, on the evidence of the writing, was shared and endorsed by the narrator are in this supposed sequel completely relinquished. The following description of Birkin's thoughts suggests the change of emphasis more concisely than any one of the narrator's several comments. The passage comes from the last chapter and thus invites comparison with Ursula's vision of the future at the end of *The Rainbow*. Birkin is pondering the death of Gerald Crich and his thoughts revert to a set of notions which he has often entertained before.

"God cannot do without man." It was a saying of some great French religious teacher. But surely this is false. God can do without man. God could do without the ichthyosauri and the mastodon. These monsters failed creatively to develop, so God, the creative mystery, dispensed with them. In the same way the mystery could dispense with man, should he too fail creatively to change and develop. The eternal creative mystery could dispose of man, and replace him with a finer created being. Just as the horse has taken the place of the mastodon.

It was very consoling to Birkin, to think this. If humanity ran into a *cul de sac*, and expended itself, the timeless creative mystery would bring forth some other being, finer, more wonderful, some new more lovely race, to carry on the embodiment of creation. The game was never up. The mystery of creation was fathomless, infallible, inexhaustible, forever. Races came and went, species passed away, but ever new species arose, more lovely, or equally lovely, always surpassing wonder.

Such a vision of the termination of human life is the prime cause of the radically altered style and visualisation in this, Lawrence's fifth novel. As Frank Kermode has observed, *Women in Love*, like *Middlemarch* is concerned "with a moment of history understood in terms of a crisis archetype".[101] Unlike all the preceding novels, with their

[101] "D. H. Lawrence and the Apocalyptic Types" in *Continuities* (London, 1968), p. 132.

confident and linear development, *Women in Love* is
concerned with antitheses, with counterforces on whose
presently uncertain and seemingly untenable balance the
continuance of human civilisation is seen to depend.

These antitheses are presented in the novel largely
through the complicated set of relationships which are at
the centre of Lawrence's story. But the contrast of the two
main love affairs is only part of this complex. The stage by
stage comparison between the increasingly doomed love
of Gerald and Gudrun and the happy though ever
tentative reconciliation between Birkin and Ursula is but
the centre of an intricate web of counterbalancing relationships. Even within the quartet of major characters,
the permutation of relationships is more involved than
the simple notion of contrasting love stories can suggest.
For although Lawrence is concerned to present the relation of Ursula to Birkin and Gudrun to Gerald, he is also,
to take a first instance, concerned to present the relation
of the two women to each other as a condition of their
response to the men.

At an earlier stage of composition *Women in Love* was
part of a novel that was to be entitled *The Sisters* and in
the form in which we have it, an important interest is
still the manner and the effect of relationships between
women. The evolving relationship of the two Brangwen
sisters as it is presented in *Women in Love* is founded on
both a long established sisterly affection and a total dissimilarity of feeling and outlook. And although Lawrence
shows the complex rhythm of friendliness and hostility
that marks their feeling for each other, their fundamental
incompatibility is what finally prevails. In the first
chapter the two sisters sit together and discuss sympathetically their misgivings about men and marriage.
In "Continental", one of the last chapters, they have their
"last talk", in which Ursula attempts to defend her
commitment to Birkin against Gudrun's criticism. The

incompatibility of feeling which is expressed and, as it were, consolidated in this scene involves one of the most important formulations of the whole issue of civilisation as the novel proposes it. The issue between the two women concerns what we may call the nature of a proper irony. Gudrun is shown as having none of Ursula's faith in life, none of her "sensitive expectancy". Her outlook is conditioned above all by her propensity to disallow and thus thwart her responses and to withhold commitment. What Birkin says of her art is shown by the novel as a whole to be true of her attitude to life: "Her contrariness prevents her taking it seriously—she must never be too serious, she feels she might give herself away. And she won't give herself away—she's always on the defensive." Vital confidence and dynamic are the very things that Gudrun is ready to admire in her sister:

> How deeply, how suddenly she envied Ursula! Life for her was so quick, and an open door—so reckless as if not only this world, but the world that was gone and the world to come were nothing to her. Ah, if she could be *just like that*, it would be perfect.
> For always, except in her moments of excitement, she felt a want within herself. She was unsure.

On other occasions this sense of deprivation that Gudrun experiences expresses itself in a certain malice in her attitude to Ursula. An important illustration of this occurs during the little ballet in the style of Pavlova and Nijinsky that is improvised by the group of people week-ending at the great country house, Breadalby. Along with some of their fellow guests, Ursula and Gudrun dance the story of Ruth, Naomi and Orpah. "Ursula was beautiful as Naomi. All her men were dead, it remained to her only to stand alone in indomitable assertion, demanding nothing. . . . The inter-play between the women was real and rather frightening. It was strange to see how Gudrun clung with heavy, desperate passion to

Ursula, yet smiled with subtle malevolence against her . . ." Later in his description of this psychologically revealing mime dance Lawrence again emphasises "Gudrun's ultimate but treacherous cleaving to the woman in her sister". And the whole episode, like so many of the others in this most intricately organised novel, refers us to another, the one in which Gudrun again dances out her fear and frustration, this time to be disturbed by the approach of Gerald's highland cattle. Again envy is the directing feeling, though now it is more intense:

> Ursula seemed so peaceful and sufficient unto herself, sitting there unconsciously crooning her song, strong and unquestioned at the centre of her own universe. And Gudrun felt herself outside. Always this desolating, agonised feeling, that she was outside of life, an onlooker, whilst Ursula was a partaker, caused Gudrun to suffer from a sense of her own negation, and made her, that she must always demand the other to be aware of her, to be in connection with her.

This sense of emotional deprivation and vacuousness is the concomitant of Gudrun's peculiarly intense self-consciousness, which in turn serves to effect a further dissipation of spontaneity. At the great climaxes of experience in the novel Gudrun is never abandoned to feeling; her responses are limited to role-playing and to the selection of appropriate notions and styles of feeling. This involves a kind of irony which is in part a matter of a wilful distancing of experience and in part a matter of a lack of genuine responsiveness. It is well exemplified when Gerald's young sister is drowned at the water-party. Gudrun's attitude to the incident has no authenticity. She merely displays a certain histrionic inventiveness.

> Gudrun had wild ideas of rushing to comfort Gerald. She was thinking all the time of the perfect comforting, re-assuring thing to say to him. She was shocked and

frightened, but she put that away, thinking of how she should deport herself with Gerald: act her part. That was the real thrill: how she should act her part.

Not even the death of Gerald has any effect upon Gudrun's submerged or, to use the word most employed in the novel, subterranean life of feeling. When Gudrun meets her sister immediately after Gerald's death in the Alpine snows her response is, as always, unreal: "Gudrun hid her face on Ursula's shoulder, but still she could not escape the cold devil of irony that froze her soul."

Irony as the counterpart of emotional impotence and of the repression and distortion of the emotions is the main thematic issue that is involved in the story of the relationship between the two sisters. However, *Women in Love* as a whole does not repudiate the need for irony; rather it tries to realise and convey what are its true proprieties. The relationship between Gudrun and Ursula is an important perspective on the relationship which Ursula and Birkin seek to establish. For though at Birkin's insistence these two come to be suspicious of all self-consciousness, of ideas and of words themselves, they nevertheless understand the undeniable necessity for conscious and intelligent human beings to be affected in these terms. They are peculiarly alert to the danger of what Ursula in her last interview with Gudrun thinks of as "word-force", the power and the tendency of words to prevent thought from being isometric with feeling. Ursula is upset by her sister's gently mocking criticism of her commitment to Birkin. "There was an insult in Gudrun's protective patronage that was really too hurting." But her discomfort also derives from a less ephemeral, a more crucial difficulty, that is to say from her sense of the vulnerability, the instability of the unstereotyped, even unformulated feeling upon which her commitment to Birkin is based. "In her soul she began to wrestle, and she was frightened. She was always frightened of words, because she knew that mere word-force could always make her believe what she did not believe." This notion of the complex and slightly comic and yet potentially dangerous interaction of words and feelings lies at the very centre of the nexus of themes with which the novel is concerned.

The relationship between the sisters corresponds to that between the two leading male characters, to that brotherhood which the two tacitly and, at one significant point explicitly, attempt to achieve. Both characters are introduced for the first time in *Women in Love*. Gerald Crich is a successful Nottinghamshire coal magnate and industrial innovator and Rupert Birkin, in terms of specific social placing, can best be described as an intellectual with a private income.[102] It is true that at the beginning of the novel Birkin is a school inspector. But this social function hardly has the authenticity or significance in the novel that Gerald's has. It enables him easily to come into contact with Ursula and it also permits him, through his decision to resign, to make his act of dissociation from modern society:

> "I shall give up my work altogether. It has become dead to me. I don't believe in the humanity I pretend to be part of, I don't care a straw for the social ideals I live by, I hate the dying organic form of social mankind—so it can't be anything but trumpery, to work at education."

Otherwise Birkin's work in education plays no further part in the novel any more than it does in his life. Rather (and this is also true of Birkin's role generally) it seems the consequence of some authorial fiat. Unlike the other three main characters of the novel, Birkin is absolved from presentation in terms of coherent social and historical causation.

[102] Any irony that may seem to attach to this statement derives from the novel itself. Questioned by Ursula about the practicability of withdrawing from "the dying organic form of social mankind", Birkin replies, "Yes—I've about four hundred a year. That makes it easy for me."

The friendship between Gerald Crich and Rupert Birkin, like that between Baxter Dawes and Paul Morel and that between Jack Caldecott and Somers, intimates the issue of the relationship between the intellectual and the man who is more disposed to action than to reflection. The course of the friendship between the two entails both more ideas and more incident than that between Gudrun and Ursula. At the beginning of the novel it is shown in a series of conversations. Towards the end of the first chapter Birkin argues for individual spontaneity against Gerald's belief in the need for control and for standards of behaviour, and in the chapter entitled "In the Train" they argue about the state of society and about the prospects for civilisation. Yet these exchanges do more than express and confirm intellectual differences. Present but unrecognised in these debates is the intimation of their unspoken friendliness to each other. "It was always the same between them; always their talk brought them into a deadly nearness of contact, a strange, perilous intimacy which was either hate or love, or both. They parted with apparent unconcern, as if their going apart were a trivial occurrence." Gerald's chief reservation in his admiration for Birkin is his sense of the extent to which Birkin's ideas are untested, merely theoretical: "Birkin was too unreal; —clever, whimsical, wonderful, but not practical enough. Gerald felt that his own understanding was much sounder and safer. Birkin was delightful, a wonderful spirit, but after all, not to be taken seriously, not quite to be counted as a man among men." What Birkin finds hard to accept in Gerald is his rigidity, his wilful and un-yielding single-mindedness:

> This strange sense of fatality in Gerald, as if he were limited to one form of existence, one knowledge, one activity, a sort of fatal halfness, which to himself seemed wholeness, always overcame Birkin after their moments of passionate approach, and filled him with a sort of contempt, or bore-

dom. It was the insistence on the limitation which so bored
Birkin in Gerald. Gerald could never fly away from himself, in real indifferent gaiety. He had a clog, a sort of mono-
mania.

Yet the main obstacle to the relationship is not so much
these reservations concerning qualities that are really
very complementary as the difficulty in finding and
agreeing upon a format for the friendship to which both
feel prompted. In broad terms the relationship may be
regarded as a homosexual one. There is evidence of homosexual feeling and on one occasion the novel records a
miming of homosexual relationship between the two.[103]
Nevertheless, the term homosexuality is not an altogether
appropriate or accurate one for what Lawrence here
presents. In part the problem is historical. More than
half a century after *Women in Love* was written homosexuality enjoys a kind of acceptability and implies
certain distinct styles of social life in a way that it did not
in the England in which Lawrence was writing. Furthermore, although there is homosexual feeling present, it
would be false to suggest that this is all there is to the
friendship or even that this is the central item in it. The
critic's problem is in great part a reflection of that of the
characters themselves. Their endeavour is to broach, to
experience, and in some way to formalise a relationship
between man and man which, it is implied, is one necessary condition of a full relationship between man and
woman. In the chapter "Man to Man" Birkin recognises
the problem that is immediately consequent upon the
establishment of his relationship with Ursula: "Suddenly
he saw himself confronted with another problem—the
problem of love and eternal conjunction between two

[103] The Prologue to *Women in Love* (see *Phoenix II*, pp. 92–108)
makes it clear that at one stage of the composition Lawrence
intended the friendship of Birkin and Crich to be unmistakably
homosexual. In cancelling this passage, Lawrence made the relationship far more complex and difficult to define.

men." To a considerable extent the history of the friendship between Birkin and Gerald can be seen as a continuing effort to find the necessary terminology. The
metaphor which Birkin offers somewhat uneasily to
Gerald is the *Blutbruderschaft* of the old German knights.

> "We will swear to each other, one day, shall we?" pleaded
> Birkin. "We will swear to stand by each other—be true to
> each other—ultimately—infallibly—given to each other,
> organically—without possibility of taking back."
>   Birkin sought hard to express himself. But Gerald hardly
> listened. His face shone with a certain luminous pleasure.
> He was pleased. But he kept his reserve. He held himself
> back.

This first attempt to negotiate a relationship between two
highly discrete male individualities is unsuccessful. But
although Gerald, like Ursula, is unable or unwilling to
accompany Birkin in a movement that is verbally
initiated, the two men do later, as a result of their
wrestling together, achieve a momentary understanding
which tacitly incorporates something of the pledge of
mutual loyalty which Birkin had originally envisioned.
This occurs in the chapter "Gladiatorial". The scene is
the high point in the relationship between the two, and
the paragraphs describing the actual wrestling constitute
one of the scenes or symbolic pictures peculiar to the
art of this novel. The scene ends with a handclasp between
the two men: "The wrestling had some deep meaning to
them—an unfinished meaning."

Thematically, all the relationships in *Women in Love* are
interrelated. And the wrestling between Birkin and
Gerald is of great importance for the relationship between
Birkin and Ursula. When the wrestling is over Birkin tells
Gerald of the fiasco of his proposal of marriage to Ursula
which had occurred immediately prior to (and which
indeed has caused) his visit to Gerald at Shortlands. In
this situation Gerald for once possesses the verbal ini-

tiative. And Birkin's inability to understand him is of considerable significance for the novel as a whole.

> Gerald stared in amazement and amusement. He could not take it in.
> "But is this really true, as you say it now?"
> "Word for word."
> "It is?"
> He leaned back in his chair, filled with delight and amusement.
> "Well, that's good," he said. "And so you came here to wrestle with your good angel, did you?"
> "Did I?" said Birkin.
> "Well, it looks like it. Isn't that what you did?"
> Now Birkin could not follow Gerald's meaning.

Although the failure of the relationship between the two men is shown to be in great part the result of Gerald's failure to relax his will and reserve, the firm coherence of Gerald's nature is also a great if unrecognised influence for good in Birkin's life. This highly beneficent influence has been neglected in the criticism of *Women in Love*, which in general has read Lawrence's portrait of Gerald as an essay in demonologising. The simple fact, however, is that Gerald is Birkin's necessary complement. And to misunderstand Gerald is to misunderstand, as Ursula does at the very end of the novel, the proportions and consequences of Birkin's loss when Gerald meets his death. When, in the chapter "Gladiatorial", Birkin wrestles, as Gerald suggests, with his good angel, he is in effect relating his own fluent responsiveness and sensibility (admirably rendered in the actual descriptions of the wrestling) to a figure of stability and order. Birkin comes to wrestle with Gerald at the very nadir of his highly eventful emotional history as related in the novel. Having been set into a panic about himself and his future, he seeks to dissolve his difficulties in a rush to action and hurries to propose marriage to Ursula. His essential incoherence is an embarrassment and an irritation to her.

Only after the struggle with Gerald is Birkin able, almost literally, to compose himself and to understand the true nature of his relationship with Ursula. To Birkin, Gerald's verbalisation of the uses of their friendship is puzzling. But to the reader who has been following its development the meaning will be plain enough. In *Women in Love* as in *Sons and Lovers* an important thematic concern is the proper and humane reconciliation of a wide and profound responsiveness with the claims of order and control.

The quality of relationship achieved between Birkin and Gerald in "Gladiatorial" is never further developed nor even repeated. There is only a deterioration. And this is the consequence of what, given the many Baudelairean terms employed in the novel, may be understood as a kind of ennui in Gerald: "There was a numbness upon him, a numbness either of unborn, absent volition, or of atrophy. Perhaps it was the absence of volition. For he was strangely elated at Rupert's offer. Yet he was still more glad to reject it, not to be committed." Birkin's inability to sustain his friendship with Gerald is conceded to be his own greatest failure. It entails a loss of necessary regenerative and formative influence upon his own life and also a limitation upon his relationship with Ursula. For Birkin's realisation at the end of the novel is that the movement towards human fulfilment requires not one but a whole nexus of relationships. While the properly established relationship between man and woman is a prime condition of a fulfilled maturity, it is but the first of a whole pattern of continually evolving and inter-related dialectics. Furthermore, the number of issues adumbrated by the Gerald–Birkin theme is considerable. It is not just a question of the nature of friendship or of pride, vulnerability or initiative. The failure of Birkin and Gerald, despite all the psychological realism in the description of the friendship, also constitutes Lawrence's examination of the disjunctions, so damaging to civilisation, between private feeling and the industrial order, between individual human needs and mass production, between feeling and sensation, between art and sociology and between humane sensibility and the social system.

The third and final kind of relationship in which the members of the central foursome are engaged and the one which makes for a complete symmetry of relationships is that between any one character and the member of the opposite sex with whom he or she is not involved in a love relationship. That is to say, the nexus of relationships at the centre of the narrative is completed by Ursula's brief friendship with Gerald and Gudrun's with Birkin. Here as in all the other types of affinity there is rhythm and development. In both relationships there is a moment of sympathy and then a falling off and a failure to achieve any lasting bond.

In the early chapters of the novel Ursula is strongly opposed, even antagonistic, to Gerald. She is suspicious of his passion for industrial efficiency and doubtful of his absolute innocence in the accidental shooting of his brother. Her early hostility to him comes to a climax in the well-known chapter "Coal-Dust" in which Gerald compels a sensitive and nervous Arab mare to stand fast at a level crossing whilst a noisy goods train goes by. The sight of the suffering that Gerald wilfully enforces upon the animal makes Ursula "frantic with opposition and hatred of Gerald". "She alone understood him perfectly in pure opposition." After this the feeling between them begins slowly to relax into a new compassion. In a conversation after Ursula's marriage, Ursula tells Gerald of her hope that he and Gudrun will come together. And even though there is in this, as in many other conversations in the novel, a tension between word and feeling, "a strange tension, an emphasis, as if they were asserting their wishes, against the truth", Ursula undoubtedly develops a new affection for Gerald. As she tells Gudrun, "There is something I *love* about Gerald—he's *much* more lovable than I thought him." Nevertheless the possibility of understanding that is suggested here is never again resumed in the novel. In retrospect this aborted friendship seems a minor version of that between Gerald and Birkin. It parallels the movement of the more prominent relationship, has the effect of making it seem less parochially masculine and again underscores the difficulties present in all Gerald's relationships. His friendship with Ursula, as with Birkin, is forfeited as a result of his strong and subsequently accelerating preoccupation with self-confirmation through the sensation and efficacy of his own will. This preoccupation conduces at the last to a destructive, fatal hysteria, in which no human or material engagement is any longer possible.

In the second of these friendships, that between Gudrun and Birkin, there is again a development of feeling. For despite her scoffing at Birkin's theories about finding "an eternal equilibrium in marriage", Gudrun is deeply offended later on when she hears a member of the intellectual set at the Pompadour give a mocking reading of a letter in which Birkin had again set out some of his ideas. Resolutely she seizes the letter from Halliday and leaves the café. It is a measure of her interest in Birkin that she is unwilling to give up the letter even to Ursula. Despite her sister's displeasure, Gudrun insists on retaining it "as a memento, or a symbol". Shortly after this, Gudrun becomes involved with Birkin in a discussion of the future of England, and her interest in his views is intense: "It was strange, her pointed interest in his answer. It might have been her own fate she was inquiring after. Her dark, dilated eyes rested on Birkin, as if she could conjure the truth of the future out of him, as out of

some instrument of divination." But Birkin's attack on
the irremediable decadence of present forms of English
life cannot finally prevent Gudrun's customary recourse
to the known gratifications of a cynical quietism. Sardonic-
ally she attempts to invalidate his criticisms by predicting
both the failure of his proposed emigration and his return
to England. The narrator here observes: "It was finished,
her spell of divination in him. She felt already purely
cynical." This marks the climax of the relationship. At
this point Birkin's words and the influence behind the
words fail to sustain the bond that might have helped to
save Gudrun and Gerald and, in consequence, Ursula and
Birkin themselves. This is the moment at which Gudrun
resumes her sado-masochistic involvement with Gerald.
It is significant that immediately after she turns away
from Birkin, Gudrun touches Gerald in a way that "was
as if she killed Gerald with that touch".

   The tight mesh of contrasting and paralleling relationships that draws together the four major characters also
extends beyond them to involve the lesser and the minor
figures. The book is characterised throughout by pattern
and symmetry. Thus a further sense of narrative balance
is created by the fact that both Gerald and Birkin must
extricate themselves from love affairs with other women
before they are free to enter into involvement with
Gudrun and Ursula. In order to come to Ursula, Birkin
must free himself from his long established but now dead-
locked relationship with Hermione Roddice, the hostess
of the great country house Breadalby and an amateur of
the arts. This relationship, which Ursula claims is based
on sham spirituality and insincere social passion, serves
in the novel as an important prelude and contrast to the
story of Birkin and Ursula. (Birkin's relationship with
Hermione in its excess of verbalisation, its unnegotiable
confrontation of wills and its dangerous repression of
actual feeling helps to emphasise the fallibility of Birkin

and also the perils inherent in his attempt to formulate alternatives to current orthodoxies of feeling.) Similarly Gerald Crich's early relationship with Pussum, the fashionable prostitute of London Bohemia, is a prelude to the cruel reductive sexuality which he will experience with Gudrun. A further element in the symmetry of the novel is Loerke, the German artist, who is both the counterpart and the extension of Gerald. At the point where Gerald's nature is no longer subtle enough to proceed with Gudrun in the cultivation of sado-masochistic sensation, Loerke offers a further progress in emotional degeneration and decadence. The implication is that the particular corruption of Loerke's art is a more refined and more advanced version of the corruption of the modern industrial order.

The symmetry, pattern and balance that are so pervasive in the novel tend to remind us, however unexpectedly, of the classical art of the eighteenth century. And this impression is confirmed and made explicit by certain specific passages in the book. The opening scene, in which Gudrun and Ursula sit together stitching and drawing and discussing marriage distinctly recalls Jane Austen. And this opening reference is further strengthened by more explicit allusions elsewhere in the novel. To Gudrun the Crich house seems very much of the period of Jane Austen and she is greatly attracted to it. Birkin is also very taken with the Georgian chair which he and Ursula see at the street market. "When I see that clear, beautiful chair, and I think of England, even Jane Austen's England—it had living thoughts to unfold even then, and pure happiness in unfolding them. And now, we can only fish among the rubbish heaps for the remnants of their old expression." What is most important in these and other references is that they are no doubt calculated to draw attention to a similarity of thematic concern between Lawrence and Jane Austen. As in Jane Austen's novels, the central issue of *Women in Love* is the equalisation and resolution of the antinomies of experience. The need for a proper balance, a proper polarity, is the burden of Birkin's argument in the many discussions that go on at Breadalby and in all his urgent attempts to come to an understanding with Ursula and Gerald. Birkin's most rudimentary concern is with a proper balance in the epistemological relationship between subject and object. Deriving from this is his particular concern (which is the most important in the action of the novel) to achieve the same balance in human relationships and to avoid the disproportions revealed in the sado-masochistic feeling that informs the way in which Gerald and Gudrun apprehend each other. The predominating nouns in Birkin's talk reveal the prime emphasis. Equilibrium is the word that he most frequently employs. What Birkin asks of Ursula is "an equilibrium, a pure balance of two single beings:—as the stars balance each other." Elsewhere he speaks of the "star-equilibrium which alone is freedom", of "the pure duality of polarisation", of "a dance of opposites". And this insistence is not confined to one character. Gerald Crich also articulates a concern with the reconciliation of opposites. For him the crucial word is harmony.

To take up Lawrence's reasonably explicit invitation to compare *Women in Love* with the work of Jane Austen is not, of course, to find or expect to find any great coincidence of aesthetic effect between the two. Although the comparison provides an interesting perspective upon the themes of Lawrence's novel and makes us more fully aware of its formal balance, of the patterned relationships of the characters and of the counterpoise of scene and episode, the more memorable effect is to reveal the insufficiency of this mode of art as a means of representing and interpreting the modern world. In the comparison that Lawrence intimates, it is the dissimilarities which are the more important for our appreciation of the themes and the art of *Women in Love*. The comparison brings out the anarchy and the scarcely suppressed violence of the England which Lawrence describes and also exposes the superannuatedness of Georgian ideas of order and reconciliation as a means of dealing with them. Birkin's moralising of experience involves him in a more radical examination of the springs and origins of feeling than was ever necessary for any of Jane Austen's characters. His passionate concern with the nomenclature of relationship is an expression of the extremity of the problem confronting his society. In part Birkin's unceasing effort to denominate and to realise existentially new notions of order and reconciliation is a critique of eighteenth-century terms or at least of the mechanistic connotations and distortions to which, in the mind of Gerald Crich for instance, these words have succumbed in the twentieth century. (Thus Gerald's notion of harmony quickly deteriorates into an unworkable piety: "He did not define to himself at all clearly what harmony was. The word pleased him, he felt he had come to his own conclusions. And he proceeded to put his philosophy into practice by forcing order into the established world, translating the mystic word harmony into the practical word organisation.") In part Birkin's struggle with words demonstrates the extremity of the situation by showing the need for a language that can evoke the deepest, most powerful and, paradoxically enough, the least categorisable forces of healing in the individual and society. Star equilibrium is a term which attempts to describe something more elemental than what is conveyed by any of the moral and social abstractions that Jane Austen as novelist was able so confidently and so subtly to dramatise and to commend. In the society described in *Women in Love*, the abstractions that were serviceable in a time less exposed to radical confusion, disorder and apocalypse no longer connect with the kind of feeling and understanding that can make for the composure of civilisation.

If the novel begins by intimating a concern with the decorous balancing of opposites, it ends by completely invalidating such expectations and conventions and by presenting a conflict that is painful, radical and absolutely beyond the possibility of negotiation or compromise. From the retrospect of the last page, the earlier Austenian features come to seem like a hollow and ironic counterpoint to the overall movement of the book. The book conveys in purely formal terms the absolute failure of eighteenth-century forms to accommodate contemporary experience. And if such a demonstration seems to be a rehearsal of the obvious, it is worth remarking upon the several conscious efforts in early twentieth-century literature to establish or at least to rehabilitate the notion of "classicism". Akin to these was the characteristic Bloomsbury predilection for the eighteenth century.[104] There are several passages in *Women in Love* that attest to Lawrence's experience of this kind of taste. And as narrator he offers this toying with superficial notions of balance and proportion as one instance of the propensity of the vital intelligence to degenerate into an evasive and trivial intellectualism. The eighteenth-century is, for example, a special bond of feeling between Gudrun and Loerke.

> They praised the by-gone things, they took a sentimental, childish delight in the achieved perfections of the past. Particularly they liked the late eighteenth century, the

[104] "Strachey, in his respect for reason and detachment, looks with admiration towards the eighteenth century, the century of Hume and Gibbon with its amazing self-sufficiency, its good manners and good taste. . . ." Johnstone, *op. cit.*, p. 114. The same attitude informs Clive Bell's *Art* and the essays of Virginia Woolf and Maynard Keynes.

period of Goethe and of Shelley, and Mozart. . . .
They delighted most either in mocking imaginations of destruction, or in sentimental, fine marionette-shows of the past. It was a sentimental delight to reconstruct the world of Goethe at Weimar, or of Schiller and poverty and faithful love, or to see again Jean Jacques in his quakings, or Voltaire at Ferney, or Frederick the Great reading his own poetry.

In its form even more than in its themes *Women in Love* is a critique of this cult of spurious enlightenment. By its last page the novel has moved far beyond any possibility of discriminating and resolving experience in terms of merely social antitheses. What begins with a reminiscence of a Georgian drawing room ends with a confrontation realised in unmistakably cosmic terms: good and evil, life and death, civilisation and (albeit sophisticated) barbarism. The former term signifies the rhythm of relationship in which Birkin and Ursula proceed with their never finished task of establishing an acceptable and mutually balancing association. The latter refers to the relationship between Gudrun and Gerald, the modern artist and the modern capitalist, who together represent the full emotional range of a society in the first stages of the process of degeneration and decay.

The eighteenth century is but one of the distinct periods in intellectual history of which *Women in Love* takes cognisance. There are several others. Indeed the book abounds in philosophical and cultural references, all of which are relevant to the main themes of the novel. The thematic role of allusion and reference in *Women in Love* is similar to that in *The Waste Land*. Eliot's view of Lawrence's ignorance and lack of education has already been amply refuted. But it still needs to be emphasised that in *Women in Love* the consciousness of Birkin is as much informed by what has been called "the mind of Europe" as that of Tiresias in *The Waste Land*.

Within the brief course of the novel Birkin actually recapitulates to himself all the traditional responses to the discontents of industrial civilisation. Indeed this is a very important, if sometimes comic, part of Birkin's education as presented in the novel. For instance, there is considerable justice in the criticism that is registered in a question which Gerald Crich puts to Birkin while the latter is delivering a root and branch criticism of the industrial order.

> Gerald took a little time to re-adjust himself after this tirade.
> "Would you have us live without houses—return to nature?" he asked.

This implicit accusation of an untenable Rousseauism is later justified by Birkin's behaviour after Hermione has attempted to kill him. He leaves the great mansion and on a hillside in the country takes off his clothes and sits down among the primroses. Nature is the sole necessary relationship for Birkin at this moment. "Why should he pretend to have anything to do with human beings at all? Here was his world, he wanted nobody and nothing but the lovely, subtle, responsive vegetation, and himself, his own living self." A very good instance of Lawrence's fidelity to the complexity of feeling is his ability to convey in this scene not only Birkin's utter world-weariness and his tremulous disgust with the claustrophobic tensions in his relationship with Hermione which prompt him to this behaviour, but also the comedy, the sense of derangement which must inevitably attend upon such an impulse. "He climbed out of the valley, wondering if he were mad. . . . It was raining and he had no hat. But then plenty of cranks went out nowadays without hats, in the rain."

The ironic recognition registered in the single word "cranks" does not mean that Birkin surrenders the idea of a return to nature. Some three chapters later he is joined by Ursula on the banks of Willey Water and though this meeting initiates Birkin's eventual restoration to human contact, his declared attitude is still the same. He still disregards all social and sexual needs. Significantly (and consistently) these are also broached in terms of French romanticism. The following conversation contrasts the idylls of Bernardin de Saint Pierre with those of Watteau.

> They landed under a willow tree. She shrank from the little jungle of rank plants before her, evil-smelling fig-wort and hemlock. But he explored into it.
> "I shall mow this down," he said, "and then it will be romantic—like Paul et Virginie."
> "Yes, one could have lovely Watteau picnics here," cried Ursula with enthusiasm.
> His face darkened.
> "I don't want Watteau picnics here," he said.
> "Only your Virginie," she laughed.
> "Virginie enough," he smiled wryly. "No, I don't want her either."

The process of Birkin's rehabilitation involves, indeed depends upon, his acceptance of Ursula. And she, of course, is as insufficiently naïve to play the role of Virginie as Birkin is to take that of Paul. Nevertheless, both sets of lovers understand and undertake the love relationship as in one very important respect a mode of release from the compromising and debilitating corruption of society. In *Paul et Virginie* and *Women in Love* we have two generations of romantic dissent. Yet the effect of the century that intervenes between them is hard to minimise. This is what explains the comparative uncertainty and stridency, the web of reservation that attaches to the enterprise of Birkin and Ursula. Baudelaire is a prominent item in Birkin's mind, and this particular reference helps to remind us of what comes between Birkin and an earlier and less complex stage of romantic feeling. Birkin's sense of the difficulty of negotiating what might be called salvation and his sense of gathering damnation are clearly put in a conversation he has with Ursula. Birkin is again insisting that the process of civilisation is no longer creative:

> "I suppose it isn't," said Ursula, rather angry.
> "Oh yes, ultimately," he said. "It means a new cycle of creation after—but not for us. If it is the end, then we are of the end—fleurs du mal if you like. If we are fleurs du mal, we are not roses of happiness, and there you are."
> "But I think I am," said Ursula. "I think I am a rose of happiness." . . .
> "If we are the end, we are not the beginning," he said.
> "Yes we are," she said. "The beginning comes out of the end."
> "After it, not out of it. After us, not out of us."
> "You are a devil, you know, really," she said. "You want to destroy our hope. You *want* us to be deathly."
> "No," he said, "I only want us to *know* what we are."

Ursula's insistence here on some notion of cyclical evolution as opposed to Birkin's expectation of apocalypse reminds us how in all such exchanges Ursula's characteristically Brangwen confidence in life serves to rebut Birkin's gloomy and often prejudiced cerebration. This is not to deny that at one point Ursula herself has a sense of the end of her "line of life" and realises, as in *The Rainbow* one would never expect her to, that "all her life she had been drawing nearer and nearer to this brink, where there was no beyond, from which one had to leap like Sappho into the unknown." Nevertheless, taken as a whole the relationship between Birkin and Ursula is in great part a dialectic between Ursula's vitality and unself-questioning dynamic on the one hand and Birkin's reflection and conceptualisation on the other. The innate concision and inflexibility of the French terms and traditions of thought to which Birkin's mind so readily reverts have the effect of underscoring this distinction between Birkin's consciousness and Ursula's. The references to intellectual and cultural history also bring out the sophistication of Birkin's endeavour. He apprehends the crisis of his society and his time not as an intellectual naïf, but as one who is tutored in the tradition of European thought and civilisation which, at the particular moment the book describes, is shown to be approaching an unprecedented crisis.

This crucial moment is depicted with a social extensiveness far greater than that accorded to any of the salient moments of time depicted in *The Rainbow*. In *Women in Love*, time and the potential of time no longer hold the same significance that they did in *The Rainbow*. The narrator is primarily concerned with the efforts of his hero and heroine to disengage themselves from a society that is on the edge of chaos and destruction, and only a full and exhaustive report on the society can make their enterprise intelligible and justified. *Women in Love* is a testing of all strata and possibilities of social life at a given moment in time. As H. M. Daleski has observed in his illuminating account of the novel, "The structural principle of *Women in Love* is locative; that is to say, there is a calculated movement from one place to another, each place being a representative unit in the social organism and serving as the focus of a local significance. . . . There are five such foci in the book: Beldover, where Ursula and Gudrun live; Shortlands, the Crich home; Breadalby, Hermione's country house; the Café Pompadour, the haunt of London Bohemians; and the Tyrolese hotel, where Birkin, Ursula, Gudrun and Gerald stay during their Alpine holiday. We are required, in each place, to register the tell-tale tremors which herald in inevitable cataclysm."[105] The story ends at the very heart of Europe; and the major characters with the exception of Ursula all have important associations with the continent. Gerald has been educated at German universities. Gudrun belongs to an international group of artists, Birkin retires to France when he is ill, and Hermione at

[105] *The Forked Flame, A Study of D. H. Lawrence* (London, 1968), p. 128.

the end departs for Italy. Nevertheless, despite these wider European implications, *Women in Love* is primarily about England. It is a survey that ranges from the country houses of the traditional and industrial aristocracies to the mining villages. And as most critics have agreed, it is an impressive and convincing account of a complete social organism at a moment of arrest in its life and culture.

Yet to dwell too much on the sociology of *Women in Love* would be to oversimplify both the art and the manifest intentions of the novel. Furthermore, Lawrence himself has pre-empted the use of the word by employing it in his own text in a pejorative sense. Sociology is a range of concern and a mode of seeing that is attributed to Gerald Crich. After his early interest in and subsequent disillusion with primitive cultures and peoples, "he took hold of all kinds of sociological ideas, and ideas of reform." Lawrence implies that these ideas are but a function of Gerald's particular quality of mind, which is "curious and cold". Sociology, he suggests, denotes merely one kind of epistemological condition and one which, in the sense he understands the word, he is far from endorsing. In proposing the issue of epistemology we come closer to Lawrence's most preliminary concern. For the crisis of society and indeed of evolution which the novel describes is but the manifestation of an original epistemological failure. The particular slant of Lawrence's social descriptions in *Women in Love* is explained by his desire to show the origin and effects of this essential failure. This, so to speak, microcosmic concern is nowhere more clearly revealed than in the series of art objects which plays such a conspicuous role in the novel. *Women in Love* is a richly intricate work, as H. M. Daleski's study of the structure and Angelo P. Bertocci's account of some of the imagery have shown.[106] And one is conscious of the

[106] Angelo P. Bertocci, "Symbolism in Women in Love" in *A D. H. Lawrence Miscellany*, pp. 82–101.

inaccuracy that can so easily attend upon the slightest false emphasis in a critical account of it. Nevertheless, in assigning thematic primacy to the paintings and statues, one is making an indispensable emphasis. Works of art play a more crucial role in this novel than in any other of Lawrence's fictions and his treatment of them reveals the ultimate and irreducible basis of concern in *Women in Love*.

9
ART, EPISTEMOLOGY AND
CÉZANNE

Within the complex economy of *Women in Love* the strikingly large number of art works functions in two different ways. Most obviously, each painting or sculpture serves to reveal something about character. It tells us something of the nature and the mode of perception of the character who created it or the quality of response in the person who admires it. Gudrun's art, for instance, is in the pristine as well as the current sense of the word, belittling. Examples of her work are "two water-wagtails, carved in wood, and painted . . ." In the view of Hermione Roddice, their owner, they are, "perfectly beautiful—full of primitive passion—". But Ursula's response is different. She is unsusceptible to the modishly primitive in Gudrun's art but is highly suspicious of her sister's predilection for the miniscule. "Isn't it queer that she always likes little things?—she must always work small things, that one can put between one's hands, birds and tiny animals. She likes to look through the wrong end of the opera glasses, and see the world that way . . ." The impropriety that is surmised here so early in the novel is abundantly confirmed later on in an incident that occurs after Gudrun has entered the Crich household as tutor to Gerald's youngest sister, Winifred. Gudrun's first idea for a drawing project is that they attempt to make a picture of Looloo, the child's pet Pekinese. 'Let us draw Looloo,' said Gudrun, 'and see if we can get his Looliness, shall we?'" This kind of undertaking—the attempt to capture the vital quick of a living being—involves an assumption about art which it is the burden of the novel, in its discrimination of aesthetics, to repudiate. The act of drawing the dog is presented quite amusingly; nevertheless the epistemological wrongness is firmly if delicately established. The child draws "with a wicked concentration in her eyes", "as if working the spell of some enchantment". The result is a picture that is entertaining but also patently reductive: "It was a grotesque little diagram of a grotesque little animal, so wicked and so comical, a slow smile came over Gudrun's face, unconsciously." The kind of art and feeling that Lawrence must have had in mind when writing this in 1916 or shortly thereafter is now widely familiar. It is that strain in modernism which evades the tensions of the adult consciousness through an oversimplification and deflation of the object. For Lawrence that is the most suspect of all modern versions of the primitive.

The deficiencies in Gudrun's art and influence are further illuminated by the contrast between this drawing of an animal which she encourages Winifred to make and the drawing which so preoccupies Birkin at Breadalby. This latter is a Chinese drawing of geese, one of Hermione's many rare and costly possessions. Birkin is so fascinated by it that he makes a copy "with much skill and vividness".[107] He regards the epistemological mode in this as in other works of art as the key to a whole civilisation: "One gets more of China, copying this

[107] The whole incident derives from Lawrence's Bloomsbury days. Lady Ottoline Morrell describes how during one of Lawrence's visits to Garsington she came upon him in the library "copying, with finest skill, a Persian miniature". See Edward Nehls, *D. H. Lawrence: A Composite Biography* (Madison, 1957), vol. I, p. 308.

picture, than reading all the books." And in this "marvellous drawing" there is expressed an apprehension of the world that is infinitely richer than that allowed by Gudrun's reductive ironies. This is how Birkin describes the effect of the picture and the sense of Chinese civilisation which it conveys:

> I know what centres they live from—what they perceive and feel—the hot, stinging centrality of a goose in the flux of cold water and mud—the curious bitter stinging heat of a goose's blood, entering their own blood like an inoculation of corruptive fire—fire of the cold-burning mud—the lotus mystery.[108]

In that they portray animals these two contrasting drawings also form part of the carefully patterned bestiary in *Women in Love*. All the animals in the novel, the dogs, cats, bullocks, horses and rabbits, also help to suggest the basic timbre and responsiveness of the human characters. The art works elicit less elemental, more complex and particular casts of feeling. Like the paintings and sculptures that are individually described, the many general references to art also further the realisation of character. Gudrun and Loerke, we are told, "talked together for hours, of literature and sculpture and painting, amusing themselves with Flaxman and Blake and Fuseli with tenderness, and with Feuerbach and Böcklin". The lack of proper discrimination in this list and the "tender" patronising of art as a form of amusement can only seem a trivialisation of art itself in the same way that Gudrun's own art is a trivialisation of life. Again, the instance of Birkin's taste provides a revealing contrast. The specification of his particular admirations involves some pictures by Picasso which reveal an "almost wizard, sensuous apprehension of the earth".

[108] Lawrence's essay "The Crown" contains a somewhat less elliptical account of this particular image. See *Phoenix II*, p. 403.

There are two other art works that do more than help to particularise the nature of characters. These are the West African statues which so profoundly engage Birkin's attention and the two works by Loerke, the factory frieze and the Godiva statuette, which figure prominently in the concluding pages of the novel. Each group distinguishes the nature of the character connected with it, but more significantly, each constitutes a major crisis in the story line of the novel and thus conduces directly to the deepest thematic strata. These art objects also form the clearest demonstration of the extent to which *Women in Love*, at the same time that it treats of the modern condition generally, is also concerned with one very dramatic manifestation of that condition, modernism in the visual arts.

The West African statues first appear in the narrative in the chapter entitled "Crême de Menthe", when Birkin and Gerald and certain members of London Bohemia foregather at Halliday's flat. The sitting room contains "one or two new pictures . . . in the Futurist manner" and also "several negro statues, wood-carvings from West Africa, strange and disturbing". These objects, so familiar to us now as an important part of the initial enterprise and the tradition of cubism, elicit contradictory responses in Gerald Crich. One of a woman in childbirth with a "strange, transfixed, rudimentary face" "reminded Gerald of a foetus, it was also rather wonderful, conveying the suggestion of the extreme of physical sensation, beyond the limits of mental consciousness". Yet Gerald refuses to admit openly this sense of wonder at the figure. Instead of conceding his interest in the decadence revealed in the statue, he keeps his true feelings private and in public resorts to a conventional comment. " 'Aren't they rather obscene?' he asked, disapproving." Birkin dissents from Gerald's view and judges them to be "very good". Yet Birkin's total response to the statues is more complicated than this. The primitive figures linger on the edge of his consciousness and at a later and crucial moment in his life move to the forefront as a partial objectification of both his own emotional state and that of his civilisation. This occurs in the chapter "Moony", in which after a period of intense opposition Birkin and Ursula start to move together again. This initial movement to rapprochement precipitates in Birkin an avalanche of feeling (highly reminiscent of a characteristic propensity in Will Brangwen) which expresses itself in an almost hysterical determination to be married to Ursula forthwith. The explicit occasion for this moment of excess, which has such damaging consequences for his relationship with Ursula, is a sudden and highly detailed memory of the negro statuettes.

He remembered the African fetishes he had seen at Halliday's so often. There came back to him one, a statuette about two feet high, a tall, slim, elegant figure from West Africa, in dark wood, glossy and suave. It was a woman, with hair dressed high, like a melon-shaped dome. He remembered her vividly: she was one of his soul's intimates. Her body was long and elegant, her face was crushed tiny like a beetle's, she had rows of round heavy collars, like a column of quoits, on her neck. He remembered her: her astonishing cultured elegance, her diminished, beetle face, the astounding long elegant body, on short, ugly legs, with such protuberant buttocks, so weighty and unexpected below her slim long loins. She knew what he himself did not know. She had thousands of years of purely sensual, purely unspiritual knowledge behind her. It must have been thousands of years since her race had died, mystically: that is, since the relation between the senses and the outspoken mind had broken, leaving the experience all in one sort, mystically sensual. Thousands of years ago, that which was imminent in himself must have taken place in these Africans: the goodness, the holiness, the desire for creation and productive happiness must have lapsed, leaving the single impulse for knowledge in one sort, mindless progressive knowledge through the senses, knowledge arrested and ending in the senses, mystic knowledge in disintegration and dissolution, knowledge such as the beetles have, which live purely within the world of corruption and cold dissolution.

The writing here, with its restlessly appraising adjectives, its carefully noted detail, its repetitions and its suggestion of the interaction of Birkin's perception and thought, presents one of the most important experiences in the novel. The work of art that is remembered and described here affords the feeling, the very sensation of the decadence which Birkin surmises in himself and in his society. The statue allows a sampling of the alternative to the synthesising and creative impulse which makes for civilisation. It serves as an analogue to a particular impulse in modern psyche and society. It is an actual and felt experience of that disjunction "between the senses and the outspoken mind" which, in as much as any half dozen words can describe it, is the central theme of the novel.

The likely imminence of "this awful African process" is extremely frightening to Birkin. His mind dwells painfully on its European form:

It would be done differently by the white races. The white races, having the arctic north behind them, the vast abstraction of ice and snow, would fulfil a mystery of ice-destructive knowledge, snow-abstract annihilation. Whereas the West Africans, controlled by the burning death-abstraction of the Sahara, had been fulfilled in sun-destruction, the putrescent mystery of sun-rays.

His sense of his own and his society's susceptibility to this "strange, awful afterwards of the knowledge in dissolution" prompts Birkin to rush into an ill-considered, panicky and unsuccessful proposal of marriage to Ursula. It suddenly occurs to him that there is an alternative to the terrifying compulsions of an evolutionary decadence: "There was another way, the way of freedom." And this

194

involves the one relationship available to Birkin that seems capable of achieving the true balance between reason and feeling, object and subject, selfhood and relatedness which can make for a disengagement from that stage in the process of history in which, as Birkin imagines it, "We fall from the connection with life and hope, we lapse from pure integral being, from creation and liberty . . ."

At this point, the concerns of character and author are very close. Nevertheless, it would be a mistake to regard Birkin as a mouthpiece for Lawrence's views, or as a *raisonneur*. Rather he is a character undergoing delusion, education and development. In the novel as a whole we are strongly conscious of the distinction between the character Birkin and the authorial voice. Lawrence as narrator of *Women in Love* is not concerned with theories and ideas in the way that Birkin is. His concern is rather with the larger experiential context of the ideas. And this is something which the incident of the African statue illustrates very clearly. The memorable aesthetic experience occurs first; the ideas which constitute Birkin's attempt to understand the experience are dependent upon it and subsequent to it. One very important role of the works of art in the novel is to establish a difference between aesthetic experience and conceptual experience. Ideas are a part, but only a part, of Lawrence's representation of Birkin's complex and tortuous development.

The two works by Loerke which play such an important part in the finale of the action at the Alpine resort hotel are recognisable as companion pieces to the two African statues. It is highly significant that Loerke's frieze and his statuette should be introduced precisely in this setting, for they are expressions of that specifically European decadence, that propensity for "snow-abstract annihilation", which Birkin had earlier surmised. Loerke's art registers the particularity of northern decadence just as the African statues specify a decadence that is of the tropics. Both express forms of abandonment to the cult of sensation, to the reiteration of a single, undeveloping and thus unliving mode of consciousness. The first of Loerke's works to be described is a great granite frieze for a factory in Cologne. It clearly recalls Gertler's "Whirligig":

> It was a representation of a fair, with peasants and artisans in an orgy of enjoyment, drunk and absurd in their modern dress, whirling ridiculously in roundabouts, gaping at shows, kissing and staggering and rolling in knots, swinging in swing-boats, and firing down shooting galleries, a frenzy of chaotic motion.

The point of the picture, Loerke maintains, is to show how modern man is worked by the machine—" . . . the machine works him, instead of he the machine. He enjoys the mechanical motion in his own body." The picture inevitably recalls a similar submission to sensation in the African mask, the face of which is "void, peaked, abstracted almost into meaninglessness by the weight of sensation beneath".

A more complex example of Loerke's art is his small statue of a nude girl on the back of a horse. Lawrence devotes three paragraphs of careful and detailed description to it.

> The statuette was of a naked girl, small, finely made, sitting on a great naked horse. The girl was young and tender, a mere bud. She was sitting sideways on the horse, her face in her hands, as if in shame and grief, in a little abandon. Her hair, which was short and must be flaxen, fell forward, divided, half covering her hands.
>
> Her limbs were young and tender. Her legs, scarcely formed yet, the legs of a maiden just passing towards cruel womanhood, dangled childishly over the side of the powerful horse, pathetically, the small feet folded one over the other, as if to hide. But there was no hiding. There she was exposed naked on the naked flank of the horse.

The horse stood stock still, stretched in a kind of start. It was a massive, magnificent stallion, rigid with pent-up power. Its neck was arched and terrible, like a sickle, its flanks were pressed back, rigid with power.

The humiliation and subjection in this gross configuration recall the earlier incident of Gerald and his Arab mare. The recollection is confirmed by the fact that Gudrun and Ursula each maintain the same attitude to the statue that they had held towards that other equally dramatic image of a horse and rider. Gudrun is fascinated by the sadism and contempt which the statue expresses: "Gudrun went pale, and a darkness came over her eyes, like shame, she looked up with a certain supplication, almost slavelike." Ursula on the other hand is as robustly hostile to Loerke's statue as earlier she had been to the ugly actuality of Gerald's attempt to subjugate the Arab mare. Ursula's initial criticism of the piece is that it constitutes an unwarranted and unacceptable distortion of reality: "Yes. *Look* how stock and stupid and brutal it is. Horses are sensitive, quite delicate and sensitive, really." In defending his sculpture against this criticism Loerke resorts to the notion of Significant Form, if not to the actual term. Addressing Ursula in a derisive and insulting way, "from the height of esoteric art to the depth of general exoteric amateurism", Loerke develops the very theory of art which in England has come to be associated with the name of Roger Fry.

"Wissen sie, [*sic*] gnädige Frau, that is a Kunstwerk, a work of art. It is a work of art, it is a picture of nothing, of absolutely nothing. It has nothing to do with anything but itself, it has no relation with the everyday world of this and other, there is no connection between them, absolutely none, they are two different and distinct planes of existence, and to translate one into the other is worse than foolish, it is a darkening of all counsel, a making confusion everywhere. Do you see, you *must not* confuse the relative work of action with the absolute world of art. That you *must not do*."

Lawrence, as we have seen, considered Significant Form to be but a name and a justification for a cult of aesthetic ecstasy which he regarded as one aspect of the general modern search for sensation. In her discussion with Loerke, Ursula makes essentially the same point. She is in no doubt as to the expressive quality in Loerke's art despite his aesthetic theory and his protestations to the contrary: "I know it is his idea. I know it is a picture of himself, really—" And concerning the quality of the sensation which Loerke's statue affords, she is confident and downright. "The horse is a picture of your own stock, stupid brutality, and the girl was a girl you loved and tortured and then ignored." It is Loerke's powers of cynicism and contempt which enable him to replace Gerald Crich as Gudrun's lover. For in comparison with Loerke's subtleties, Gerald's cult of sensation is crude and rudimentary. For all his comic charm of speech and manner (he is no more to be seen in terms of simple villainy than Gerald is), Loerke is the most malevolent character in the book. And Loerke's art, even through the intervening medium of Lawrence's words, renders the essence of his sensibility.

A further function of Loerke's art and of the decadence which it signifies is to constitute a comparison with the kind of epistemology that Ursula and Birkin try to propose and to validate. The evolution of this alternative vision begins very early in the novel. In the third chapter, entitled "Class-Room", Birkin observes one of Ursula's lessons in which the children are asked to draw catkins in their exercise books. There then occurs a brief but highly important disagreement between Birkin and Ursula. Indeed, of all the many art works and discussions of art that we have been considering few are more fraught with significance for the novel as a whole than the children's drawings in question here and the argument which they elicit. Birkin suggests that instead of drawing the outlines of the flower the scholars should make colourings that show "the gynaecious flowers red, and the androgynous yellow". Ursula, as is so often the case in such exchanges, rejects the idea. But Birkin pursues his point, arguing that the colours are the main fact of the phenomenon and that fact is what the children should learn to register. "Outline scarcely matters in this case. There is just the one fact to emphasise." Ursula's continuing resistance prompts Birkin to make what is, for their relationship and for the novel as a whole, a crucial distinction:

> "It's the fact you want to emphasise, not the subjective impression to record. What's the fact?—red little spiky stigmas of the female flower, dangling yellow male catkin, yellow pollen flying from one to the other. Make a pictorial record of the fact, as a child does when drawing a face— two eyes, one nose, mouth with teeth—so—"

One term in Birkin's contrast is clear enough by virtue of being exemplified in Loerke's sculpture. To convert phenomena into what Birkin calls "subjective impression" is to force them, whether animate or inanimate, to subserve and even to gratify and to cater to the condition of the subject. This, as we have seen in the case of Gudrun and Gerald, is to deny any possibility of the dialectic or interchange of feeling that makes for life and growth. All that is possible as a result of this emphasis is a friction that allows only the sadistic or masochistic sensation which Gerald and Gudrun experience.

Commenting in 1907 upon the art of Cézanne, Rainer Maria Rilke employed terms very similar to Birkin's notions of "fact" and "subjective impression". He observed that "It is indeed natural for one to love every one of these objects, if one has made it: but if one shows that, then one makes it less well, because one forms an opinion of it, instead of stating it. One paints 'I love this', instead of stating 'here it is'."[109] This distinction between the thing as it is and as it may be seen and thought and felt to be, is a major issue in Birkin's life and in Lawrence's novel. The point is resumed several times in the book, but its most important development and elaboration occur in a conversation between Birkin and Ursula in which Birkin attempts to persuade Ursula to regard their relationship in the same terms that he does. Ursula insists on the idea of love, while Birkin, like Rilke in the passage just cited, tries to explain the idea and the necessity of another mode of relationship:

> She pondered along her own line of thought.
> "But it is because you love me, that you want me?" she persisted.
> "No it isn't. It is because I believe in you—if I *do* believe in you."
> "Aren't you sure?" she laughed, suddenly hurt.
> He was looking at her steadfastly, scarcely heeding what she said.
> "Yes, I must believe in you, or else I shouldn't be here saying this," he replied. "But that is all the proof I have. I don't feel any very strong belief at this particular moment."
> She disliked him for this sudden relapse into weariness and faithlessness.
> "But don't you think me good-looking?" she persisted in a mocking voice.
> He looked at her to see if he felt that she was good-looking.
> "I don't *feel* that you're good-looking," he said.
> "Not even attractive?" she mocked bitingly.
> He knitted his brows in sudden exasperation.
> "Don't you see that it's not a question of visual appreciation in the least," he cried. "I don't *want* to see you. I've seen plenty of women, I'm sick and weary of seeing them. I want a woman I don't see."
> "I'm sorry I can't oblige you by being invisible," she laughed.

[109] Quoted in Werner Haftmann, *The Mind and Work of Paul Klee* (London, 1967), p. 88.

"Yes," he said, "you are invisible to me, if you don't
force me to be visually aware of you. But I don't want to
see you or hear you."
"What did you ask me to tea for, then?" she mocked.

This, like many other passages in the novel, suggests
the comedy that is perhaps attendant upon any story
of the philosopher in love. Yet underlying and informing the comedy there are some crucial issues. One way to
define the epistemological implications of this conversation is to refer to Lawrence's own discussion of the art and
achievement of Cézanne in the essay "Introduction to
these Paintings". For in pursuing Lawrence's account of
Cézanne we discover not only an interesting resumé of the
themes of *Women in Love* but also what is effectively a
commentary on some of its less immediately intelligible
episodes. It is significant that it was the work of a painter
that prompted Lawrence to this articulation of his own
deepest concerns as a writer. His interest in Cézanne is a
good instance of the way in which the work of painters
serves as the best, the most serviceable metaphor for his
own art and concerns. As Jack Lindsay has remarked,
"What is striking is that Lawrence can . . . find his pre-
decessors in art as he cannot find them in literature."[110]
"Introduction to These Paintings" is a lengthy preface to
a volume of reproductions of Lawrence's own paintings,
but his main concern in the essay turns out to be with the
state of modern art generally and in particular with the
achievement of Cézanne. What Lawrence commends
most of all in the work of this painter is an insistent refusal
to acquiesce in preconception and cliché. "To a true
artist, and to the living imagination, the cliché is the
deadly enemy." "Cézanne was a realist, and he wanted to
be true to life. But he would not be content with the
optical cliché." "Cézanne's early history as a painter is a

110 Jack Lindsay, "The Impact of Modernism on Lawrence" in
Paintings of D. H. Lawrence (London, 1964), p. 39.

history of his fight with his own cliché. His consciousness wanted a new realisation."[111] There follows a paragraph which could well stand as a footnote to Birkin's simultaneous repudiation of the platitudes of love and conventional vision. It is also, implicity, a major statement of Lawrence's own aesthetic.[112] The painter Cézanne is for Lawrence an exemplar of the artistic function in a way that no modern novelist or poet is.

Without knowing it, Cézanne, the timid little conventional man sheltering behind his wife and sister and the Jesuit father, was a pure revolutionary. When he said to his models: "Be an apple! Be an apple!" he was uttering the foreword to the fall not only of Jesuits and the Christian idealists altogether, but to the collapse of our whole way of consciousness, and the substitution of another way. If the human being is going to be primarily an apple, as for Cézanne it was, then you are going to have a new world of men: a world which has very little to say, men that can just sit still and just be physically there, and be truly nonmoral. That was what Cézanne meant with his: "Be an apple!" He knew perfectly well that the moment the model began to intrude her personality and her "mind", it would be cliché and moral, and he would have to paint cliché. The only part of her that was not banal, known *ad nauseam*, living cliché, the only part of her that was not living cliché was her appleyness. Her body, even her very sex, was known nauseously: *connu, connu*! the endless chance of known cause-and-effect, the infinite web of the hated cliché which nets us all down in utter boredom. He knew it all, he hated it all, he refused it all, this timid and "humble" little man. He knew, as an artist, that the only bit of a woman which nowadays escapes being ready-made and ready-known cliché is the appley part of her. Oh, be an apple, and leave out all your thoughts, all your feelings, all your mind and all your personality, which we know all about and find boring beyond endurance. Leave

[111] *Phoenix*, p. 576.
[112] The metaphorising of love and perception recurs in Lawrence's later works. It explains, for instance, Mrs. Witt's notion of "visual philandering" in the novella *St. Mawr*.

it all out—and be an apple! It is the appleyness of the portrait of Cézanne's wife that makes it so permanently interesting: the appleyness, which carries with it also the feeling of knowing the other side as well, the side you don't see, the hidden side of the moon. For the intuitive apperception of the apple is so *tangibly* aware of the apple that it is aware of it *all round,* not only just of the front. The eye sees only fronts, and the mind, on the whole, is satisfied with fronts. But intuition needs all-aroundness, and instinct needs insideness. The true imagination is for ever curving round to the other side, to the back of presented appearance.[113]

The last few sentences of this paragraph provide a remarkably succinct explanation of Cubism, and the essay as a whole is an important apologia for the characteristic vision and art of this century. It is a criticism of an epistemology that perceives the world merely optically and statically. Lawrence especially admires Cézanne because, like Picasso and Braque, he concedes the complex ontology of the object.[114] Instead of trying to capture it, he allows its movement, its dimension in time as well as space, and its involvement in process. ". . . he set the unmoving material world into motion. Walls twitch and slide, chairs bend or rear up a little, cloths curl like burning paper. Cézanne did this partly to satisfy his intuitive feeling that nothing is really *statically* at rest— . . . and partly to fight the cliché, which says that the inanimate world *is* static, and that walls *are* still."[115] Again we are reminded of Birkin's admiration for the Picasso pictures. Lawrence's art in *Women in Love,* Birkin's exasperated

[113] *Phoenix,* pp. 578, 579.
[114] A similar epistemological concern and viewpoint are to be found in the poetry of one of Lawrence's earliest admirers, William Carlos Williams, whose imagination was also strongly visual. Williams's chief metaphor for the relationship between the perceiver and the object was the dance. See Sherman Paul, *The Music of Survival, A Biography of a Poem by William Carlos Williams* (Urbana, 1968), pp. 68–76.
[115] *Phoenix,* p. 580.

demand that Ursula be invisible and Picasso's cubist paintings all have in common the radical purpose of apprehending a range of richness and complexity in life which is no longer to be perceived in the familiar terms of simple appearances. In *Women in Love*, as in none of the earlier novels, there is a striking sense of the imperfect coincidence of the visual and the optical. The seen world, which had been so confidently assumed and so finely rendered in the earlier novels, is here a subject of doubt. The uncertainty pervades the novel as a whole. It is there in the almost simultaneous manysidedness in the depiction of English society, which contrasts so strongly with the traditional linearity of the narrative of *The Rainbow*. It is also there in the discontinuous, slide-like series of scenes which provides a background of dying forms as a context for the living impulse of Ursula and Birkin. This same uncertainty also makes itself felt in individual episodes. It explains, for instance, a major difference between Birkin and Gerald. In the wrestling scene we read: "Birkin was more a presence than a visible object; Gerald was aware of him completely, but not really visually. Whereas Gerald himself was concrete and noticeable, a piece of pure final substance." By the same principle, in the scene at the end of "Excurse" Ursula and Birkin eventually gain a freedom from the delimitations of what Lawrence in his discussion of Cézanne calls the "mental-visual consciousness". The long evocation of this important moment in their experience is presented in terms that are explicitly non-visual. It is realised as "the fingers of silence upon silence, the body of mysterious night upon the body of mysterious night, the night masculine and feminine, never to be seen with the eye, or known with the mind, only known as a palpable revelation of mystic otherness". Just as many of the individual words in this description are given meaning and justification by earlier passages in the novel, so the prime emphasis refers back to the comic exchange between Ursula and Birkin that we have already cited. In *Women in Love* episodes as well as images and concepts enjoy a significance that is incremental. And only at the end of "Excurse" is the earlier debate resolved experientially. The implication is that traditional categories of perception have become too rigid and thus deny phenomena their actuality, their appleyness, their Looliness, their otherness. Familiar modes of visualisation (even, we may suspect, those in *The Rainbow*) are no longer capable of doing justice to the life in things. For Lawrence, as for the Cubists and the Dadaists, to see things in terms of the long established Renaissance conventions of time, space and progress is to be encumbered with a platitudinous and sterile view of the world. And to adhere to such dead forms is to deny the full texture, mobility and unpredictability of man's human and material circumambience. A vital issue proposed in *Women in Love* is Birkin's quest for a means of restoring the autonomy of the object. His endeavour, which is at the same time theoretical and practical, comic and yet momentously serious, is to become disengaged from the gathering decadence that is the inevitable consequence of superannuated epistemologies and to see the world in such a way as to make for an enriched and enriching perception.

Thematic description of a novel of the density of *Women in Love* must inevitably simplify and thus to some extent falsify the actual reading experience that the novel affords. The most important part of this larger effect is a matter of language, of the actual words used. And as with the earlier novels, the most obvious appeal of the language in *Women in Love* is a visual one. Nevertheless, in this particular respect as in others, the contrast with *The*

Rainbow is profound and thoroughgoing. The writing, as well as the story calls in question the conventional idea of the visual. Even in the simplest instances, visual similes and references establish the irrelevance of traditional visual categories and configurations. Hermione's country mansion as it is described at the beginning of the chapter "Breadalby" is a charming but trite image; it is "like an English drawing of the old school" and "as final as an old aquatint". Also, certain characters appear as visual clichés. Halliday is "like a Christ in a Pieta". Hermione looks "as if she had come out of some new, bizarre picture". Her long, pale face is "somewhat in the Rossetti fashion". This concern with the visual cliché also accounts for one very striking feature of the writing—the many detailed descriptions of the dress and appearance of Gudrun and Ursula. Their brightly coloured stockings and their everchanging style of dress constitute one of the significant visual effects of the book. Fashion can be said to be a theme of *Women in Love* in so far as both Brangwen girls perceive contemporary chic as a restriction on their freedom as individuals: "In England it was chic to be perfectly ordinary." In conversation with Ursula, Gudrun develops the point at greater length: "But you'll find that the really chic thing is to be so absolutely ordinary, so perfectly commonplace and like the person in the street, that you really are a masterpiece of humanity, not the person in the street actually, but the artistic creation of her—" The novel and arresting dress of Gudrun and Ursula is their rejection of this idea of the fashionable and the feeling that underlies it. Of the two, Gudrun dresses more strikingly and adventurously. This is, at least in part, because of her hypersensitivity to the cliché. We remember, just to take one instance, how quickly and depreciatingly she converts the prospect of marriage to Gerald into a visual banality of a picture: "She suddenly conjured up a rosy room, with herself in a beautiful gown, and a handsome man in evening dress who held her in his arms in the firelight, and kissed her. This picture she entitled 'Home'. It would have done for the Royal Academy." Yet Gudrun's keen awareness of the cliché is little more than repudiative. It is rather like the attitude which Lawrence discerns in some of Cézanne's less successful landscapes, which are not creative realisations of the subject but merely conscious denials or omissions of the predictable:

> Sometimes Cézanne builds up a landscape essentially out of omissions. He puts fringes on the complicated vacuum of the cliché, so to speak, and offers us that. It is interesting in a *repudiative* fashion, but it is not the new thing. The appleyness, the intuition has gone. We have only a mental repudiation.

Gudrun's appearance is always this kind of determined and ostentatious denial of the modish. However, since it is not founded on anything more than denial, it also testifies to her ultimate involvement, in however negative a way, with the known and the predictable. The point is made, perhaps unwittingly, by Hermione when she judges Gudrun's get-up to be "at once fashionable and individual". And in the following example, a similar judgment is made by the narrator himself. On this occasion she is leaving the Café Pompadour after seizing Birkin's letter from Halliday.

> She was fashionably dressed in blackish-green and silver, her hat was brilliant green, like the sheen on an insect, but the brim was soft dark green, a falling edge with fine silver, her coat was dark green, brilliantly glossy, with a high collar of grey fur, and great fur cuffs, the edge of her dress showed silver and black velvet, her stockings and shoes were silver grey. She moved with slow, fashionable indifference to the door. The porter opened obsequiously for her, and, at her nod, hurried to the edge of the pavement and whistled for a taxi. The two lights of a vehicle almost immediately curved round towards her, like two eyes.

The substance of this passage exemplifies the complex artifice of Gudrun's sensibility, and the actual writing provides a good illustration of the visual prose in *Women in Love*. And this is considerably different from that in *The White Peacock*, *Sons and Lovers* or *The Rainbow*. The description shows the same alertness to colour, design and texture that is typical of Lawrence's previous writing, but there is also a new quality or, to put it more accurately perhaps, the absence of an old one. Unlike those in the earlier books, the colours and textures presented here are not continuous with the mood and feeling of the narrative voice. They give us little sense of Gudrun as one understood and appreciated and accommodated within the subsuming consciousness of the narrator. Rather she is seen as a discrete and exotic object. In the description there is a paramount sense of the metallic, the cold and the unliving. It is caused by the insistent repetition of the word "silver", by the use of words such as "sheen", "brilliant" and "glossy" and by the prominence of adjectives suggesting the sombre and the dark. This paragraph indicates Lawrence's attitude to Gudrun and to the fashionable and wealthy artistic world of which she is an adherent and in which there are so many precious things that have no real function. (One thinks, for instance, of all the "silk robes and shawls and scarves, mostly oriental, things that Hermione with her love for beautiful extravagant dress, had collected gradually".) But the passage also expresses something other than a point of social criticism or an authorial distaste for wanton luxury. The narrator does not perceive the living nature of Gudrun. Rather he sees her, as the syntax of the first long sentence suggests, as a series of bizarre and unliving attributes. The insect simile, of course, belongs to one of the image strands of the novel, but here it also has its own intrinsic quality. It suggests something that is in texture uninviting, even repellent. This impression is also confirmed and extended by the second and clinching simile of the paragraph in which the headlights of the curving vehicle are seen as two eyes. For here there is a further suggestion of something bizarre and alarming. There is a subtle but distinct breakdown of sympathetic feeling between the writer and the subject that is represented. By sympathetic feeling I do not mean moral or intellectual approval but rather a responsive appreciation on the narrator's part. To compare the above passage with, for instance, the description of the young Anna Brangwen going to church with her cousin Will in *The Rainbow* is to underscore what I have in mind. In the earlier novel Anna's appearance is recorded in similar detail, but there is also something else, the sense of a living individual, which derives from the narrator's sympathetic understanding for her. In *Women in Love*, except in certain passages dealing with Birkin and Ursula, this compassionate vision is broken. Lawrence's eye sees less sympathetically. Objects and people are more alien, more distant.

There are many passages that one could cite in order to demonstrate this change in the action of Lawrence's visual imagination. The following description of a landscape has the same essential quality as the earlier description of a human figure. The sentences come from the first chapter, in which Ursula and Gudrun, having discussed marriage, go on to initiate a characteristic narrative rhythm of the novel by walking to a nearby church in order to watch an actual wedding.

> The sisters were crossing a black path through a dark, soiled field. On the left was a large landscape, a valley with collieries, and opposite hills with cornfields and woods, all blackened with distance, as if seen through a veil of crape. White and black smoke rose up in steady columns, magic within the dark air. Near at hand came the long rows of dwellings, approaching curved up the hill-slope, in straight lines along the brow of the hill. They were of darkened red brick, brittle, with dark slate roofs. The path on which the

sisters walked was black, trodden-in by the feet of the recurrent colliers, and bounded from the field by iron fences; . . .

The fact that this description itself introduces the word "landscape" suggests how Lawrence's visual perception has lost something of its old, direct responsiveness and become self-conscious. The seen world is here relegated to comparative insignificance through notation of one simple and broad category. This dismissiveness is possibly justified by the depressing mediocrity of the scene. Nevertheless, one can recall similarly unpromising sights in, say, *Sons and Lovers* that the Lawrentian vision was able to illuminate and memorably to redeem. Here the powers of creative visualisation are less energetic and insistent. Lawrence can still see and identify the saving item (the columns of black and white smoke, "magic within the dark air") but as a whole the passage emphasises the tedium, the unlivingness of the scene. Most remarkable of all is the absence of colour interest in the writing. Black is the dominant and most repeated adjective in the passage; everything is "blackened with distance, as if seen through a veil of crape". The simile serves less to describe the phenomenon than to subordinate it to that sense of the ghastly unliving which in *Women in Love*, as in none of the earlier novels, obscures the colliery landscape.

The feeling, in the most literal sense of the phrase, of *déjà vu* which informs the book is enhanced by the unquestionably subordinate role that the evocation of the phenomenal world in general and the visual world in particular plays in this novel. Conversation, argument, debate and reflection are the words which best describe the writing that predominates in the book. The implication of some of the imagery in *Women in Love* also weakens our sense of the actuality of the phenomenal world. Images of hell and the underworld, for example, are a highly important strain in the book. One effect of this particular imagery is that the reader is uncertain whether he should see a given milieu as an actual place or as a correlative of torment, pain and suffering. The Pompadour is a good instance of the point at issue. Literally, it is an intellectual café after the fashion of the Café Royal in the early years of the century. But it is also described as "this small, slow, central whirlpool of disintegration and dissolution". And to enter it is to enter "some strange element", to pass "into an illuminated new region, among a host of licentious souls". The result of such twofold implications is that at times the book seems a fantasia in which setting, character and event serve as objectifications of authorial feeling. Again the contrast with *The Rainbow* is striking. Reality as apprehended by both the narrator and the characters of *Women in Love* is no longer directly, confidently or creatively ascertained. And feeling is subject to involution, fragmentation and an analytical self-consciousness which make impossible the great synthesising energy that we find in *The Rainbow*.

Here we come upon something which can only be regarded as an imperfection in the novel. Essentially it is a matter of the role of the narrator, which is here very different from that in *The Rainbow*. In the earlier book, the narrator was present in an appropriate and functional rhetoric and stood in a relationship with the characters and situation of the novel that was both balanced and intelligible. In *Women in Love* the role of narrator is often uncertain. Formally he is more distanced from the stuff of the novel, less of an ordered and definable presence. But occasionally, although there is no formal provision for such an intrusion, the emotions of the narrator impinge on the novel in ways that are damaging to its narrative consistency and verbal texture. Most obviously, the narrator tends to inveigh against characters such as Hermione, Gudrun and Gerald and the result is both a regrettable stridency in the writing and an obscuring of the complexity of the nature and role of the characters in question.

Anything like a full account of the effect of *Women in Love* must involve some notion of authorial mood. For there are feelings and concerns which seem to haunt the book but which are not accommodated in the basic categories of fiction such as character, episode or story. And the effect of this unassimilated authorial feeling is to detract from the primacy, the interest and the effectiveness of the created fictional world. In *Women in Love* for the first time we sense a serious breakdown of continuity between Lawrence and the subject matter of his art. The faltering of his confidence in traditional visual categories and in his own traditional and visual art (brought about presumably, by his removal from the social and cultural milieu which validated this kind of seeing) makes for an imperfect objectification in fictional terms of concern and feeling. The most important example of this is the climax of the Birkin–Ursula relationship as described in the final pages of the chapter "Excurse". It is the great apogee of the novel. Nevertheless, the success of the rendering of this moment of experience that is "never to be seen with the eye, or known with the mind, only known as a palpable revelation of mystic otherness" is highly questionable. The sedulous avoidance, in the last seven paragraphs of the chapter, of all recourse to social or cultural or visual terms may achieve the desired effect of avoiding the cliché, yet it conveys at the last only a sense of verbal complexity and is in no way experientially convincing. We are left with authorial assertion rather than fictional realisation.

The pictorial in the novel provides a further instance of the changed art of *Women in Love*. For here, as in *The Rainbow*, there are certain scenes, certain moments in the action, that constitute such a marked retardation of the narrative and that are endowed with so much visual detail and heightening that they appear to us as pictures. Indeed, in *Women in Love* there are many more than the five we identified in *The Rainbow*. It may even be the increased use of such configurations which makes them seem less impressive here than in the earlier work. Undeniably, some of the tableaux do approach the same order of achievement. One thinks of the portrayal of Gerald and Birkin wrestling or of the vivid scene (singled out by E. M. Forster in *Aspects of the Novel*) in which Birkin stones the moon's reflection in the lake. But there are other instances of manifestly pictorial writing in which the seeing is less immediate and in which the texture and implications of the image are coarsened or diminished. An example of this is the well known tableau in which Gerald forces his Arab mare to stand close to a level-crossing whilst a long and terrifyingly noisy goods train passes by. Though part of the horrific effect of this scene is auditory, it is primarily a visual experience for the reader, as it is for Ursula and Gudrun who look on. For Gudrun, as for the reader, the long awaited approach of the guard's-van gives to the terrible scene the order and impact of a composed picture. "The guard's-van came up, and passed slowly, the guard staring out in his transition on the spectacle in the road. And, through the man in the closed wagon Gudrun could see the whole scene spectacularly, isolated and momentary, like a vision isolated in eternity." Yet despite the succinctness of the image as an expression of brutalising industrialism, its effect is limited and obvious in comparison with that of the great tableaux in *The Rainbow*. In the writing there is a trend towards allegory of the kind that Lawrence once greatly deplored when discussing the painting of Watts:

> But I say, all mysteries and possibilities lie in things and happenings, so give us the things and happenings, and try just to show the flush of mystery in them, but don't begin with a mystery and end with a foolish concrete thing, like

taking Death and making a figure with "yellow topaz eyes —each a jewel", or a vulgar, bestial "Mammon", with long teeth, as Watts does. Some of Watts's pictures are commonplace, and a trifle vulgar. But look at his "Love and Death"—its beauty lies in the aesthetic unknowable effect of line, poise, shadow . . .[116]

The comparative lack of texture and complexity in the presentation of the image of animal and machine can be ascribed to its subservience to the abstractions that threaten to dominate *Women in Love* and which give it some resemblances to a morality play.

In certain other tableaux there is a converse kind of deficiency. In these the visual writing is too intense rather than too schematic. We are faced not with the mere decoration of ideas but with a richness in colour, light and texture which appears in no very immediate way endemic or necessary to the situation described. In these scenes there is a conscious importation of visual glamour and even, one might say, a kind of poeticising. One good example of what I have in mind occurs in the chapter "Water-Party". Ursula and Gudrun sail off to a little island in the lake where they swim naked and then dance. This part of the scene, with its Watteauesque implications, is well managed and is, of course, intricately involved in the organisation of the book. (The episode recalls Birkin's essay in nudity, for instance, and also relates to the long succession of groups dancing that the novel contains.) But the next part of the scene, in which the great boat-lanterns are lit and exchanged, seems somewhat overwritten. Each lantern contains a brightly coloured image the significance of which is intelligible in general terms. But the scene with the lanterns is a falling off in the verbal texture of the novel. It seems an exotic insertion rather than something continuous and integrated with the general style of the novel. There is something

[116] *Letters*, p. 47.

similar in the scene at Breadalby in which Ursula and
Gudrun do a mime dance of Naomi and Ruth. The scene
is a very important one, for it is here that Gerald and
Birkin first become fully aware of Gudrun and Ursula,
and the picture of the dance is finely presented. Nevertheless, there is an element of artifice in the writing as in
the occasion itself. In considerable part the scene is
endowed with significance by being made unusual.
Significance is, as it were, imposed rather than revealed.
(It is interesting to note that the scene derives from art
rather than from experience. For the dance is an imitation
of one of the influential and, at the time presented in the
novel, modish achievements of early modernism. It is a
little ballet "in the style of the Russian Ballet of Pavlova
and Nijinsky".) In scenes such as these, Lawrence's art
appears to lose contact with its native culture. Moments
of rich and memorable awareness are here less a matter
of matured and experiential perception than of authorial
assertion and insistence.

A distinction often encountered in the published discussion of Lawrence's novels is one in which *Sons and Lovers*
is seen as a belated work of the nineteenth century while
The Rainbow, in contrast, figures as Lawrence's first
modern novel. This view has always seemed to me to be
unhelpful because, both in the writing and in its major
assumptions, *The Rainbow* has much more in common
with its predecessor than it does with its supposed sequel,
which in publication it predates by some five years. And
if the ascription of the adjective modern is to be something more than a casual academic exercise (and in my
view it is a necessary means of defining a major change in
Lawrence's art and also the way that change was affected
by historical circumstances), it is to *Women in Love* that

the word and the crucial distinction must be applied. The most obvious way in which *Women in Love* points forward rather than back in Lawrence's career is that it is his first novel to deal with the effects of the Great War. Like every one of the subsequent novels, it deals with the breakup of England's imperial faith, culture and style. It differs from all the preceding novels in that it no longer sees the individual life or that of society as a whole borne along by a process of growth and creative development. Characters such as Gerald Crich and Hermione Roddice represent the decline of an industrial, social and cultural imperium. And this ending of an old order is what enjoins a new kind of art. Narrative fragmentation replaces the old vital continuum. Many-sided social analysis replaces the confident recognition of the heroic or what Lukacs called the "typical". And there is an altogether new uncertainty in the relationship between the authorial consciousness and objects, characters, events and story. Most significant of all, there is a radical alteration in what we have identified as one of the most innate and determining characteristics of Lawrence's major fiction, his pre-eminently visual style.

In his study of Ruskin, John D. Rosenberg has said of his subject that he was "eye-driven, even photoerotic". "All the forms of the visible world leaped into animate life before his eyes; nor could he resist recording the play of light upon the life of things. His medium was a prose charged with the sudden clarity of first sight."[117] These same words go a long way towards defining the primary characteristic of Lawrence's mind and art. Yet vision involves more than an innate capacity. It is cultural as well as, so to speak, retinal. And Lawrence's early novels attest to the traditions of visualisation that moulded his singular capacity for perception. In his early prose it is

[117] John D. Rosenberg, *The Darkening Glass* (New York and London, 1961), p. 4.

easy to see the presence, either by implication or by overt reference, of certain images and configurations that we associate with Blake, the English landscape painters, Rossetti and some of the Italian painters commended by Ruskin himself. Lawrence's mind was marked by the peculiarly visual sensibility of the Victorian period, but *Women in Love* reveals the abrupt superannuation of this tradition of seeing. The condition of England which it presents is now no longer amenable to this mode of vision. Lawrence's interest in Cézanne must in fact be seen as part of his conscious, discursive effort to become rid of dead, invalidated forms of perception. But *Women in Love* constitutes his first imaginative apprehension of the new situation.

Women in Love has the two qualities that mark all novels that we recognise as modern—a diminution of cultural density in subject matter and, in consequence, an enforced experimentation in style. And from these the several strains and imperfections in the writing in *Women in Love* can be seen to stem. In this, Lawrence's first distinctively modern work, the new strains are for the most part accommodated and do no irreparable damage. *Women in Love* is the major representation of a momentous crisis in English experience. Thematically it is rich, intricate and profound; aesthetically, despite the blemishes we have considered, it is well ordered and sustained. To compare it with other works of literature dealing with the crisis of England brought about by the Great War is not only to recognise its supremacy but also, if one bears in mind that it was written at the very moment of historic change, to appreciate Lawrence's remarkable powers of insight, adaptability and improvisation as a novelist. In the novels originating after *Women in Love* the new and profound difficulty confronting the novelist was not to be so successfully overcome. The recession in cultural continuousness and particularly in sympathetic visual imagination and the corresponding growth in conscious artifice, which in *Women in Love* are still held in an aesthetically acceptable balance, point forward to the conspicuous absence in Lawrence's last novels of the synthesising vision that constitutes his great, albeit somewhat anachronistic, gift to modern literature and culture.

FOUR
EPILOGUE

Myself, I suffer badly from being so cut off. But what is one to do? One can't link up with the social unconscious. At times, one is *forced* to be essentially a hermit. . . . One has no real human relations—that is so devastating. . . .

Men were never, in the past, fully societal—and they never will be in the future. But more so, more than now. Now is the time between Good Friday and Easter. We're absolutely in the tomb.

LETTER TO DR. TRIGANT BURROW,
3 AUGUST 1927

10

THE NOVELS OF THE
TWENTIES

AT the time *Women in Love* was completed exactly half of Lawrence's career as a novelist still lay before him. But his achievement in the novel form shows no corresponding symmetry. As the great majority of Lawrence's critics have agreed, the novels written in the twenties constitute a distinct anti-climax. And to seek to characterise these works, whether in terms of the total effect that each has or in terms of the particular role and quality of the visual imagination at work, is often to find oneself proposing negative definitions of the achievement represented by the earlier books. But it is also necessary to guard against overstating the unsatisfactoriness of Lawrence's last five novels. For the often remarked falling-off is very much a comparative matter. Only because they must inevitably be compared with *Sons and Lovers*, *The Rainbow* and *Women in Love* do these later works seem disappointing. Considered on their own, the last five novels all have life and interest, and some of them deserve a better reputation and a wider currency. However, to make the full case for these later books is beyond the scope of this essay. In a study of the crucial phase in the history of realism that is signified by Lawrence's changing modes of representing the seen world, the latter half of the canon can figure only as a series of instances of the unviability and the weakening of the visual imagination. Nowhere in the later novels do we find that pitch of creative energy which distinguishes the novels of the 1910s.

There are other reasons for this besides the important one considered at the end of the last chapter. The disastrous reception of *The Rainbow* and the years of poverty during which it was impossible to find a publisher for *Women in Love* must have lessened Lawrence's readiness to dedicate to another full length work of fiction the profound commitment and energy that are in these two books. Furthermore, it would seem that with the completion of *Women in Love* he had brought to a conclusion his long evolving concern to render the modern consciousness in its historical course and origins. Certainly after *Women in Love* there are no very new concerns, themes or perspectives in Lawrence's novels. Those that follow comprise but reiterations of some of the themes raised by the history of English industrial consciousness to be found in the Brangwen books. In the later novels there is, comparatively, a lack of thematic evolution, a certain repetition and a sense of weariness. These are already intimated as early as *Women in Love*. At one point in that novel Birkin momentarily tires of his ambitious efforts to find some comprehensive experience of order and meaning. His irritation evokes what is, when one comes to look at the later novels, a most interesting simile: "Why bother! Why strive for a coherent, satisfied life? Why not drift on in a series of accidents—like a picaresque novel? Why not? Why bother about human relationships? Why take them seriously—male or female? Why form any serious connections at all? Why not be casual, drifting along, taking all for what it was worth?"

The lassitude in the three novels that follow immediately after *Women in Love* is most conspicuously a matter of a lack of firm organisation and coherence. The narrative development in each of them seems fortuitously incremental rather than creatively directed. Each strikes us as evidence of the propensity of Lawrence the novelist to follow Birkin's inclination to lapse into the irresolute and easy picaresque. There is, for instance, less and less tendency for Lawrence to employ what was formerly his most characteristic fictional device, the counterpointing of scenes and episodes. What unity there is in these three books derives less from the narrative and stylistic texture and more from the authorial voice, which comes to dominate the writing in a way that it never did in the previous novels. One indication of the extent to which Lawrence's most creative energies are absent from these novels is the lack of development in the outlook, tone and manner of this authorial voice as we encounter it in *The Lost Girl*, published in 1920, *Aaron's Rod*, published in 1922 and *Kangaroo*, of 1923. Compared with the very striking mutations in the narrative voice in the novels that precede these three, the manner here is static. The characteristic tone is an irony which is sometimes sardonic and sometimes flippant. And in all three of these novels of the early twenties we sense that the chief function of this voice is to assert however casually the formal unity of what is really a multiplicity of disconnected subjects and concerns.

Each of these books "drifts on", in Birkin's words, "like a picaresque novel". That the last phrase happens to be a simile is also helpful, for the term "picaresque novel" is here more appropriate as a resemblance than as a category. It is true that each novel treats of a hero or, in one case, a heroine who sets out on a journey that also involves a moral, psychological and cultural quest. Alvina Houghton in *The Lost Girl* learns to travel beyond the sterile restrictions of her native town, first to achieve her independence in London and then to attempt a renewal of her life in the south of Italy. Geographically, the story of Aaron Sissons is somewhat similar. Forsaking his wife, child and home in order to avoid stagnation both as a man and as an artist, Aaron also journeys from the Notts. coalfield to London and thence to Italy. His story is more episodic and more a continuing progress than Alvina's. And so is that of Somers in *Kangaroo*. This novel is essentially about one highly articulated journey that occurs within the context of a larger and continuing journey. The book begins with the arrival in Australia of the leading character, treats of his brief stay there, of his superficial political involvements and of his ultimate departure. In each of these books the journey conduces, usually in a negative way, to the education of the leading figure. Nevertheless, the term picaresque novel does not adequately describe any of them. For Lawrence readily wanders from what is ascertainably the main and directing concern of each book. At times this is a matter of switching, for no very convincing reason, from one mode of fiction to another. For example the social satire in the first hundred or so pages of *The Lost Girl* is suddenly abandoned in favour of a new and relatively unsatirical concern with a troop of travelling performers called the Natcha-Kee-Tawaras and with their mysterious invocations and ritual. The sudden prominence of these characters jeopardises the verisimilitude of the novel and also damages the textural consistency of the style. A sudden shift of interest also occurs in *Aaron's Rod*. In the middle of the book, Aaron, who is the initial focal interest, is suddenly relegated to a secondary position so that prime attention can be directed to Lilley, Aaron's friend and tutor. It is often said that this shift from a working class refugee's progress through the fashionable cosmopolitan world to the comic difficulties of a bourgeois moralist gives the effect of two novels in one. In my view the novel is more successful than critical opinion customarily allows. Its account of the breakdown in the twentieth century of traditional forms of power and authority is subtle and relaxed. Nevertheless, the central inconsistency suggests Lawrence's difficulties at this stage of his career in sustaining a given fictional commitment.

These novels are also impaired by something more than an inconsistency of fictional modes, that is to say, by a propensity temporarily to abandon the conventions of fiction altogether. In the concluding section of *The Lost Girl* where Lawrence describes Alvina's journey through Italy, he abandons his role as novelist and reproduces what is patently his own experience of returning to Italy after years of absence. The writing is extremely good, but it strikes us primarily as travelogue or autobiography rather than as a continuation of the novel we have been reading. A more flagrant example of Lawrence's new and cavalier indifference to the proprieties of the art of fiction is the novel *Kangaroo*. In fact, judged as a novel it frequently seems a very trumped up affair. Here, at a moment's notice, Lawrence is prepared to abandon his characters and their experience in order to set out upon some extra-fictional venture. At one point, as for instance at the beginning of the chapter in which he enters on a discussion of the mob and the "mass-spirit", Lawrence writes as an essayist. And at another, say in the well-known chapter entitled "The Nightmare" in which he describes Somers's painful experiences during the Great War, he obviously writes as an autobiographer. In terms of the novel as a whole, the significance and effect of this passage are quite disproportionate. For the events and issues described in the chapter are incomparably more important to the narrator and in consequence more interesting to the reader than the accounts of the imaginary Australian political party which is the ostensible subject of the novel. The chapter is a major work of prose in its own right and an important first-hand description of the decay in English ethical culture during the first

World War. It is an important historical as well as auto-biographical document. But the effect of its somewhat contrived presence in *Kangaroo* is to expose the paucity and superficiality of Lawrence's imaginative interest in the world that he has invented in order to write a novel.

The Lost Girl, Aaron's Rod and *Kangaroo* each contain elements that have not been fully accommodated by the central fictional design. Often the original design is changed. Sometimes it is abandoned altogether and replaced by thinly disguised autobiography, essays in social, cultural and psychological speculation and chapters of travelogue. It is in this last kind of writing that we can observe the continuing history of Lawrence's visual imagination in his novels of the early twenties. For along with the dissipation of imaginative commitment to the novel form there also occurred a separation, a specialisation of his visual powers as a writer. There are undoubtedly some striking passages of visual writing in these three novels. One thinks of the description of the Plain of Lombardy in chapter xv of *Aaron's Rod* or of the description of the Australian bush in the final chapter of *Kangaroo*. But the fact that one recalls them as such discrete items is a clue to their essential insignificance. The visual writing in the earlier novels was much more central to their overall effect and meaning. But Lawrence no longer perceives in terms of a given social, psychological and visual complex. The old simultaneity is now fragmented and diffused. His visual art now figures as a set piece, an adornment, as one kind of prose item in a series of prose items. Usually the visual passages are well done; but they belong less in a novel than in a travel book. And Lawrence's most unified, sustained and successful book during these years was in fact his travel book, *Sea and Sardinia*. This is a record of a brief visit which Lawrence made to the island in 1921. And this relaxed and modest undertaking seems perfectly in accord with

Lawrence's state of mind in a way that his fictional enter-
prises of the time do not. It is entertaining and free from
the difficulties of uncertain authorial predisposition. The
visual quality and detail are particularly impressive; and
they seem even more so when one recalls that Lawrence
did the writing several weeks after the actual visit. Of all
his works, none provides clearer evidence of his singular
powers of visual insight and retentiveness.

There is a marked difference between the novels that
Lawrence wrote in the early twenties and those composed
in the later part of the decade. For in his last two novels,
The Plumed Serpent and *Lady Chatterley's Lover*, we find
something of a reintegration of his visual powers with a
fictional purpose. At the same time (and it seems legiti-
mate to say, in consequence) there is something of a
renewal of Lawrence's earlier, serious commitment to the
art of fiction. The genesis and the actual writing of these
last two novels as revealed in the letters recall the protracted composition of the early and major novels. Unlike
Kangaroo, which was virtually completed within some five
weeks, these last two novels were, like the Brangwen
books, extensively revised and even completely rewritten.
And this new involvement and care are apparent in their
style. In *The Plumed Serpent* there is a verbal density, a
poetic richness and a coherence of theme and organisation that are not to be found in any of Lawrence's novels
since *Women in Love*.

One of several likely reasons for Lawrence's renewal of
interest in the novel form seems to have been his experience of Mexico and his intense interest in its life, history
and art. *The Plumed Serpent* shows Lawrence engaged with
a culture and a whole way of life for the first time since
his self-imposed exile from England in 1919. The life of

Mexico is a central subject in this novel in a way that the life of Australia in *Kangaroo* or of Italy in *Aaron's Rod* were not. And this new interest and engagement in a culture dissipates the sense of merely personal or casual concerns which pervades the writing in the earlier novels of the twenties. It permits an objectification of feeling which revives and gives meaning to Lawrence's innate intensity of visualisation. In *The Plumed Serpent* we have again a book which is pre-eminently visual in style as well as in the matrix and context of its themes. As in some of the earlier novels, certain great tableaux stay in the reader's mind; one thinks of Kate's journey down the lake or of the ceremonial dances or of the removal of the Christian images from the church by the revolutionaries. And everywhere in the book there is the old visual style which integrates character and incident with the forming and informing landscape and milieu. Here are a few paragraphs that typify the writing in the novel. They describe a part of Kate's journey to Sayula.

> The boy said they must go in the tram-car, so in the tram-car they went. The driver whipped his mules, they rolled in the still, heavy morning light away down an uneven, cobbled road with holes in it, between walls with falling mortar and low, black, adobe houses, in the peculiar *vacuous* depression of a helpless little Mexican town, towards the plaza. The strange emptiness, everything empty of life!
>
> Occasional men on horseback clattered suddenly by, occasional big men in scarlet serapes went noiselessly on their own way, under the big hats. A boy on a high mule was delivering milk from red globe-shaped jars slung on either side his mount. The street was stony, uneven, vacuous, sterile. The stones seemed dead, the town seemed made of dead stone. The human life came with a slow, sterile unwillingness, in spite of the low-hung power of the sun.
>
> At length they were in the plaza, where brilliant trees flowered in a blaze of pure scarlet, and some in pure lavender, around the basins of milky-looking water. Milky-dim the water bubbled up in the basins, and women,

bleary with sleep, uncombed, came from under the dilapidated arches of the portales, and across the broken pavement, to fill their water-jars.

The tram stopped and they got down. The boy got down with the bags, and told them they must go to the river to take a boat.

They followed obediently down the smashed pavements, where every moment you might twist your ankle or break your leg. Everywhere the same weary indifference and brokenness, a sense of dirt and of helplessness, squalor of far-gone indifference, under the perfect morning sky, in the pure sunshine and the pure Mexican air. The sense of life ebbing away, leaving dry ruin.

In *The Plumed Serpent* this kind of writing is more than description or décor. The appearance and condition of this landscape and of the figures in it register both the need and the difficulty of social and political renewal (the major themes of the novel) with a specification that is too dense for thematic summary.

Although the mood of this landscape is indissolubly central to the events and concerns of *The Plumed Serpent*, one discerns an element in the description that is nowhere to be found in the similarly functional evocation of milieu in Lawrence's Nottinghamshire novels. There is in the passage a very distinct sense of distance and excludedness on the part of the narrator. This effect may derive in part from the fact that Lawrence is describing the perceptions and thoughts of Kate, who is very much a traveller; but a second look at the writing shows that there is a strong sense of the alien in the narrative consciousness within which the consciousness of the character is contained. This sense is immediately established in the first paragraph by the designation of the town as "Mexican". And it is present again in the sudden recourse to the second person in the description of the "smashed pavements, where every moment you might twist your ankle or break your leg". This appeal to familiar expectation reinforces our impression of authorial uncertainty in the face of strange and perilous conditions. The apprehension of something foreign, of something that is seen but not sympathetically understood is resumed even more strongly in the last paragraph. Again the adjective of nationality occurs and again the idiom of the traveller is emphasised by the fragmentary nature of the last two sentences. Perception and judgment are here rendered in a short-hand that suggests the tourist's journal.

This discontinuousness between narrator and subject recurs throughout the novel and develops into a serious imperfection. *The Plumed Serpent* has none of the formal and stylistic diffuseness of the three novels that precede it, yet it is not a completely unified or successful fictional entity. The fault in the quoted passage is fundamentally the same fault that occurs in the larger matters of characterisation, theme and narrative organisation. In *The Plumed Serpent* there are essentially two stories which the author has attempted, not altogether successfully, to dovetail and to integrate. First, there is the account of the visionary attempt at a renewal of Mexico by a brotherhood devoted to the old gods of the country. Secondly, there is the story of Kate Leslie, a middle-aged European widow who is weary of her own way of life and of her native civilisation and who seeks a personal renewal. The notion of renewal which is common to both stories might seem to unify the two narrative concerns, but the compatibility is apparent rather than real. For the vision of the Mexican renaissance necessitates a mode of language that appertains to myth, while the account of Kate's career and situation requires another and less opulent language that is proper to psychological realism. The enforced conjunction of these two modes in *The Plumed Serpent* is as unsatisfactory aesthetically as the relationship between Kate and Cipriano is morally. Lawrence was an incorrigible realist, and a single-minded and exclusive devotion to myth was beyond his powers in fiction. (A particularly clear-cut illustration of this is the second part of "The Man Who Died" in which the mythical frame of reference established in the first part is completely destroyed by Lawrence's insistence on pursuing the psychological, sexual and social consequences for Jesus of a physical and mundane resurrection.) In *The Plumed Serpent* the presence of the realistic perspective only serves to make us conscious of the luridness and the certain element of hysteria which are the great defects of the mythical writing.

Lawrence was greatly taken with Mexico as a visual experience and as a culture; nevertheless he was inevitably a tourist there and the image of cultural possibility which the book presents is largely a projection of an alien prophecy. It is basically the same undertaking that we find in Joseph Conrad's *Nostromo*, in which a Latin American culture also serves as a backdrop for the articulation of crucial issues in European civilisation. Conrad, however, uses the horror-comedy of Costaguana's political instability to mock his English reader. For Conrad the disjunction of cultures is a serviceable irony. But in Lawrence's altogether non-ironical, indeed sympathetic, account of a quest for affirmation, the disjunction between theme and setting illuminates the lack of real social objectification. The vision of renewal, we feel, is as implausibly foisted on to Mexico as on to Kate. It is only a highly coloured presentation of certain "problems" obtaining in the England and the Europe of that time. For instance, the meaning of nation and culture and the nature of the bonds that make for a social organism had all become topical and distinguishable as "issues" in the years around 1922 when the secession of Ireland as an independent state created the first break in the imperial order. It is noteworthy that Kate's first husband was a fighter for Irish independence. In this way Ireland serves as an important, albeit negative, reference in the concern with national liberation and with cultural renaissance which Lawrence ascribes but does not successfully transplant to Mexico. These same concerns figure prominently, of course, in *Women in Love*. But there they are presented in the social context to which for Lawrence they truly belonged. In *Women in Love* they were apprehended with a profound imaginativeness. Here they are rendered more abstractly and superficially, as issues.

In *The Plumed Serpent* there is at root the same lack of continuity between themes, milieu and event that we find in the immediately preceding novels. The difficulty is less apparent, but it is there. Lawrence's new social and cultural attentiveness is in the last resort of little service to his art. The milieu, however intrinsically interesting, is not adequately coincident with Lawrence's deepest preoccupations. Lawrence observes but does not see; that is to say, Mexico is closely observed but not registered or understood in the way that both the rural and the industrial landscapes of Nottinghamshire were in the early novels. In *The Plumed Serpent* as in all Lawrence's other novels about foreign countries there is the same lack of unified perception. Speaking of the Australian landscape in *Kangaroo* Lawrence says: "You feel you can't *see*—as if your eyes hadn't the vision in them to correspond with the outside landscape." This sentence suggests the basic failing in all the novels written during Lawrence's ten years of global wandering.

Lawrence's last novel, *Lady Chatterley's Lover*, is an inevitable exception to the generalisation that the novels about his native region are his best. The failure of this book demonstrates that his genius as a novelist was particular to a given time as well as to a given place. In this last book the old achievement is beyond recovery, even though there is still some evidence of Lawrence's profound familiarity with the conditioning milieu. Here, to take just one instance, is Lawrence's description of the wood at Wragby Hall as Connie sees it just before her relationship with Mellors begins:

> Little gusts of sunshine blew, strangely bright, and lit up the celandines at the wood's edge, under the hazel-rods, they spangled out bright and yellow. And the wood was still, stiller, but yet gusty with crossing sun. The first wind-flowers were out, and all the wood seemed pale with the pallor of endless little anemones, sprinkling the shaken floor. "The world has grown pale with thy breath." But it was the breath of Persephone, this time; she was out of hell on a cold morning. Cold breaths of wind came, and overhead there was an anger of entangled wind caught among the twigs. It, too, was caught and trying to tear itself free, the wind, like Absalom. How cold the anemones looked, bobbing their naked white shoulders over crinoline skirts of green. But they stood it. A few first bleached little primroses, too, by the path, and yellow buds unfolding themselves.

This lyrical evocation of landscape (which relates very obviously to the theme of tenderness which at one stage in the protracted composition of the novel provided its title) constitutes something entirely beyond the conventions of vision represented either by the Royal Academician and clubman who is Connie's father or by the conspicuous modernism of her friend Duncan Forbes. But in this, as in so many other descriptive passages in *Lady Chatterley's Lover*, the visible world is not seen with the same fullness or intensity that we find in the books written fifteen years earlier. There is here some faint sense of the premeditated poetic, even perhaps of the precious. The easy recourse to literary quotation and allusion also suggest a mind that is now directed inwards rather than outwards. In the above passage the externalisation is highly selective. And as with *The Plumed Serpent*, the stylistic weakness is the clue to the general weakness. For in *Lady Chatterley's Lover* the phenomenal world is not granted its autonomy or its intrinsic interest. It is, as it were, co-opted into a system of symbols. Country house, park and industrial landscape, for instance, are there primarily to subserve a too explicit schematic order.

The skeletal conspicuousness of the themes in *Lady Chatterley's Lover* is a worse fault than the programmatic solemnity in the notorious choice of vocabulary. Ideas play too prominent a role in this novel because neither Mellors nor his author possess the quick, energetic irony about ideas that we encountered in Birkin and in the Lawrence who wrote *Women in Love*. Furthermore, in the articulation of some of these ideas, there is a confusion and also (ironically, given the reputation of the novel) a certain reticence. The criticism of female sexual rapacity in this novel is no clearer or more precise than it was in *The Plumed Serpent*, where it also served as a heavy but unparticularised emphasis. The thematic significance of the concern with unorthodox sexual practice is similarly obscure. Whether this is due to Lawrence's reluctance further to antagonise convention or to his own ethical or psychological uncertainty is here only an academic issue. But the fact that the issue occurs to the reader at all is an index of the extent to which the novel's leading effect is an agitation of ideas. Early in the 1920s, in the Foreword to *Fantasia of the Unconscious*, Lawrence commented on the relationship between his art and his ideas:

> This pseudo-philosophy of mine—"pollyanalytics", as one of my respected critics might say—is deduced from the novels and poems, not the reverse. The novels and poems come unwatched out of one's pen. And then the absolute need which one has for some sort of satisfactory mental attitude towards oneself and things in general makes one try to abstract some definite conclusions from one's experi-

ence as a writer and as a man. The novels and poems are pure passionate experience. These pollyanalytics are inferences made afterwards, from the experience.[118]

Abundantly true though this is of the early novels, it is the very reverse of what we have in this last novel. *Lady Chatterley's Lover* treats mainly of the secondary experience that Lawrence terms "inferences". The novel suggests an author who is no longer intimately and specifically engaged with the fluid actualities of experience. He seems rather to be a solipsist, using setting, character and story to embody private concerns that have long since lost flexibility of categorisation and thus consolidated into mere issues. Lawrence's native region no longer exists in its earlier fullness as landscape, society and culture. It merely provides symbols and also certain perceptions which are transmuted into the delicate lyricism which is one aspect of the private, personal quality of the novel.[119]

Of all the novels of exile, none has a more poignant effect than *Lady Chatterly's Lover* in pointing up the particular and unrepeatable occasion of Lawrence's genius as a novelist. For the alienation in the writing in this last novel demonstrates the singular richness of the early works. Above all it was a cultural richness. The contrast between *Lady Chatterley's Lover* and, say, *The Rainbow* is a good illustration of the extent to which authorial involvement and concern with a culture of some density are prerequisites for a major novel. In *Lady Chatterley's Lover* we see the loss of the mutually enhancing

[118] *Fantasia of the Unconscious* (New York, 1960), p. 57.
[119] A late expression of Lawrence's visual imagination was the series of paintings which he began at about the same time that he started *Lady Chatterley's Lover* and which were exhibited in London in 1929. The more ambitious works such as "Resurrection", "Fight with an Amazon" and "Flight Back into Paradise" are all extremely autobiographical. They show the same preoccupation with self, personal feeling and personal history that so obviously inform the novel. But there is little more to them than this. Judged as paintings they have only slight merit.

correspondence between artist and society which had distinguished Lawrence's early novels. The essential commitment to realism has gone and we have here, by contrast, a modern work. The loss of interest and energy in the representation of society, the concern with private feeling, the schematisation and the insistent provocative-ness all recall the art which is characteristic of the period after the Great War. Yet these features of the novel occur, we feel, more by default than by design or prevision. For Lawrence was no more a fluent or natural modernist than England was a natural breeding place for Dada, surreal-ism or existentialism. In Lawrence's career the modern signifies the loss of the particular cultural synthesis that his greatest novels record.

Inheriting the forms and traditions of the realistic novel, one of the great devices for perception and understanding created by the nineteenth-century bourgeoisie, Lawrence brought to them a simultaneously moral and visual sensibility which was in part his innate gift and in part the special product of the Victorian culture in which he grew up. The result was a series of major works which, though clearly works of realism, are without any of the narrow-ness of concern that we usually associate with the term. Lawrence's intensity of perception, which refers back ultimately to Blake and intermediately to various English painters and critics of the nineteenth century, makes his early novels the great flowering of the pre-eminently visual mode of fiction which we know as realism, of the phase in the history of narrative in which story telling was used for the modelling and analysis of society. For the early novels render an actual human and material reality as opposed to the merely personal feeling which is the chief subject of *Lady Chatterley's Lover*. They reveal a rich social and cultural order which, despite its manifest brutalities, nourishes and confirms the intensity and subtlety of the authorial perception. And the significant particulars of this cultural and intellectual background force us to widen our view of the provenance of Lawrence's art. His greatest novels refer us to a European literary tradition. They also compel us to formulate our response in terms larger than strictly literary ones. Lawrence's histories of industrial England are a continuation of the great English romantic vision which we can follow in the work of Blake, Turner, Ruskin and William Morris. All were sustained by an awareness of both literature and painting. But this synthesis occurred within a larger synthesis. For they were also directed by a vision of heroic possibility for the individual, for society and for life itself.

INDEX

"Study of Thomas Hardy", 18, 61, 82, 83n, 84, 88n, 129–30, 142, 145

Tillyard, E. M. W., 117
Trespasser, The, 5n, 144n
Turner, J. M. W., 14, 63, 237
Twilight in Italy, 18, 20n, 144–6

Van Ghent, Dorothy, 37
Verga, Giovanni, 53, 107
Voysey, C. A. F., 115

Watteau, 184
Watts, 5, 142, 213–14
Wells, H. G., 99, 151
  Ann Veronica, 99
Weiss, Daniel A., 24n

White Peacock, The, 4–15, 16, 21, 33, 40, 50, 127, 142, 144n, 162, 163, 208
Williams, William Carlos, 203n
Wint, Peter de, 144
Women in Love, 4, 49n, 57, 64–5, 75, 93, 96, 98, 103, 113, 115n, 139–41, 149, 151, 154–5, 157, 159–61, 162–218, 221, 222, 232, 234
Woolf, Leonard, 150
Woolf, Virginia, 150, 151, 181n
  Night and Day, 150
Wordsworth, William, 14
Worringer, William, 87–8, 94

Yeats, W. B., 91

Zola, 38n, 49, 50, 57, 110